FICTIONS OF

FREEMASONRY

FICTIONS OF
FREEMASONRY

FREEMASONRY AND THE GERMAN NOVEL

SCOTT ABBOTT

Wayne State University Press   Detroit

Library of Congress Cataloging-in-Publication Data
Abbott, Scott H.
   Fictions of Freemasonry : Freemasonry and the German novel / Scott
Abbott.
      p.   cm.
   Includes bibliographical references (p.   ) and index.
   ISBN 0–8143–1992–0 (alk. paper)
   1. German fiction—History and criticism. 2. Freemasonry in
literature. I. Title.
PT749.F74A23   1991
833.009—dc20   90–12739
                                                          CIP

Designer: Mary Krzewinski

For Timothy, Samuel, Benjamin, Nathan, Thomas, Maren, and Joseph

The syllables of the word *Araby* were called to me through the silence in which my soul luxuriated and cast an eastern enchantment over me. I asked for leave to go to the bazaar on Saturday night. My aunt was surprised and hoped it was not some Freemason affair.
—James Joyce, "Araby"

Contents

Illustrations

Preface

Freemasonry. Yet another cause of the revolution. The initiation is a fearful ordeal. Cause of dissension among married pairs. Distrusted by the clergy. What can its great secret be?
—Gustav Flaubert, *Dictionary of Accepted Ideas*

In Günter Grass's *Dog Years* (*Hundejahre*, 1963), when officials accuse Oswald Brunies of un-German conduct, interviews with his students reveal that he may be a Freemason: "The students had written down things their teacher had said, maxims which seemed demoralizing and negative. Suddenly everyone was saying: He was a Freemason. But then no one knew what that was: a Freemason."[1] Concerning Freemasonry, Brunies' students are strongly influenced by rumor and remain unencumbered by facts; and as modern fictional characters, they are not alone in their ignorance. In Thomas Mann's *Magic Mountain* (*Der Zauberberg*, 1924), Hans Castorp is likewise shocked to learn that his mentor Settembrini is a Freemason: "Once again he had been extraordinarily surprised to hear that there was, in all seriousness, still such a thing."[2]

These twentieth-century responses would have been anomalies in literature of the late eighteenth century, a time when Freemasonry was a powerful institution and Freemasons were a staple of German fiction. Freemasons (or members of similar secret societies) appear, for instance, in novels by Schiller, Goethe, Wieland, Jean Paul, Tieck, and Hölderlin. But literary conventions shift with historical circumstances, and as early as the mid-nineteenth century, when one character in Karl Gutzkow's *The Knights of Spirit*

11

(*Die Ritter vom Geiste*, 1850–1851) admits that he has always skipped over Masonic passages in the German classics, a friend assures him that it is only natural: "You have probably always felt that these Masonic speeches do not, in fact, reflect what we admire of Herder and Goethe. . . . The great, omnipotent Olympian . . . has nothing in common with the lodge. Once in Weimar someone showed me Goethe's Masonic apron; it did not edify me."[3]

Goethe's actual Masonic apron may remain unedifying to the modern reader as well; and certainly Hans Castorp and Brunies' students find it odd to visualize their mentors in such aprons. But Goethe's (and Herder's and Frederick the Great's) symbolic aprons represent a complex Masonic culture that Goethe and his contemporaries knew intimately, a culture reflected repeatedly in their novels and in those of their nineteenth- and twentieth-century successors as well.

The first chapter of this book sketches the history of Freemasonry through the eighteenth century, focusing on issues and figures most intimately related to the novels I discuss.[4] The list of eighteenth-century Masonic topics, spheres of influence (imagined and real), and their manifestations is impressive: nonpolitics and revolutionary conspiracies, Jesuits and anti-Jesuits, the private opening of a public sphere, political landscape gardening, ritual education, debates on natural vs. arbitrary language, radical biblical criticism, alchemy, confidence men, learned academies, occult societies, and novels of every description. Running through both history and fiction is a basic Masonic story, a ritual tale told in many ways but with recurring motifs. It is in part the myth of the magus E. M. Butler describes so well. It is a story of esoteric education in the East. It involves a symbolic ritual route that challenges with trials of courage and teaches through pedagogical architecture. It features a secret society with the power and will to direct the affairs of an individual or a state. Historically, the story serves to found new secret societies, attract new members, or fuel theories of conspiracy. Fictionally, various motifs and themes may coalesce as a subgenre, the *Geheimbundroman* or league novel, or, more commonly, they form a subplot of a *Bildungsroman* or perhaps a social novel.

In this welter of historical and fictional Freemasonry, two issues recur regularly: politics and ritual symbolism. As told by some, the Masonic story reflects on its own ritual sign system. Both Schiller's *Ghost-Seer* (*Der Geisterseher*, 1787–1789) and Goethe's

Wilhelm Meister's Apprenticeship and *Travels* (*Lehrjahre*, 1795–1796; *Wanderjahre*, 1821, 1829), for example, examine esoteric and exoteric signs and the Masonic semiotic transformation from reality to symbol and back to reality. The story can be represented as historically true to gain wealth from and political power over the credulous. Hund and Cagliostro told this version, as do Schiller's narrators in *The Ghost-Seer*. It can be a story of frustrated democracy, as told in Gutzkow's *Knights of Spirit* and Heinrich Mann's *The Subject* (*Der Untertan*, 1918). Hofmannsthal's characters in *Andreas* (1932) succor one another in their belief and disbelief in a transcendent Masonic sign system. The story can be presented as myth: a dangerous ritual descent into a romantic fascination with death as in Thomas Mann's *Magic Mountain* or a mythicization of history, a semiotically effected will-to-power like that decried in Grass's *Dog Years*. In any case, this intriguing story about politics and semiotics is just as attractive to readers of the late twentieth century as it was to the seventeenth-century readers of Andreae's Rosicrucian fictions.

In my book I aim to provide historical contexts in which to read selected German novels written over the course of three centuries. This has been done before, of course, in excellent books by Ferdinand Josef Schneider, Marianne Thalmann, Heinrich Schneider, Reinhart Koselleck, and most recently Michael Voges, just to name the most prominent. I am much indebted to these sources and frequently refer to them.

Historical context is indispensible; and a strictly historical survey of literary Freemasonry would provide its own satisfaction; that is clear. Such studies, however, invariably leave one wishing for closer analysis of individual works. To meet my own preference in that matter, this book features focused, interpretive studies of Schiller's *Ghost-Seer*, Goethe's *Wilhelm Meister* novels, Gutzkow's *The Knights of Spirit*, Hofmannsthal's *Andreas*, Thomas Mann's *Magic Mountain*, and Grass's *Dog Years*. I substantially reevaluate and reinterpret these major novels in Freemasonic contexts. Because of the emphasis on individual novels, this book is not a comprehensive history of Freemasons in literature. It lacks, for instance, a thorough description of the popular late eighteenth-century league novel; little is said about important novels by Wieland, Jean Paul, Moritz, Tieck, and many others well worth discussing in this context; and Russian, French, English, American, Spanish, and Italian "Masonic novels" are virtually ignored. Recent publications, however, fill in many of those gaps,[5] and supplementary studies will surely result.

I would like to thank Heinrich Schneider, librarian of the Bayreuth Masonic Library, and Inge Baum, librarian of the House of the Temple in Washington, D.C., for their extraordinary helpfulness. Contrary to my expectations, Freemasons share their documents freely and welcome scholars working in their field. Thanks are also due to Hans Wysling of the Thomas Mann Archive in Zürich, to Alfred Bush of Princeton's Firestone Library, and to the Interlibrary Loan Services of Vanderbilt Library.

Research for this book was supported by Vanderbilt University's Research Council and by the National Endowment for the Humanities. I am grateful for their assistance.

Of those who have read and criticized my work, I owe special thanks to Susan Abbott, Frederick Amrine, Wilfried Barner, Thomas Heine, Bruce Kieffer, James K. Lyon, Hans Schulz, Hinrich Seeba, and Guy Stern. In Kathryn Wildfong and Lisa Nowak Jerry I was fortunate to find sensitive, helpful editors. And finally, my largest debt is to Theodore Ziolkowski, who has supported this project from its inception.

CHAPTER ONE

Eighteenth-Century Freemasonry: Politics and Semiotics

Es ist wohl denkbar: daß die öffentliche Geschichte sich
aus der geheimen werde erklären lassen können.
—Fichte, *Philosophie der Maurerei*

If history be no ancient Fable / Free Masons came from
Tower of Babel.
—"The Freemasons; an Hudibrastic poem,"
   London, 1723

FREEMASONIC HISTORY

An early description of Freemasonry declares it an "ancient and
honourable institution: ancient no doubt it is, as having subsisted
from time immemorial; and honourable it must be acknowledged to
be, as by a natural tendency it conduces to make those so who are
obedient to its precepts."[1] Both assertions make sense: for Freemasonry has roots in stonemason guilds that date back through the
centuries; and the moral precepts of the order are indeed conducive
to an "honourable" life. But in both cases one can affirm the opposite as well: for Freemasonry is a distinctly modern institution,
closely tied to the eighteenth century in which it experienced its
greatest successes; and in reference to its honor, like most institutions Freemasonry has given rise to its share of scandals, having, in
fact, harbored some of the great charlatans of the last three centuries. These and related dualities—ancient and modern, moral and
immoral, secret and public, literal and symbolic, democratic and authoritarian—characterize a complex, constantly shifting Freemasonic movement.

15

Freemasons trace their official beginning to a historical act: at a 1717 meeting in London several Masonic lodges joined to form a Grand Lodge. The lodges represented in the 1717 merger had developed out of guilds of "operative" stonemasons which began to admit aristocrats, intellectual and business leaders, and men of other trades as honorary or "speculative" masons. The purely speculative, nonoperative lodges that finally resulted lost contact with the actual building trades, retaining the compass, square, trowel, apron, columns, steps, and other masonic and architectural tools and structures as symbols of their new enterprise. The building of Solomon's temple became an allegory for the inner, moral development of a brother; and the stone-by-stone erection of Europe's cathedrals was ritually evoked as initiates ceremonially established harmonious inner edifices.

Six years after the Grand Lodge was formed, Anderson's *Constitutions of the Free-Masons, containing the History, Charges, Regulations etc. of that most Ancient and Right Worshipful Fraternity* (London, 1723) presented a blueprint for the moral structure of the growing fraternity. In the document's first "Charge," Masons are directed to obey moral laws and to subscribe to that religion on which all men can agree. On that basis, the document promises, Masonry will emerge as a harmonizing influence, promoting friendships among those whom sectarian religion separates. The second charge asserts that the Mason is a peaceful subject of civil authority and that he must never take part in conspiracies against the freedom and welfare of his nation. The promised consequence is that rulers will support and promote the brotherhood in times of peace. The third charge requires that only free-born, mature men of good reputation be admitted as members of a lodge; women are explicitly excluded. Further charges address how Masons should relate to one another within and outside the lodge: there should be no arguments over religion or politics in the lodge, all Masons are brothers and should be treated equally, and brothers should aid one another whenever possible.

The organization this document helped to foster appealed strongly to men of the Enlightenment; and soon Freemasonry could claim influential members throughout Europe and America. Even an abbreviated list of eighteenth-century Freemasons is truly extraordinary. Wren, Pope, Hogarth, Scott, Boswell, and Burns were all Masons. Franklin, Washington, and Revere were American Masons. Lafayette, Voltaire, Montesquieu, Beaumarchais, and the

Montgolfier brothers were among the many influential French Masons. And Klopstock, Klinger, Nicolai, Moritz, Kotzebue, Iffland, Forster, Mesmer, Haydn, Mozart, Wieland, Claudius, Lessing, Herder, Fichte, Goethe—and dozens of monarchs and princes, including Frederick the Great and several of his successors—were German-speaking Freemasons.

Frederick's initiation into the brotherhood in 1738, less than a year after the Hamburg lodge had been founded as the first on German soil, was a key event for German Freemasonry. Frederick became the master of his own lodge and took an active part in Freemasonry for years after assuming the throne in 1740. During his reign he protected and supported the order, writing, for example, of Maria Theresia's intermittent attacks on Freemasonry: "The Empress is exactly right, for if she cannot know what is occurring in the lodges she is not required to put up with them. I, however, who know [the lodges], should not only put up with them, but must also justly protect and maintain them."[2] In a 1777 correspondence with the lodge La Royale York de l'Amitié, Frederick renewed his commitment to the brotherhood, while issuing a veiled warning: "A society whose only work is to fruitfully bring forth all the virtues in my states can always count on my protection. This is a laudable task for every good ruler, and I will never cease fulfilling it." Frederick's participation in the lodge underscores its social importance, and his need to limit its functions to advancing moral virtues indicates the political potential of the secret society.

In the decade following establishment of the first German lodge, further lodges were founded in Dresden, Berlin, Bayreuth, Leipzig, Frankfurt am Main, and Vienna, usually with English permission. In the early years, following the English pattern, German lodges raised their members to three degrees: Apprentice, Journeyman (or Fellow Craft), and Master. But as early as 1742, French-inspired "Scottish" lodges were established in Berlin and Hamburg, introducing degrees beyond the original three; and that break from tradition set off an explosion of changes and competing systems. Some orders accepted women. Others developed rituals based on Rosicrucian lore, stories of the Knights Templar, and Catholic doctrine. Among the more notorious of these were the Clermont System (a "Catholic" order), the occult *Gold- und Rosenkreuzer* (whose proponents Wöllner and Bischoffwerder were influential advisers to mystically inclined Frederick Wilhelm II, Frederick the Great's successor), the *Mopsorden* (an order of "adoption" that accepted women and gave rise to much gossip), and the powerful Strict Observance. Perhaps the best known of all the Masonic offshoots was the order of Illuminati, a radical political order founded in Bavaria by Jesuit-educated Adam Weishaupt.[3]

With the rise of such widely diverse systems (many of them spectacularly opposed to the rationalist, nonpolitical, nonsectarian early order), with a rapid increase in membership, and with growing public belief that Freemasons were involved in conspiracies against church and state,[4] attempts at reform were inevitable. Leading Masons gathered in Wilhelmsbad in 1782 to rectify the brotherhood, an effort that met some success. After that reform, throughout the nineteenth and into the twentieth century, Freemasonry continued to grow in terms of pure numbers, but it has never again reached the levels of influence it enjoyed in the eighteenth century. Why, then, was Freemasonry so attractive in that century? And why did it become the Enlightenment institution *par excellence*?

THE ATTRACTION OF FREEMASONRY

In the fall of 1792, the idealist philosopher Johann Gottlob Fichte responded to a friend's questions concerning his Masonic affiliation:

> I am not a Mason. Irrespective of the many inducements to become one, I had important reasons to avoid them. . . . As a means to acquire acquaintances and helpful connections it is excellent, and for this purpose I recommend it strongly. . . . It seems to me, namely, that in our age, brought by luxury to slavery and by slavery to all manner of corruption, we are in dire need . . . of a society as a seed of goodness; and for that purpose Freemasonry—not in its present form, but at least in its already authorized husk—could qualify. . . . If you become a Freemason, then, we shall, God willing, one day meet.[5]

Despite his reservations, Fichte did become a Mason, and during the seven years he was active in the brotherhood, he used lodges in various cities to establish contact with influential Masons. He also expanded and specified (most specifically in the Masonic lectures he gave in Berlin)[6] his view of the brotherhood.

Fichte's lectures begin with a short description of recent events, emphasizing the persecutions the order has suffered from hostile governments and the Catholic church. He then discusses the chaos caused by competing sects of Masons and reminds his listeners of recent public disclosures and ridicule. In the face of all this, however, talented, intelligent men of character continue to gather in Masonic lodges. Why? Fichte's answer, put most simply, is that Freemasonry provides educational opportunities not available elsewhere. In society at large each man trains for a certain profession and receives a one-sided education. The separate professions are at odds with one another and work to fragment rather than unify society. Freemasonry's purpose, Fichte states, is education of the *whole* man.[7] Masonry is a "training ground for versatility." As such it supplements religious education by teaching the nonsectarian essence of religion; and it perfects political education by uniting patriotic and cosmopolitan views, making Masons good citizens of their states and the world as well.

These themes—of unification and wholeness, of Freemasonry as a counterweight to sectarian religion, of healing a split between nationalism and cosmopolitanism, of moral education— reiterate a view of Freemasonry set forth two decades earlier by a character in Lessing's *Ernst and Falk, Dialogues for Freemasons (Ernst und Falk, Gespräche für Freymäurer,* 1778, 1780). Falk, a Mason conversing with his non-Mason friend Ernst, points out that humanity is divided into warring states, competing social classes, and various religions. Freemasons work to lessen the negative impact of these three destructive divisions. In the lodge Masons learn to be cosmopolitan, socially equal, and nonsectarian.[8]

Fichte's and Lessing's descriptions of Freemasonry as cosmopolitan *and* nationalistic, democratic *and* nonpolitical reveal a series of tensions that may provide a key to the order's phenomenal eighteenth-century success. In assessing that tension, Reinhart Koselleck describes Freemasonry as a "specific answer to the system of absolutism" prevalent in eighteenth-century Europe.[9] According to Koselleck's theory, men of intellect and economic influence, denied direct political power by the prevailing system, found in Masonry an avenue to indirect power. Masons appropriated the only sphere available to them, "den ausserstaatlichen geistigen Innenraum" (56), setting themselves off, in this "moral innerspace outside the state," from church and state to form a third axis of power in society. The secrecy by which the new moral realm was set apart, so antithetical to the openness of the Enlightenment, draws Koselleck's special attention, for the Masonic secret leads, in his analysis, into the center of the dialectic between morality and politics.

19

The mystery promised by the secret society was different in each Masonic system; but in the secrecy protecting that mystery "lay the promise of . . . a new, better, and previously unknown life. The initiation meant 'the discovery of a new world hidden in the midst of the old one'" (61). Such promises appealed, of course, not only to advocates of the Enlightenment but also to men interested in alchemy, mystical religion, and hierarchical power; many of the systems that sprang up played on such desires. In this sense, the new secret societies threatened advances Enlightenment thinkers believed they had made. But Koselleck is interested in another sort of mystery, a moral, political "critique" that leads to an eventual "crisis": the overthrow of absolutist governments.

From the beginning, Freemasons separated themselves from any overt political activity, expressly forbidding politics in their lodges. Their task, they said, was not to reform the state but rather to change the individual. This moral focus, along with the secrecy cloaking the lodges, gave Masons various freedoms unavailable outside the lodge. In the lodge "Noblemen, gentlemen and working men" met and dealt with one another on an equal social footing, an impossibility in a state that recognized and legitimized differences in class. Such moral freedom, Koselleck suggests, undermined the rule of the state and became the secret of Freemasonry. And that secret was very attractive: "Under the sign of the Masonic mystery arose the social structure of the moral internationale. . . . The lodges became the most powerful social institution of the moral world in the eighteenth century" (64).

As an institution of the *moral* world, Freemasonry's political influence was necessarily indirect, but nonetheless potent:

> Directly, the Masons have nothing to do with politics, but they live according to a law which, when it prevails, makes an overthrow superfluous. They withdraw from the state and from the government and form an indirect power which threatens sovereignty, but only morally. . . . Morality is the presumptive sovereign. Directly unpolitical, the Mason is, in fact, indirectly political. Morality remains indeed non-violent and peaceful, but in that very mode, through its polarisation to politics, it calls the state into question.(68)

Koselleck's theoretical construct makes sense of, and in return is legitimized by, various ritual practices that served as vehicles or expressions of Freemasonry's politically subversive moral law. One of the most interesting expressions was Masonic landscape gardening.[10]

The eighteenth-century change in taste from highly formal, geometrically designed baroque gardens to more natural "English" gardens was in part an expression of changes in political preference.[11] Baroque gardens, of which Louis XIV's gardens at Versailles were the most prominent, were seen by Shaftesbury, Addison, Pope, Rousseau, Herder, Schiller, and others as allegories of absolute monarchies: "Where nature seemed alienated from its own being, as in the baroque garden, it came to be a symbol of political oppression and arbitrariness, a synonym for the despotic order" (Buttlar, *Der Landschaftsgarten*, 11). English liberals, influenced in part by architectural symbols in the Freemasonic ritual many of them knew, developed gardens in which the architecture of the landscape was intended to reflect and inspire a moral, naturally human, nonabsolutist pattern. Tracing a ritual route in a Masonic initiation, or following the "belt-walk" or "circuit" of an English garden, the initiate was meant to undergo a moral education.[12] Other Europeans followed the English lead; and the Wirlitz gardens near Dessau, for example, were constructed with such Masonic pedagogical practice in mind.[13]

These gardens, like other manifestations of Enlightenment Freemasonry, are still *indirect* political statements. The Illuminati, however, provide Koselleck with an excellent historical example of the progression from a moral concern to *direct* criticism of the state. Considering themselves more qualified morally to lead the state than those in power and protected by the secrecy of their lodges, the Illuminati planned to take over the state by gradually filling the state bureaucracy with worthy members of the order. The time would eventually come, then, when they would, de facto, be the state. The plan never came to fruition, for the Bavarian government exposed the Illuminati and exacted harsh penalities from the conspirators. But, as Koselleck points out, there were still significant results.

In the polemics against secret societies that followed the Bavarian crackdown, "the first political camps driven by the consciousness of being in a latently critical situation formed" (106). Warring factions joined together to defend the structure of the absolutist state against the enemy supposedly lurking in secret societies. Secret societies were branded states within states (which, in a sense, they were), and in the struggle for power between the state and the secret state it harbored revolution was (correctly) foreseen.

21

Contemporary fears were not only limited to the sphere of politics but also to religion. Official Masonic policy required lodges to accept anyone who professed some belief in the "Great Architect of the Universe," a practice indirectly undercutting sectarian religion in the same way democratic ideals in the lodge undermined state authority. Friedrich Schlegel made this point while warning against Freemasonry in his *Philosophy of History* (1828): "For this reason, in a Revelation imparted to all, there can be no secrecy. . . . This would be to constitute a church within a church—a measure to be as little tolerated or justified as an *imperium in imperio* . . . such a secret parasitical church would unquestionably . . . be very soon transformed into a secret directory for political changes and revolutions."[14] But just why, Koselleck asks, did indirectly exerted power, both political and religious, arouse such great fears of overthrowing throne and altar?

The moral emphasis alone would not have raised fears of imminent political change. But a philosophy of history developed in part in Enlightenment secret societies indeed caused anxiety. From the beginning Freemasons reinterpreted the history of the world, highlighting masonic events (e.g., great architectural achievements) that led from Adam to the Masonic success in eighteenth-century England. The newly written history gave legitimacy to Masonic plans for the future. In Germany, Koselleck argues, this involves transforming the Leibnizian theodicy. Masons themselves, working in secret (as had divine providence), become the new gods who guide history: "It is, henceforth, the Masonic order which provides that the harmony of the cosmos really rules on this earth" (109). Schiller touches on the (fictional) replacement of gods by emissaries of a secret society in a letter to Goethe about the Society of the Tower in *Wilhelm Meister's Apprenticeship*: "The novel . . . approaches the epic in several ways, among them, in that it has machines that, in a certain sense, represent the gods or ruling fate."[15] The Illuminati finally fulfilled this sort of thinking, combining Rousseauian ideas about nature, a moralized Christianity, and the contemporary ideal of progress into a philosophy of history. A knowledge of the Illuminati's role in bringing that philosophy of history to fruition was the final secret toward which initiates of that order worked.

Despite Masonic protestations to the contrary, then, the seeds of revolt were nurtured in Freemasonry and its offshoots, most clearly in the Illuminati. Exposés like Ernst August Anton von

Göchhausen's "Disclosure of the System of the Cosmopolitan Republic" ("Enthüllung des Systems der Weltbürger-Republik," 1780), despite their misreadings of the Jesuits' role in the process, are correct in revealing the political implications of Freemasonry's moral goals: that "the existence of the secret society would lead to the dissolution of the existing order, irrespective of what the Masons themselves have in mind."[16]

In terms slightly different from those with which Koselleck works, Jürgen Habermas describes Freemasonry as one of several seventeenth- and eighteenth-century institutions—including coffee houses in England, salons in France, and language societies in Germany—which met the developing need for a public sphere (*Öffentlichkeit*). The social equality ruling in Masonic lodges, as well as their open discussions, could occur only outside the absolutist political arena. According to Kant, the limitation of the public sphere was "the effective cause of all secret societies. For it is a natural function of humanity to communicate with one another, primarily about what concerns humanity in general" (Habermas, 133). Ironically, then, these early steps toward a public sphere took place in a jealously guarded private sphere. The rational communication that marks a public sphere is normally furthered by open publication; but in the eighteenth century that communication required the protection *from* publication afforded by the secrecy of the lodge. Habermas points out that Lessing's character Falk draws attention to a secret origin of the public sphere when he claims that Freemasonry is just as ancient as bourgeois society, "if bourgeois society is not, in fact, but a descendant of Freemasonry" (51).

In the historical development Habermas and Koselleck describe, the gradual development of the public sphere lessens the need for secrecy and isolation. Exclusive, ritualistic Freemasonry becomes an anachronism attracting those who are fleeing rather than pursuing an increasing public sphere. Among others, Herder recognized and welcomed changes in Freemasonry. In his "Dialogue on an Invisible-Visible Society" ("Gespräch über eine unsichtbar-sichtbare Gesellschaft," 1793), written as a continuation of Lessing's *Ernst and Falk*, he argues for opening up the Freemasonry that, as a secret society, helped prepare for the Enlightenment. Now that it has achieved its goals, he writes, Masonry should become a German Academy or Humanitarian Society. The lodge should become a library to propagate truth openly.

But Herder's progressive attitude toward the new public sphere was not universally shared. Friedrich Schlegel, for example, continued Lessing's Masonic dialogue in quite another vein in his "Ernst and Falk, Fragment of a Third Dialogue on Freemasonry" ("Ernst und Falk, Bruchstück eines dritten Gesprächs über Freimaurerei," 1804). Angered by the increased democracy inspired by the French Revolution, he argued for a renewal of secrecy. Scientific, artistic, and mystical knowledge, he suggested, should be kept from the democratic hordes. But even while arguing opposite sides of the question, both Herder and Schlegel show the contemporary secret society to be the institution of political opposition (whether reactionary or progressive) Koselleck and Habermas describe.

Throughout this discussion of Freemasonry as a nonpolitical political institution, the focus has been on moral laws taught under the cover of secrecy. By changing that focus slightly, from the moral laws to the semiotic system through which they are taught, we can open up a second area of investigation, one quite different from, yet related to, the first.

In 1810 Karl Christian Friedrich Krause, a philosopher and leading Dresden Freemason, published a book very much in the spirit of Herder's recommendation for Masonic progression from a secret society to a German Academy.[17] Krause sees Freemasonry as a necessary step toward a universal *Menschheitsbund* (league of humanity). To move toward this final goal, he makes public what he calls "The Three Oldest Documents of the Craft of the Masonic Brotherhood" ("Die drei ältesten Kunsturkunden der Freimaurerbrüderschaft"), pointing out that the rituals contained therein have already been published in England. The "secret" symbols involved are not the essence of Freemasonry, he argues, and the (political) oath of secrecy sworn as part of the ritual is a lamentable intrusion. It is a disservice to both the brotherhood and humanity to pretend there is a great secret—whether political, alchemical, or theosophical—hidden behind a final ritual curtain. To cure such esoteric tendencies, Krause presents a "higher spiritualization of the most important symbols and customs of old-English Freemasonry handed down in the three oldest documents of the craft." This "spiritualization" of symbols is presented in the catechetical form of Freemasonic ritual.

Krause first discusses the main symbols of Freemasonry, the "three great lights"—Bible, square, compass—which teach, respectively, to live faithfully, to make one's actions lawful, and to unite

24

brothers within certain boundaries. The Bible is a good symbol, he writes, because it depicts pious people in *"accurate* images." The square is called a natural, old figure of the law; and the compass is shown to work architecturally in ways that can be seen as analogues for society. Krause continues in this vein, explaining or "spiritualizing" the three smaller lights (sun, moon, and master mason) and many other symbols of Freemasonry. As Krause's liturgical explanations illustrate, much of Masonic ritual consists of presentation of various symbols followed by explanations relating them to the moral education of the initiate.[18]

According to Krause, the symbols drawn from the craft of masonry are somewhat arbitrary. Any other craft or art (he mentions music, painting, and medicine) could likewise supply figures portraying and affecting human development. The symbols are not the essence, but they act as does the word for thought or a sound for emotion. But even as he stresses the arbitrariness of these signs, he wants to ground or motivate them, calling them *"accurate images"* (*"treue* Bilder") and emphasizing their "natural, sincere, honorable origin" (31). By calling attention to the arbitrariness of Masonic symbols, Krause can discredit the nonexistent esoteric treasures so many seek in Freemasonry; and by emphasizing the natural suitability of the same symbols, he gains natural, moral authority for the teachings presented through the symbols.

In Lessing's *Ernst and Falk*, as Alice Kuzniar has pointed out, Falk similarly "disparages masonic symbolic language because the essence of what masonry means cannot be revealed by its signs, texts, and customs," and yet he also "delights in uncovering unconventional etymologies and shifting meanings in order to arrive at the true meaning of the word masonry."[19] "In the process," Kuzniar concludes, "the initial mystery is necessarily lost, for the hidden origins of Freemasonry are disclosed as linguistic play. The letter replaces the spirit" (17).

There is, of course, a logical problem set up as Krause (or Lessing's Falk) plays both sides. He tries to deal with this by describing a development from the arbitrary symbol, which is but a crutch, to an unmediated truth, which must nevertheless be poetically mediated. The seed that Freemasonic ritual presently is, he writes, will grow to maturity

when this representation is no longer only symbolic and allegorical, but also, most substantially, immediately artful and representative; when it does not, as a product of the understanding, merely
affect the understanding, but also, as a direct, substantial,
nonfigurative expression of a human, beautifully modulated heart,
affect the heart, and move and elevate the whole person; which is
only possible through the help of the most beautiful arts. (36)

As Krause's historical-liturgical essay draws to a close, he stresses
again the arbitrariness of Masonic symbolism; "for a man is a Freemason because of his entire, human, universally healthy life, not
through the arbitrary choice of his signs. He is a Freemason, independent of all symbols" (41). And Krause calls for the Mason to
"spiritualize" his symbols: "that he seek to discern clearly what they
intimate figuratively, but to do so without a figure, and to come to
love what has been discerned in a pure heart" (43).

Krause's struggle with this problem represents one side of
the ongoing debate in Masonic circles over the status of the fraternity's symbols. The other side of the discussion is well portrayed in
the oath Krause prints, an oath that protects the brotherhood's symbols with threats of violence, demonstrating in the process a linguistic idolatry from which Krause wants to free the institution: "I furthermore do swear, that I will not write it, print it, cut it, paint it, or
stint it, mark it, stain or engrave it, or cause it so to be done, upon
anything moveable or immoveable, under the Canopy of Heaven,
whereby it may become legible or intelligible, or the least Appearance of the Character of a Letter, whereby the secret Art, may be
unlawfully obtained" (164). The threatened penalty fits the crime,
for the brother who reveals the Masonic symbols (raised to the status of magical signs by the oath) will have his throat cut and his
"Tongue torn out by the Root, and that to be buried in the Sands of
the Sea" (165). Krause's point is that there are no "secret mysteries,"
as the oath calls them, in Masonic symbolism, only moral teachings.
And if there are no "secret mysteries" behind or in the signs, then
the oath that protects the signs is superfluous, or to put it more
strongly, politically and religiously misleading.

Krause's discussion of Masonic symbols fits into a more
general debate about signs and sign systems that took place during
the seventeenth and eighteenth centuries. Michel Foucault discusses some of the changes in how language was viewed in his *The
Order of Things*,[20] pointing out that signs seen as natural, akin with
things, representative of the world, marks of truth, become arbitrary

fictions that may or may not translate that truth. Where knowledge had earlier "always resided in the opening up of a discovered, affirmed, or secretly transmitted sign" (59), where knowledge had divined "signs that were absolute and older than itself" (60), it now became "a network of signs built up step by step in accordance with a knowledge of what is probable" (60). This discovery of probability in place of the absolute, of the necessarily arbitrary sign, has political as well as epistemological implications.

David Wellbery describes this shift in emphasis: "The desacralization of language is the extrication of language from its place within the ceremonies of religious and absolutist authority and its transformation into a medium of communication and debate among equal subjects."[21] This is exactly Krause's project. By publishing several Masonic rites he hopes to desacralize symbols that, hidden and mystified, work to set Masonry up as a particular absolutist power. Contending that the various symbols are arbitrary, he argues (in Wellbery's words), that "it is only the ideas that count and they must exhibit rational coherence if they are to be acceptable" (36). No fear here of writing it, printing it, cutting it "whereby it may become legible . . . whereby the secret Art, may be unlawfully obtained." There simply is no secret art, and no signs that could absolutely reveal it.

Nevertheless, Krause insists on a natural, affective ritual, appealing to both reason and emotion "with the aid of all the fine arts." Much of Masonic appeal comes through the aesthetic quality of its ritual; and it is no accident that literary figures like Friedrich Ludwig Schröder and Adolph Freiherr von Knigge were involved in creating and recreating various rites. In the wake of competing mystical systems, Schröder, one of the century's leading theater directors, simplified the ritual, making it more nearly resemble the original English system. Knigge, a popular novelist, worked in the opposite direction as he added Freemasonic symbolism to the stark, rationalistic system originally outlined by Weishaupt for the Illuminati, stimulating sudden growth in what had been a tiny fraternity. Whether simplifying or embellishing, whether desacralizing or mystifying, whether publishing or keeping secret, the philosophers, novelists, theatrical directors, educators, and others involved in forming Masonic symbolism were all intensely aware of the power residing in the semiotic systems they were creating.

By focusing on the secrecy that separates Freemasonry from the state and the church, and by emphasizing Masonic practices (social equality, insistence on nonsectarianism, practiced democracy, moral criticism of the state) that question all absolutist states and religions, Koselleck and Habermas enable us to see Freemasonry as a particularly influential Enlightenment institution responsible, in part, for political advances made during the eighteenth century. And Krause, with his insistence on Masonic ritual as an arbitrary semiotic system, likewise places Masonry in a desacralized, nonabsolutist context. However, opposing these "enlightened" tendencies toward political and religious "democracy," the various hierarchical systems, unknown heads, fearful oaths, alchemical practices, and esoterically interpreted rituals promising absolute knowledge and power exerted semiotic and political forces of their own.

The political and semiotic oppositions found in eighteenth-century Freemasonry are thematic strands that can be followed from Schiller's *Ghost-Seer* through Goethe's *Wilhelm Meister* and Gutzkow's *Knights of Spirit* to Hofmannsthal's *Andreas*, Mann's *Magic Mountain*, and Grass's *Dog Years*. Before they became operative in major works of fiction, however, these themes were given early literary form by developments in Masonic historiography and the "Masonic novel," developments that, more often than not, left history and fiction productively intertwined.

FREEMASONIC (HI)STORIES

Although the formation of the Grand Lodge in 1717 and Anderson's *Constitutions* of 1723 give Freemasonry convenient and incontrovertible historical monuments, and although historians have many facts at their disposal as they seek to explain the social and political causes and effects of the eighteenth-century institution, much of the century's Masonic activity is inextricably entwined with various legends, stories, novels, and even frauds. Specific stories served specific needs.

Anderson's fanciful history stretching from Adam to his own time (he claims, for example, that "Grand Master Moses often marshaled the Israelites into a regular and general lodge whilst in the wilderness") is an attempt to lend the weight and glory of all known history to the new institution; and as Koselleck suggests, the resulting philosophy of history may have been a factor in challenging absolutist rule. Such a history, however, ultimately satisfies only the credulous. As Fichte pointed out in an exchange of letters with

Ignatius Aurelius Fessler, perhaps the leading Freemason in Berlin as the nineteenth century began, Masonic "history" must be transformed into legend if it is to continue to be taken seriously by intelligent men. Fessler was writing a conjectural history of Freemasonry that linked the order with the Knights Templar and other earlier secret societies; and Fichte suggested that Fessler would do better to write his "history" in such a way that intelligent readers could recognize it as allegory. Fessler admitted that such a fiction, as fiction, would then be historically unassailable; but he insisted on history: "No *Fiction*!"[22]

Unlike Fessler, Lennhoff and Possner's *Internationales Freimaurer-Lexikon* ends its discussion of Anderson's fanciful chronicle by pointing out its fictionality—and also its worth: "It is a chronicle, not history, which Anderson has passed on to us. Whoever discards the good Reverend entirely, wrongs him. And whoever takes him perfectly seriously goes astray" (35). Such an admission of nonhistoricity turns attention away from a potentially ridiculous chronicle and focuses it on a symbolically significant story.

But the desire for supporting, indeed legitimizing, historical roots was strong in the eighteenth century, as it always has been. This is evident in the eight competing, variously influential theories concerning the origin of eighteenth-century Masonry listed in the *Internationales Freimaurer-Lexikon*. The first, and clearly most authentic, is the theory that Freemasonry arose from guilds of operative masons. The second theory, and already the waters grow murky, states that Freemasonry is a continuation of Renaissance scientific academies, German Baroque language societies, the union of academies proposed by Comenius, and so on. According to the third theory, Deists created Freemasonry as an organ to promote their ideas. The fourth theory claims that Freemasonry is a descendent of Rosicrucianism; Elias Ashmole, a leading Rosicrucian and also a Freemason, is the most direct connection between the two. Freemasonry is linked by the fifth theory with the Kabbala, by the sixth with Knights Templar, and by the seventh with ancient secret societies of the Egyptians, Hebrews, and Greeks. The racist eighth theory finds Freemasonic origins exclusively in Germany. Each theory, including the largely historical first, is more or less a fictional construction, and each has its own power over certain types of people. In some ways, the more fictional the story and the more fantastic the claims, the more effect the story has. Of all these theories, for instance, the spurious Rosicrucian and Knights Templar connections evoked the most excitement in the eighteenth century (along with rumors of a Jesuit takeover of the lodges). So in one sense Fessler was justified in rejecting Fichte's recommendation that his "history" be labled story, although in the process Freemasonry lost support from Lessing and Fichte and others desiring a more strict separation of fiction and history. Like many religious innovators, the founders of the most successful Freemasonic branches used Fessler's kind of (hi)story to establish legitimacy and to express their principles. In search of power, they began with Anderson's fanciful chronicles and built ever more elaborate narratives. The history of the Strict Observance, the Freemasonic order established by Karl Gotthelf von Hund, is a good case in point.

Hund claimed, while at the court of the pretender Charles Edward Stuart in 1742, to have been initiated by a mysterious Knight of the Red Feather into an ancient order of Knights Templar. Hund said he had been named the grand master of the province of Germany, and he produced a coded charter to prove his claim. As the system of Strict Observance developed under his leadership, Hund elaborated his fiction, claiming that the order was led by unknown heads who demanded unconditional obedience; and he developed a colorful ritual that emphasized Templar origins and extended hierarchical grades of initiation.

The new order grew steadily until 1763, when a man calling himself Georg Friedrich von Johnson-Fünen appeared in Jena, claiming to be a Scottish noble and head of the *true* order of Knights Templar. He had been sent to Germany, he said, to purify and renew various systems, including Hund's, which had strayed from the true order. Johnson's legitimating story appealed strongly to the same people who had believed Hund's account, and Johnson expanded his claims: the order supposedly controlled vast sums of money; it had a large, secret army preparing for a conquest of Cyprus; and it possessed the alchemical formula for making gold from base metals. Hund consequently found it necessary to place his own order under Johnson's leadership.

But the fictions Johnson had used to displace Hund's own fictions could not long pass muster. Hund eventually learned details of Johnson's past life which disproved his claims, and he challenged him to a duel. Johnson fled, and Hund once again controlled the Strict Observance. For a time the order flourished. Many prominent Masonic lodges affiliated with the Strict Observance, and by 1775 twenty-six German princes belonged to the order. Questions about

Hund's original story began to cause unrest, however, and after he died in 1776 the Strict Observance rapidly lost influence. Finally the assembled Masonic lodges at the Wilhelmsbad Congress (1782) adopted a rectified system dispensing with Hund's higher grades and Templar legends. The story of the Knight of the Red Feather had born tremendous fruit; but as the stakes rose and competing stories grew ever more outrageous, mainstream Freemasonry retreated to stories that seemed historically possible or that could be raised to the figurative level of admitted fiction—a step neither Hund nor his imitators were willing to take.

Hund and his narratively talented allies and rivals dominated organized German Freemasonry during the third quarter of the eighteenth century. But the two true masters of this confidence game were Saint-Germain and Cagliostro.

Saint-Germain, who died in 1784, could tell his story in several languages and buttress it with a seemingly comprehensive knowledge of history. He awakened the desires of his audiences with pretentions of vast alchemical knowledge, including the ability to prolong life indefinitely with a secret liquid he possessed. Freemasonic ties validated these credentials by linking him to legitimate moral and intellectual leaders of the age and simultaneously to the arcane knowledge and practices of the exotic Orient. For several decades he titilated the courts of Europe with the occult possibilities he represented. His successor, "Count" Alessandro Cagliostro (1743–1795), became even more notorious. The story Cagliostro told about himself describes "a mysterious Eastern origin, a tutelary sage, a far-flung journey, initiation into the ancient wisdom of Egypt by the anachronistic priests of the temples, association with the Knights of Malta," and a life spent in study and dissemination of the mysteries.[23] With his alchemy, healings, demonstrations of clairvoyance, and a new system of Egyptian Freemasonry, Cagliostro toured the capitals of Europe and found people everywhere anxious for initiation into his system. In England, France, Holland, Germany, Poland, Russia, and Italy he invariably gathered wealthy disciples and stirred up controversy, most infamously in the affair of the diamond necklace.[24]

While Hund, Saint-Germain, Cagliostro, and others like them were telling their exquisitely crafted stories to build their systems and to gain access to the richest courts of Europe, they were also providing novelists with priceless material. The story they lived and propagated, however, was anything but new. It had been told, for instance, in a seventeenth-century Rosicrucian version by Johann Valentin Andreae.[25]

THE ROSICRUCIAN FICTIONS

Universal and General Reformation of the whole wide world; together with the *Fama Fraternitatis* of the Laudable Fraternity of the Rosy Cross, written to all the Learned and Rulers of Europe; also a short reply sent by Herr Haselmayer, for which he was seized by the Jesuits and put in irons on a Galley. Now put forth in print and communicated to all true hearts.
—Printed at Cassel by Wilhelm Wessel, 1614.

The Rosicrucian manifesto printed under this baroque title —along with its two companion works, *Confessio Fraternitatis* (1615) and *Chemical Wedding of Christian Rosencreutz* (1616)—was interpreted by many of its seventeenth-century readers as an irresistible invitation to join a select, secret society of infinitely wise and benevolent men. Others read it as a utopian fiction, with timely barbs aimed at contemporary science and scheming Jesuits. But received as fiction or fact, *Fama Fraternitatis* caused an uproar in the seventeenth century; and over the next three centuries it served as a model for several real secret societies and for reams of fiction.

Fama Fraternitatis proclaims a general reformation of thought, a marvelous illumination about to transform "the whole wide world." Christian Rosenkreutz, the instigator of these changes, traveled as a young man to the East, where he learned the secrets of the universe. When the scientific community remained closed to his remarkable ideas, Rosenkreutz gathered seven men around him, "all bachelors and of vowed virginity," and together they made a compendium of all "that man can desire, wish, or hope for." They agreed that they would profess no "other thing than to heal the sick, and that *gratis*." They would wear no distinguishing clothing. They would each find a worthy person to succeed them after death. And they would keep the fraternity secret for one hundred years.

Christian Rosenkreutz finally died, not of infirmity, for he had overcome sickness, but "according to the plan of God." Two generations later the narrators of the *Fama* accidentally found Rosenkreutz's grave in a curiously shaped vault behind a hidden door. The room, built to represent the universe, was divided into three symbolically adorned parts. Among the books lining the walls the narrators discovered Christian Rosenkreutz's life story, from which most of the *Fama* narrative is said to be taken. Now in possession of a true compendium of the universe, the newly instructed Rosicrucians have written the *Fama*, they say, to enlighten the world.

Andreae repeatedly referred to the fraternity as ficticious.[26] But despite such direct disavowals, the story was seen as literal truth by many who read it. Learned men began to publish responses as the *Fama* directed, and a flood of Rosicrucian literature appeared.[27] As the Thirty-Years War began to lay waste to German-speaking countries, the number of Rosicrucian publications declined precipitously. But the fiction of a secret brotherhood dedicated to transforming the world was to find new life in the eighteenth century, for motifs introduced in *Fama Fraternitatis* would serve well the needs of later organizers and writers. The secret society founded by a man who gained wisdom in the East, the room whose proportions and contents act as a memory system of all knowledge, the archive with the life history of the order's founder, the simultaneous invisibility and power of the society's emissaries, the desire for public disclosure versus the secrecy dictated by social and political conditions—each of these motifs figure prominently in scores of novels and actual secret societies over the next three centuries. The motifs appeal politically to those limited by various governmental systems; and they appeal semiotically to those who want to teach moral lessons through ritual, to the mystically inclined who find in the symbols keys to supernatural wisdom, and, most important for us, to novelists who wish self-reflexively to examine their own production of signs.

THE FIRST "MASONIC NOVELS"

Fénelon's *Aventures de Télémaque* (1699), describing the educational adventures of Télémaque under the guidance of Minerva (disguised as Mentor), is generally considered the first novel with Masonic ties. Freemasonic allegory often has Minerva leading the Mason along an educational path; and Masons found in Fénelon's description of moral education close parallels to their own practices and aspirations. Soon after Anderson published his *Constitutions*, a more explicitly Freemasonic novel appeared in France: Andrew Michael Ramsay's *Les Voyages de Cyrus* (1727), an admitted imitation of *Télémaque*.[28] Ramsay, a friend of Fénelon and a leading

Freemason, likewise depicted the education of a young, traveling hero as he described Cyrus's initiation into the mysteries of Persian, Egyptian, Pythagorean, and Hebrew secret societies.

In 1730 Terrasson's *Sethos* appeared,[29] openly proclaiming its relationship to both *Télémaque* and *Cyrus*. All three have a moral focus, the preface says, but unlike the previous two, *Sethos* is more than a didactic fiction; it aims to depict the "entire life" of the hero. Whether or not the novel achieves that goal is debatable; but, reiterating and developing figures, themes, and motifs from Andreae's Rosicrucian fictions, the novel had a tremendous impact on Masonic fictions that followed. Any post-1730 work of fiction that describes a ritual education owes at least an indirect debt to Terrasson's novel; and in fact, several actual secret societies have drawn their rituals from this fictional account.

Sethos is a novel in three long volumes, supposedly written by a Greek who lived in Alexandria during the reign of Marcus Aurelius. As the novel commences, Amedes, a member of a powerful secret society of priests, begins to educate Sethos, a young prince whose mother has just died. Following several preliminary tests Amedes finally decides that Sethos is ready for the trials of the great pyramid.

After dark Amedes leads Sethos from the palace to the pyramid. Through a small passageway they reach a seemingly bottomless well, and, climbing a circular stairway, they find a frightening, yet promising inscription:

> Whoever traverses this path alone and without looking back will be purified by fire, water, and air, and if he can overcome the terror of death he will pass from out of the womb of the earth, will see the light again, and will have the right to prepare his soul for revelation of the secrets of the great goddess Isis.

Sethos bravely presses on until he finds piles of wood burning fiercely in a high room. Racing through this dangerous room, he undergoes the promised trial by fire. Next comes the trial by water, a broad canal across which he swims. Then an attempt to open an ivory door sets machinery in motion which raises him into the air— his third trial. Finally the machinery allows him to pass through the door, and he enters a room into which early morning sunlight falls.

Having successfully concluded the trials of fire, water, and air, Sethos is now embraced by the head priest and congratulated. Priests who seem to know everything about him teach him lessons.

34

He learns, for example, that "there is hardly a stronger desire among men than to achieve the honor of being accepted into a select, small society on the basis of merit and virtue." After taking a horrible oath of secrecy, he learns more about life in the pyramid. He sees priests' children participating in an elaborate pedagogical system, a scene reflected in the pedagogical province of Goethe's *Wilhelm Meister.* Those studying to be priests wear black, judges wear red, and physicians dark blue. Sethos is also shown the theatrical tricks used by priests to "oracularly" answer petitioners' questions; and although it originally strikes him as a fraud, he concludes that as pedagogical art it is for the people's ultimate good.

Finally Sethos is introduced to the outside world as an initiate. Wearing the order's distinctive vest he undertakes a long series of adventures, including retaking his family's throne, a political task for which his initiation has prepared him. The various battles and voyages along the African coast are of passing interest and great length; but the political aspect of the secret society through which Sethos regains his power and the exotic symbolic system that teaches moral lessons while uncovering pretended esoteric practices brought the novel a wide readership.

Especially in France, *Sethos* was taken as historically accurate, despite specific disclaimers in the preface which contrast history with fiction. Freemasons were pleased to find supposed origins in Egypt; and some branches of Freemasonry, notably the Misraim system, based their rituals in part on those described in *Sethos.* The imaginative French architect Lequeu found the progression through ritual space described in *Sethos* so intriguing that he made fanciful drawings of the pyramid and the various machines used in the initiation. And the most famous work of art based in part on *Sethos,* Mozart's and Schickaneder's opera *The Magic Flute,* reproduces the trials by fire, water, and air administered by a priestly secret society.[30]

Hundreds of works of fiction followed *Sethos,* especially as the century drew to a close, reflecting the eighteenth-century obsession with Freemasonry. In the following chapters I will take up the most important of these, but first two nearly forgotten texts and a vigorous written debate in a leading journal present interesting case studies in the theological and political uses of Masonic fiction.

Carl Friedrich Bahrdt's demythologizing *Explanation of the Plan and Purpose of Jesus* (*Ausführung des Plans und Zweckes Jesu,* 1784–1792) is a multivolume fictional history of Jesus Christ. After reading his friend Starck's book *On the Old and New Mysteries* (*Über die alten und neuen Mysterien*, 1782), a discussion of contemporary Freemasonry in the context of ancient mysteries, Bahrdt wrote that he thought again of his initiation into Masonry in London, where he was sponsored by Georg Forster and father, and had "the idea that Christ must have had the plan to establish a secret society in order to preserve and transmit to mankind the truth which had been thrust aside by clerics and temple priests."[31]

In his book, after an imaginative account of Jesus' boyhood (lived according to the designs of a secret, enlightened group of men), Bahrdt describes the formation of a secret society around Jesus which aimed to destroy superstition and unite all mankind in a rational faith in God. He explains Jesus' miracles as machinations of this secret society. The feeding of the five thousand, for example, is done by accomplices who supply ever-new baskets of bread from a cave behind Jesus; and after the staged crucifixion, members of the society nurse Jesus back to health so he can appear to have resurrected. Like the priestly oracles in *Sethos*, these "miracles" are wrought to gain power over the superstitious, power that can later be used to wean them from their superstitions. After his resurrection Jesus works quietly in the Grand Lodge, directing the fraternity "until it pleased God to call him."[32]

Paradoxically, Bahrdt's attempt at demythologizing the biblical life of Jesus involves a new myth. Like the conspirators in the novel, he must play on the nonrational sensitivities of his readers to gain the power he needs to direct them to a more rational worldview. As a result, any power the book had toward effecting the more rational view of the Bible Bahrdt desired was at least balanced by its propagation of the new myth of a Freemasonic conspiracy manipulating world history. Two centuries later Günter Grass makes much of this sort of mythical demythologizing.

A second example of the dynamic relationship between Masonic history and fiction can be found in Johann Heinrich Jung-Stilling's autobiography. Having published (with Goethe's help) his sensitive, pietistic *Heinrich Stilling's Youth* (*Heinrich Stillings Jugend*, 1777), *Journies* (*Wanderschaft*, 1778), and *Domestic Life* (*Häusliches Leben*, 1789), having healed hundreds of people of blindness with cataract operations, and having reached out to the pietistically religious in his novel *Homesickness* (*Das Heimweh*, 1794, 1796), Jung-Stilling could open his *Heinrich Stilling's Apprenticeship* (*Heinrich Stillings Lehrjahre*, 1804) in which the following story is told, with the confident phrase: "Dear readers and friends of Stilling."

36

Early in 1796, Stilling writes, he was visited at home by a young, wealthy, well-educated man who claimed that he was there on behalf of a friend suffering from cataracts. Soon, however, the visitor began to cry and then kiss Stilling's hand. "You wrote *Homesickness*?" the young man asked; and when Jung-Stilling said that he had, the still crying young man said: "'You are, then, one of my secret leaders!'" Although *Homesickness*, a defense of monarchies threatened by revolution, indeed portrays the activities of a secret society with secret heads and ties to the Orient, Stilling explained that he was no one's secret leader and, in fact, belonged to no secret society. Thinking this was part of a test, the young man continued to insist, but finally Stilling convinced him. Then came the incredulous question:

> "But tell me, how do you know about the great and honorable league in the Orient which you describe in such detail in 'Homesickness'? You have even exactly determined their meeting places in Egypt, on Mount Sinai, in the Canopic monastery, and under the Jerusalem temple."
>
> Stilling. "I know absolutely nothing about any of that, for these ideas and mental images appeared vividly in my imagination. Thus it is merely fiction, pure fabrication."

The young man continued, telling Stilling about the actual secret society, revealing things, Stilling assures his readers, that he cannot make public. None of it, however, he hastens to point out, had "a relation of the most distant kind to political conditions."[33] Neither Jung-Stilling nor his young visitor would have marveled so at the coincidence of fiction and reality if they had realized that much of what passed for ancient, ritual esoterica had in fact been drawn from the public pages of fictions like *Fama Fraternitatis, Sethos,* and *Homesickness.*

FREEMASONS AND JESUITS IN THE *BERLINISCHE MONATSSCHRIFT* (1783–1796)

Another set of pages helped spread the last of the stories to be discussed in this first chapter. Like the Rosicrucian fictions and *Sethos*, the story had a strong effect on subsequent fiction (especially Schiller's *Ghost-Seer*); like Bahrdt's story, it involves a myth of religious conspiracy; and like Jung-Stilling's, it represents an intriguing interweaving of fact and fiction.

The *Berlinische Monatsschrift,* one of the most widely read German periodicals of the late eighteenth century and a major organ of the Enlightenment, descending from the moral weeklies Habermas discusses as another step toward a public sphere,[34] was edited by Friedrich Gedike and Johann Erich Biester, both members of the Masonic National-Mother-Lodge "Zu den drei Weltkugeln" in Berlin. Prominent contributors to the journal included Moses Mendelssohn, Friedrich Schlegel, and Immanuel Kant, and Masons Friedrich Nicolai, Georg Forster, and Karl Philipp Moritz. Kant's essay "Answer to the Question: What is Enlightenment?" ("Beantwortung der Frage: Was ist Aufklärung?") appeared there in December 1784, after Mendelssohn had written "On the Question: What does it Mean to Enlighten" ("Über die Frage: Was heisst aufklären?") in September of that same year. Enlightenment is a broad program for a journal, but in a preface to the first number the editors proclaimed just that as their aim: "Enthusiasm for truth, passion for the dissemination of useful enlightenment and for the banishment of injurious and erroneous ideas" (Eifer für die Wahrheit, Liebe zur Verbreitung nützlicher Aufklärung und zur Verbannung verderblicher Irthümer).

From the beginning the journal was a lively public forum. Issues, persons, and subjects include a homage to Benjamin Franklin, a report on social security ("Proof, that the Royal Prussian General Widow's-Aid Foundation will not Become Bankrupt Before at Least 1803"), discussions of bees, deaf-mutes, the class system, universities, animal magnetism, and other topics fitting generally under the first two rubrics of the editors' programatic statement: "Enthusiasm for truth" and "passion for the dissemination of useful enlightenment."[35] But the third rubric, "the banishment of injurious and erroneous ideas," proved, finally, the negative heart of the journal.

Several essays in the fourth number (April 1783) show the first tendencies in this direction, arising out of the impulse to expose and ban prejudice, superstition, delusions, and false traditions. "The Moon Doctor in Berlin," for example, is an investigative article aimed at uncovering the natural causes of the so-called miracles performed by an astral healer. Later articles expose treasure hunters, miracle healers, messiahs, and alchemists with single-minded zeal. And in this context, "deviant" offshoots of Freemasonry soon became the journal's driving concern. The Masonry to which Biester, Gedicke, Nicolai, and friends subscribed was closely linked to the government of their fellow Mason Frederick the Great (or "Friedrich August" as a "Masonic Ode" published in the journal in 1784 calls him). As Freemasons, they had sworn to be peaceful subjects of civil authority and to take no part in any conspiracy against that authority; but they also belonged to an institution which, by its very nature, questioned the absolutist state. Made uneasy by that tension and alarmed by anti-Masonic reports like Göchhausen's *Disclosure of the System of the Cosmopolitan Republic* (1780), which called attention to the political potential and alleged aims of the secret society, Biester reacted by latching on to the aspect of Göchhausen's exposé least damaging to his own Freemasonry: Jesuit infiltration of Protestant lodges for religious and political purposes.

In the January 1785 issue, Biester published a "Contribution to the History of Contemporary Secret Proselytization" ("Beitrag zur Geschichte itziger geheimer Proselytenmacherei"), an article describing proselytizing Catholic monks who, incognito, are supposedly gaining control of various Masonic lodges to undermine English and German Protestantism. In July 1785 Christian Garve, a popular philosopher and an early favorite of Schiller's, wrote an almost fifty-page response, "On the Worries of Protestants Concerning the Spread of Catholicism" ("Über die Besorgnisse der Protestanten in Ansehung der Verbreitung des Katholicismus"), addressing his remarks to "Herrn Doktor Biester." Garve argues that the Jesuits have been banned by the Pope since 1773. Why should one fear them now that their public power is gone? Their secret actions are no more frightening than the secrecy of the Freemasons. Secret societies, Garve states finally, be they Jesuit or Freemasonic, will have little actual effect on the affairs of the world. In a thirty-page response, Biester expressed a different opinion, for from his perspective the Jesuits and high-grade Freemasons directly threaten gains made by the Enlightenment.

In the next issue of the journal, Biester printed a fifty-page letter that expresses more worries about Catholic gains in Protestant countries. The letter describes an initiation ceremony, questions the secrets of higher levels of initiation, and discusses the unknown Jesuit heads of secret societies who exploit naive believers for political and religious purposes. The purpose of the letter, he assures his reader, is to return Freemasonry to its original purity. In his introduction to the letter, Biester claimed he was printing the document because he thought people should know about the phenomenon it describes. But then, miscalculating how important the theme was to himself, he wrote that this, in August 1785, would be the last article he prints on the subject.

As early as October of that year there appeared a "New Contribution to Some Knowledge of Different Contemporary Secret Societies" ("Neuer Beitrag zu einiger Kenntniss verschiedener jetzt existirenden Geheimen Gesellschaften"), as well as "Superstition and Enthusiasm as They Act and React on One Another" ("Aberglauben und Schwärmerei in Wirkung und Rückwirkung auf einander"). Introducing the "New Contribution," Biester explained his renewed interest: "The existence of numerous secret societies in D., about which many know nothing and many do not even want to know anything, is, for us, the most important aspect of the essay." In the November issue there are three articles on Jesuits and/or secret societies; in December three more appeared, including another protesting letter from Garve and Biester's fiery answer stating that the Enlightenment must be defended against the Jesuits. From this new beginning, after the judicious attempt to end the discussion, until the journal's final number in December 1796, Biester printed more than thirty articles (several of which run more than a hundred pages) on various secret societies and the malevolent Jesuitical influence on and through these societies.

The fact that *the* Enlightenment journal in Germany would engage in such a substantial crusade against what its editors saw as aberrant forms of Freemasonry indicates the passions the subject aroused. It also attracted parodists. Claiming to be the author of the *Cosmopolitan Republic,* one such author wrote a "disclosure" of the extraordinary Jesuit or Freemasonic influence on everything from the fashionable wearing of wigs (introduced so Jesuits incognito could hide their tonsured heads) to a proof that corsets are a defense against Jesuits.[36] And alongside the historical debates and the parodies, there was also a strong literary response to the theory of Jesuit infiltration of Freemasonry. In the following chapter I discuss how Schiller used the story he read in the pages of the *Berlinische Monatsschrift* to fashion a novel in which he examines the political misuse of art. In many ways Schiller's novel serves as a paradigm for all later novels in which Freemasons play a role, for it features the politics and semiotics this introductory chapter has identified as key to the interdependent relationships between historical and fictional Freemasonry.

CHAPTER TWO

"Art Viewed as an (Im)moral Institution": Schiller's *The Ghost-Seer*

"Das Schlimmste und eigentlich Gottlose an der *Frei-maurerei* ist, dass sie die *Vorsehung* auf Erden spielen wollen."
—Friedrich Schlegel

"I must inform you further," said the tyler, "that our Craft promulgates its teaching not by word only but makes use of certain other means which may perhaps have a more potent effect on the earnest seeker after wisdom and vir-tue than merely verbal explanations. . . . Our Craft fol-lows the usage of ancient societies which explained their teaching through hieroglyphs. A hieroglyph," said the ty-ler, "is the image of an abstract idea, embodying in itself the properties of the thing it symbolizes."
    Pierre knew very well what a hieroglyph was, but he did not venture to speak.
—Tolstoy, *War and Peace*[1]

Schiller's only novel, *The Ghost-Seer* (*Der Geisterseher*), was written to boost circulation of his journal *Thalia*, or so he wrote to his friend Körner. In response to the highbrow material Körner had suggested to him, Schiller listed the proper subjects for a journal: "Cagliostros and Starks, Flamels, ghost-seers, secret chronicles, travel reports, in any case piquant stories, fleeting journies through the contemporary political world and into the ancient world of history—those are ob-jects for journals" (12 June 1788).

41

After Schiller himself so trivially situated his novel, it is no wonder that *The Ghost-Seer* has long been neglected as a minor embarrassment.[2] At best, scholars have labored in introductions or comprehensive surveys to draw wisdom from the novel's "philosophical conversation,"[3] or they have focused on how well Schiller mirrored the times,[4] or they have pointed out the novel's importance in establishing the subgenre of the league novel or *Geheimbundroman*.[5] *The Ghost-Seer* was indeed popular, it did make money for Schiller, it provides a telling depiction of the time, and it certainly occupies a pivotal position in the rise of the league novel. But one of the novel's most significant dimensions, the questions it raises about the morality of art, has been virtually ignored.

Work on *The Ghost-Seer* began in 1786, and the first installment appeared the next year in *Thalia*. That same issue also contained the third act of *Don Carlos*, the last of Schiller's plays before his six-year hiatus in literary production, the six years in which he studied Kant and wrote on aesthetics and history. *The Ghost-Seer* thus stands between a predominantly literary period and an equally distinctive historical/philosophical period in Schiller's life. That chronological position, the admitted use of popular subject matter to sell a journal, and, most important, provocative questions raised in the novel about artists, all point to *The Ghost-Seer* as a key manifestation of Schiller's thoughts on the ambivalent morality of art.[6]

SCHILLER AND FREEMASONRY

These years, as noted in the previous chapter, were marked by a public uproar over the purported Jesuit infiltration of Freemasonic lodges in Protestant Germany. That articles about the subject in the *Berlinische Monatsschrift* strongly influenced *The Ghost-Seer* has been well documented.[7] In lieu of repeating that information, two of Schiller's letters—the first about an early contact with Freemasonry, the second a response to a conversation with one of Europe's leading Freemasons—provide a representative sense for Schiller's Masonic contacts.

Like other influential men of the time, Schiller was marked for membership in the fraternity, as he wrote to Henriette von Wollzogen:

> We once spoke together about Freemasonry. A few days ago a travelling Mason visited me, a man with most extensive knowledge and with a great, hidden influence who told me that I am already on several different Masonic lists, and who implored me to let him know about every step I might take in this capacity; he assures me also, that I have extraordinary prospects in that regard.[8]

The second letter, sent to Körner in 1787 while *The Ghost-Seer* was being written, expresses Schiller's interest in the Masonic activities of Johann Joachim Christoph Bode, a leading Freemason, translator, and publisher of the time, especially Bode's account of Jesuits and Freemasons and the recent politically forced demise of Weishaupt's Illuminati in Bavaria:

> Bode told me that he had brought along something weighty from Paris concerning Freemasonry. He heartily agrees with the Berliners about the threatening danger of Catholicism. . . . The present anarchy of the Enlightenment, he thinks, is primarily the work of Jesuits.
>
> Weishaupt is now the topic of discussion of the whole world. All Masons whom I have yet heard condemn him and want him destroyed socially, without mercy.
>
> Bode sounded me out as to whether I might not want to become a Mason. Here he is thought to be one of the most important in the entire order. What do you know about him?[9]

Schiller never became a Freemason; but as these letters show, he had contact with and a ready interest in the controversies surrounding Freemasonry. In that environment, with a keen sense for public taste, and with questions about his own profession, Schiller wrote *The Ghost-Seer*, a novel fragment in two books.

THE STORY

As the story begins, the Count von O. ., whose memoirs constitute the novel, joins a young Protestant prince in Venice and finds himself immediately involved in a rather perplexing mystery. An Armenian accosts the two men on the street one evening and, just before disappearing, says without context: "He died at nine o'clock." Several days later the prince receives news that a cousin standing between him and the throne died at nine o'clock on the day the Armenian appeared.

Soon thereafter the prince takes part in an elaborate pseudo-Masonic ceremony during which a Sicilian conjures up a ghost. At a crucial moment the Armenian steps in, discloses the séance as a fraud, and delivers the Sicilian to officers of the inquisition. The prince and Count von O. . visit the Sicilian in prison, and he tells them about the Armenian, claiming that the mysterious man has lived everywhere—especially in Egypt, where he gained his boundless wisdom. He is supposedly ageless. Poison, daggers, and fire are said to have no effect on him. He never touches food or women, and he never sleeps. The prince, naturally a little sceptical, asks if the Sicilian has more than second-hand information on this man of marvels. The Sicilian then tells a story of a complicated and skillful confidence scheme broken up by the Armenian in a manner reminiscent of the present case.

The prince detects a serious flaw in the story, and after they leave he lectures the count at length on rational explanations for the mysterious events related by the obviously conniving Sicilian. By now, the narrator writes, the credulous prince has become an outright sceptic, sure of his ability to unmask superstition and fraud.

In the second book the count describes a pseudo-Masonic secret society into which the prince is initiated. Associations there lead him from his once simple mode of existence. Soon the count has to leave Venice, but he continues his account by inserting letters from the Baron von F. . ., who tells of parties, concerts, gambling, and ever greater expenses. When the prince rescues the nephew of a rich and powerful churchman from "certain death" he finds a welcome answer to his money problems; but even so he approaches ruin as he borrows huge sums of money from the grateful uncle and mindlessly gambles them away.

Finally the prince falls in love with a beautiful woman he knows only by sight, and he pursues her madly. The Baron writes frantically about lost letters, intrigues, and radical changes in the prince, and he calls for help. The count rushes back to Venice, but he arrives too late. A letter informs him that the prince is a newly christened Catholic, embraced now by the scheming arms of the Armenian. Only now does he sense that the Armenian has directed the actions of the Sicilian, the beautiful woman, the secret society— in fact, nearly every influence on the prince throughout the book— all in an effort to make the young ruler a Catholic and thus gain influence in another Protestant country. The novel ends a fragment as the count promises to tell the story in full.

44

THE LEAGUE NOVEL

The story just related could be straight from the pages of the *Berlinische Monatsschrift*. A Jesuit with Freemasonic connections and uncanny abilities craftily leads a Protestant prince away from his religion and political indifference to scepticism, to a will to power, and finally into the Catholic church. The novel fragment proved extremely popular, as numerous editions, both legal and pirated, show. Friedrich Wilhelm II, with his penchant for ghosts and mysteries, never forgave Schiller for leaving the novel a fragment; and when it became apparent that Schiller had no desire to finish it, several lesser writers stepped in to try.[10]

Besides those continuations, various popular novels of the time, as Marianne Thalmann has shown, slavishly borrow the Armenian's characteristics for their mentor figures: flashing eyes, non-European appearance and Eastern education, powerful presence, and paradoxical traits.[11] Although not central to even the worst of these novels, such motifs often accompany a common theme—the education, for better or worse, of a young man at the hands of powerful emissaries of a secret society. This is, of course, the story of the Rosicrucian fictions, of much Freemasonic ritual, and of various confidence men.

Although *The Ghost-Seer* (1787–1789) was not the first eighteenth-century literary work to exploit this theme (cf. also novels by Terrasson, Stark, Knigge, Jung-Stilling, Bahrdt, Wieland, and Moritz in preceding years), it acted as the primary model and catalyst for the flood of novels that began to appear even before Schiller brought his novel to its fragmentary close. The following list contains representative novels that incorporate the theme and motifs of what has come to be known as the *Geheimbundroman*, *Bundesroman*, or league novel:[12]

1787–1789 Schiller, *Der Geisterseher*
1787–1791 Meyern, *Dya-Na-Sore* (Schiller reviewed this very critically in the *Allgemeine Literatur-Zeitung* in 1788)
1789 Naubert, *Hermann von Unna*
1789–1792 Fessler, *Marc-Aurel*
1790–1793 Tschink, *Geschichte eines Geistersehers*
1791 Wieland, *Peregrinus Proteus*
       Mozart and Schickaneder, *Die Zauberflöte*
1791–1792 Grosse, *Der Genius*
1793 Jean Paul, *Die unsichtbare Loge*

1793–1794   Hippel, *Kreuz- und Querzüge des Ritters A.—Z.*
1794–1795   Vulpius, *Aurora*
1795   Tieck, *Abdallah*
1795–1796   Goethe, *Wilhelm Meisters Lehrjahre*
             Tieck, *William Lovell*
1796   Follenius, *Der Geisterseher* (continuation of Schiller's novel)
1797–1799   Hölderlin, *Hyperion*
1799   Wieland, *Agathodämon*
1800–1803   Jean Paul, *Titan*

This partial list represents well the rash of league novels appearing in the twelve years following publication of *The Ghost-Seer*.[13] There is no claim here that Jesuitical and Masonic secret societies and their emissaries dominate these works, although some slavishly follow what has already become a pattern; but in each novel a secret society acts in some way to guide the hero through an emissary or emissaries corresponding to the Armenian. It seems natural that popular novels of the time would exploit this sensational topic. Why, however, would Wieland, Jean Paul, Tieck, Hölderlin, Goethe, and Schiller use the characters, motifs, and themes of this new subgenre in their more serious fiction? The next chapter will take up the question concerning Goethe; but first, just what drew Schiller to the specific material of *The Ghost-Seer*, besides the practical considerations already mentioned?

THE CONFIDENCE MAN AS ARTIST

Even on first reading one recognizes that *The Ghost-Seer* is about power: a secret emissary of the Catholic church, with unlimited resources, forcefully converts a Protestant prince in an apparently successful attempt to gain power in a Protestant country. But more specifically, the novel focuses on *how* the emissary gains control of the prince, a point largely ignored in criticism. What really interests Schiller here is the artistry of the fraud, for the persuasive methods employed in winning over the prince involve the very theatrical, rhetorical media in which Schiller himself had been working for a decade.

Several years after *The Ghost-Seer* was written, Schiller's essay "On the Necessary Limits in the Use of Beautiful Forms" ("Über die notwendigen Grenzen beim Gebrauch schöner Formen," 1795) directly questioned the place of art in the moral realm:

> The moral destiny of the human race demands total independence of the will from all influence of sensuous stimuli, and taste, as we know, works unceasingly to make the bond between reason and the senses more and more intimate. Taste does thereby bring the desires to refine themselves and become more in harmony with the demands of reason, but even out of this can arise, in the end, great danger for morality. (NA XXI, 21–22)

Of course, Schiller elsewhere deals with a positive moral role of art —in, for example, "The Stage Viewed as a Moral Institution" ("Die Schaubühne als eine moralische Anstalt betrachtet," 1784), or "On the Aesthetic Education of Humanity in a Series of Letters" ("Über die ästhetische Erziehung des Menschen in einer Reihe von Briefen," 1795). There is no need to take issue with that. But as the statement just quoted demonstrates, and as the following interpretation makes clear, Schiller was also concerned with the powerful negative force art can exert.[14]

One need only compare the Prince's simple life-style with the prodigious artistic skill of those plotting against him to recognize that this novel pits a rather simple man against artistic genius. In the terms of "The Necessary Limits" essay, the prince's already weak moral will, under extraordinary attack by sensuous artistic forces, loses its power as the novel progresses.

Early descriptions of the prince depict him as modest, retiring, continent, politically unambitious, self-sufficient, and a man of few words.[15] The people banded together to gain control of the prince, however, have a different set of proclivities. The Armenian, for example, far from retiring, exerts a powerful influence on everyone around him: "'The physiognomy of the latter had something very unusual which drew our attention to itself. Never in my life have I seen so many *features* and so little *character*, so much seductive well-meaning dwelling together with so much repelling frost in *one* human face'" (NA XVI, 53–54). Note here especially the phrases referring to this man as *formally* powerful but lacking *substance*: "so many *features* and so little *character*." The straightforward prince, "[who] wanted to live by and for himself" ([der] sich selbst leben wollte), at least as the novel begins, thus contrasts severely with the Armenian, the ultimate artist, for whom pliable appearance means power.

The men and women who aid the Armenian share his ability to control form and manipulate reality; and the prince responds to the features, the dress, the lingustic facility, and the other formal attributes of the men who seek to influence him. Even the reading material he chooses, or is led to choose, formally undermines his already suspect powers of reasoning: "the blinding style of the one pulled his imagination in that direction, while the sophistry of the other entangled his reason" (NA XVI, 106).

The emphasis on form continues as the prince is drawn into a secret society. Early in the story several servants of the state inquisition mysteriously lead the prince to the canal, transport him in a gondola, blindfold him before he gets out, lead him up a large stairway and through a long winding passageway until he reaches twenty-six steps which take him down into a hall where the blindfold is removed. There sits a circle of "honorable old men, all dressed in black, the entire hall hung with black tapestries" (NA XVI, 50). Such a ritual route—with blindfolding, long hall, numbered steps, and a circle of men in a symbolically decorated hall—proves a major factor in my interpretation of two of Goethe's novels. Here it serves as an early acclimatization of the prince to the powerful symbols of Freemasonry. This is not to say that the prince is standing in a Freemasonic lodge but rather that these men of the state inquisition impress the prince with "Masonic" ritual in order to make the supposedly enlightened prince more susceptible to the elaborate ritual with which the Sicilian conjures up the ghost.

In that scene, which follows shortly, the prince and his companions take off their shoes and outer clothing and enter a circle drawn with charcoal on the floor:

> An altar, hung with black cloth, was errected in the center of the circle, and under the altar a rug of red satin was spread. A Chaldean Bible lay opened on the altar near a skull, and a silver crucifix was fastened to it. . . . Like us, the conjurer was dressed, but barefoot. Around his naked neck he wore an amulet on a chain of human hair, around his loins he had tied a white apron which was marked with secret chiffres and symbolic figures. (NA XVI, 60)

The disrobing, Bible, skull, and symbolic apron of this scene are clearly Freemasonic. The Sicilian later admits that these ritual details were designed "'merely to give the performance yet more ceremony and to excite your imagination through the unusual'" (NA XVI, 73).[16]

Thus the "secret ciphers and symbolic figures" that make up Freemasonry's semiotic system are used to excite the prince's imagination. The signs promise a (nonexistent) mystery behind themselves while concealing the real mystery of political manipulation.

Describing another scheme in which he was involved, the Sicilian mentions a second way Freemasonry has been useful to him. He first gained some fame among Masonic lodges, he reports, and then used that fraternal base to increase the trust of the old man who was his mark (NA XVI, 81). The prince now has two examples, one semiotic and one fraternal, of how the Sicilian has used Freemasonry to influence him and others. Nonetheless, he unconcernedly lets himself be led into a secret society that further binds him to the Armenian:

> a certain closed society, named the "Bucentauro," with the outward appearance of a noble, rational freedom of intellect, promoted the most unbridled licence of opinion and of morals. . . . The society prided itself on the finest tone and the most cultivated taste, and in fact really had this reputation in all of Venice. This, as well as the *appearance* of equality which prevailed there, attracted the Prince irresistibly. (NA XVI, 106; emphasis added)

It is clear that in this society "the necessary limits in the use of beautiful forms" have been crossed, that the "influence of sensuous stimuli" has affected the prince's tender morality. Freemasonry's enlightenment and equality, which helped undermine the very authoritarian political and religious system the Armenian wants to reaffirm, are now the means to attract the prince. But in the Bucentauro the *semblance* of enlightenment and the *appearance* of equality are masks for unchecked immorality. The effect on the prince is disastrous, according to the Count von O. .: "But already, through the mere familiarity with this class of people and with their ways of thinking . . . the pure, beautiful simplicity of his character and the delicacy of his moral feelings were lost" (NA XVI, 107). As a result, the prince loses his sense of self: "He feels that he is not what he otherwise was—he seeks himself—he is dissatisfied with himself" (NA XVI, 120). Now that the prince has been maneuvered from his original wish "to live by and for himself" (NA XVI, 45) to the declaration "everything that distracted me from myself was welcome" (NA XVI, 125), he is ready for the final twist in the Armenian's plot, a scene in which the prince's aesthetic education reaches a climax, in which he meets the last conspirator, a woman whose beautiful form will overwhelm him.

About to leave Venice and finally to escape the intrigues there, the prince enters a church one conspirator has pointed out and there undergoes a grand aesthetic experience.[17] Already stimulated by that vision, by the beauty surrounding him, he finds a beautiful woman praying in a side chapel and is overwhelmed. Later, hoping to help the prince gain some distance from the event, Baron von F. . . suggests that the prince had been understandably susceptible to the woman's beauty: "'what was more natural than that your inflamed imagination created something ideal, something divinely perfect out of it?'" (NA XVI, 133). This tendency toward (unearthly) perfection, analogous to the expectation of final disclosure of mystery set up by the séance and the accompanying secret Masonic symbols, finally proves the prince's undoing. Responding to a question about why he wants to see her again, the prince expresses how strongly this woman's *beauty* affects him and how little he cares who she *is*: "'I shall see her. I shall seek out her residence. I shall discover who she is.—Who she is?—What can that matter to me? What *I saw*, made me happy'" (NA XVI, 135). This final turn from being to appearance results, of course, from one more strand in the web of artifice the Armenian has spun around the prince, for the woman too is his tool. The Freemasonic/Jesuitical characters who so skillfully carry out this plot have full confidence in their artistic abilities and the reasons for their performance. The Sicilian, for instance, insists that "doubt of my art . . . was the only obstacle which I did *not* have to overcome" (NA XVI, 844). But how must the artist feel who portrays such Machiavellian use of art? How does Schiller feel about his own novel? The answer, as well as the question, lies ultimately in *The Ghost-Seer* itself. But first, a passage from another story illuminates Schiller's views on history and art during this time of transition from belles lettres to history and philosophy.

THE ARTIST AS CONFIDENCE MAN

"The Criminal Because of Lost Honor—A True Story" ("Der Verbrecher aus verlorener Ehre—Eine wahre Geschichte") appeared in Schiller's *Thalia* in 1786, the same year he began writing *The Ghost-Seer*. The introductory paragraphs ask how the enormous gap between the strong passion of the acting character and the quiet mood of the reader can be lessened so as to avoid a negative reaction. Two possibilities exist, the narrator states:

Either the reader must grow warm like the hero, or the hero must grow cold like the reader.

I know that of the best writers of history of recent time and of antiquity many have held to the first method and have seduced the heart of their reader through overpowering rhetoric [durch hinreissenden Vortrag]. But this style is a usurpation of the rights of the (creative) writer and wrongs the republican freedom of the reading public, which has the right to judge for itself; it is, at the same time, an infringement on the rights of genre, for this method belongs exclusively and specifically to the orator and poet. Only the latter method remains for the writer of history. (NA XVI, 8)

At a time when Schiller was choosing history over literature, this identification of "overpowering rhetoric" with an attack on republican freedom and its relegation to orators and poets is telling.[18] The phrase "overpowering rhetoric" has close parallels in *The Ghost-Seer's* repeated references to the confidence-artists' powerful but morally questionable facility with language:

an heroic confidence in himself and an overpowering eloquence [eine alles niedersprechende Beredsamkeit]. (NA XVI, 112)

Imagine the most enchanting figure . . . a flattering tone of voice, the most fluent eloquence [die fliessendste Beredsamkeit]. (NA XVI, 118)

She passed away like a saint, and her final, dying eloquence [Beredsamkeit] exhausted itself leading her beloved on the path which she was traversing to heaven. (NA XVI, 158)[19]

Such persuasion destroys the prince's republican freedom in favor of "Catholic" despotism. But these artistic confidence men and women have no monopoly on morally reprehensible rhetoric. The narrators who tell the story are just as guilty.

The novel's opening paragraph, from the pen of the Count von O. ., inadvertently reveals similarities between his project and the fraud being perpetrated in the story he tells:

I am recounting an event which will seem unbelievable to many, and of which I was, for the most part, myself an eyewitness. . . . [It is] a contribution to the history of fraud and of errors of the human spirit. . . . Pure, strict truth will guide my pen; for when these pages appear in the world, I will no longer exist and will stand neither to gain nor to lose through the report which I am making. (NA XVI, 45)

Comparing this statement of purpose with the Sicilian's assertions concerning his own clever story, one finds some surprising congruences:

> [Count von O. .] I am recounting an event which will seem unbelievable to many, and of which I was, for the most part, myself an eyewitness. . . .
> [Sicilian] . . . so I want to recount to you a peculiar event concerning this Armenian, of which I was an eyewitness.

Both stories indeed recount a noteworthy event, but the Sicilian dissembles throughout his story, and the count is hardly truthful about how much of the event he saw himself, for almost the entire second half of the story is told in letters by a friend of the count. The similarities continue, for where the count claimed that he had nothing to gain by publishing his account, the Sicilian says, "'I am ready to answer, for I have nothing more to lose.'"

The Sicilian's statement is a lie, for his imprisonment is nothing but a ploy to allow him to tell the prince his story. The count's claim of disinterestedness is also less than true. He knows well that prizes remain to be won after death, especially in the literary world, for he has in hand the Baron von F. . .'s report on a conversation with the prince in which they discussed "planting seeds for the future" (NA XVI, 124, 161) and also spoke of the immortality achieved by Lycurgus, Socrates, and Aristides (NA XVI, 162).[20]

Once it is clear that the Count von O. . and the Sicilian are involved in the same tricky business as they tell their respective stories, there is good reason to examine the count's motives. The count reveals his purpose when he states that he wants to defend and purify the prince's historical image by exposing the extraordinary plot against him (NA XVI, 102). He wants to "guide justice," to change the world's image of his dearest friend (a man the reader recognizes as weak, easily swayed, fickle, conceited, disloyal, and an enthusiast who lets himself be "misled" into commiting a political crime against his own family). After observing powerful artists working to change the prince's beliefs, can the reader now fail to see similar forces at work in this report from the Count von O. .?[21] The count wrote as he began that his readers would be amazed at the "peculiarity of the *means*" and the "boldness of the goal" which the characters use and pursue in the course of the story. As his narrative unfolds, the count does disclose the artistic methods the conspirators employ in their plot, but he also unwittingly reveals his own clever narrative means. And while he portrays the conspirators' cunning goal, he simultaneously exposes his own "enlightened" bias against Freemasonry and its offshoots.

When, in the opening paragraph, the count calls his work "a contribution to the history of fraud and of errors of the human spirit," he sets himself up as an enlightener á la Nicolai and Biester. As noted in the first chapter, Biester proclaimed a similar goal for the *Berlinische Monatsschrift*: "banishment of injurious and erronious ideas." In practice this goal soon led Biester to a fanatical crusade against Jesuitical Freemasonry; and Hans Heinrich Borcherdt ascribes this same paranoia to Schiller:

> Jesuitism is for Schiller an intellectual and social form that, like the courtly element in "Kabale und Liebe," must be opposed in its inner mendacity. Also making this necessary was the union of the Jesuits with the magicians and secret societies. . . . Thus originated the beginning of the "Ghost-Seer," with the intention of holding up a mirror to that time and showing it where it would arrive if it would continue along that path, thowing itself credulously into the arms of frauds like Cagliostro, Schrepfer and Saint Germain. (NA XVI, 392)

There is little doubt that Schiller was concerned with the Jesuits and their excesses. *Don Carlos* and *The Ghost-Seer* both manifest his preoccupation with the subject during these years. But a jump from that recognition of interest and concern to a statement like Borcherdt's in which Schiller supposedly wrote the novel to warn against the wicked plots of Jesuitical Freemasons misses a major point of the novel. For the Count von O. ., not Schiller, hates Jesuits and Freemasons and devotes his memoirs to defaming them. That can be made clear by focusing for a moment on a few specific references to Freemasonry.

After the count's opening paragraph and a second paragraph in which he explains how he came to live in Venice, he sets out to describe the prince in some detail. Two paragraphs portray a man with strengths and weaknesses: the weaknesses allow the manipulations to follow; the strengths provide a firm basis for the count's loyalty. The whole description ends with a very short paragraph admitting that the prince was once a religious enthusiast but abruptly denying that he was ever a Freemason: "He never became a Freemason, as far as I know" (NA XVI, 6). Why this as the closing statement (for the moment) about the prince's character? Why does the count find it necessary to assert here that the prince was never a Freemason?

Richard Weissenfels refers to this as "a defence of Freemasonry in Körner's, Biester's, and Bode's sense" (SA II, 417). In other words, the Enlightenment Freemasonry to which Schiller's friends belonged was to be spared the stigma of identification with the Jesuitical secret society portrayed in the novel. But when one looks at the Count von O. . as a prejudiced observer, when one recognizes his wish to clear the prince of as many embarrassing entanglements as possible, the denial takes on quite another meaning. The rest of the story shows the prince drawn, in fact, ever closer to the heart of Jesuitical Freemasonry. Hedging against that reality, the count wants to deny as far as possible any involvement the prince may have had with Freemasonry.

Later, after admitting that the prince indeed became a member of Bucentauro, the count hastens once again to save his prince's reputation: "The society had its secret degrees, and I want to believe, considering the Prince's honor, that he was never deemed worthy of the most inner sanctum" (NA XVI, 107). As he promised in the beginning, the Count von O. . writes here and elsewhere in his memoirs to purify the prince's reputation and to disclose the hated Jesuitical and Freemasonic conspiracy which leads him astray. Despite the count's repeated protestations of noninvolvement, however, it is clear that the prince is overwhelmed by the artistry of Freemasonry.

As stated, the bias against Jesuitical Freemasonry was the Count von O. .'s, not Schiller's. Although little has been made of the conventional separation of author and narrator in previous readings of *The Ghost-Seer*, it is of utmost importance in this interpretation that seeks to read the novel as a comment on art as an immoral institution. *The Ghost-Seer* has, in fact, multiple narrators. As already pointed out, the Count von O. . promises to tell a true story "of which I was, for the most part, myself an eyewitness" (NA XVI, 45). Early in his tale, however, he must let the Sicilian speak. The Sicilian, in almost the same words, likewise promises a true story by virtue of having been an eye witness. Not long thereafter the Count von O. . admits that at this point he had to leave Venice and that the rest of the story will come through citations from letters written to him by the Baron von F. . . In turn, large parts of the baron's account are retellings of stories related by the prince (his "vision" of the beautiful woman in the church), by Civitella (his observation of the scene between the woman and the Armenian), and by Biondello (whose story "proves" what a faithful servant he is). And as if this chasm between deed and final telling were not already wide enough, an editor of the Count von O. .'s memoirs also makes himself known, as in these two examples: *"From the memoires"* (NA XVI, 45), or "—the Count von O. . continues—" (NA XVI, 102). Finally, one more narrator appears at the end of the original, long version of the philosophical conversation, signing a footnote "S" (NA XVI, 184). This ever expanding string of people bent on telling a true story about events they saw with their own eyes effectively removes the reader four and even five times from the event.[22] "S," a narrator, the Count von O. ., and the Sicilian—or later "S," a narrator, the Count von O. ., the Baron von F. . ., and the prince form chains so uncertain as to give certain pause to any reader.[23] Although the reader inevitably senses a distance from the actual events, the various narrators work hard to relieve that unease and lead onward. They claim to be eyewitnesses, promise truth, and awaken a host of expectations that keep the reader following their story in search of satisfaction. And while the Baron von F. . ., the Count von O. ., S., and the other narrator play on the reader's sensibilities, the Sicilian, the Armenian, Biondello, Civitelli, and the beautiful woman spin out a fiction for the prince.

One of their most effective ploys is to stimulate a series of expectations in him, which they themselves cleverly fulfill. This sequence of expectation and fulfillment, as it acts on both prince and reader, provides a final insight into the morality and proper use of art. The Armenian first raises an expectation in the prince by mysteriously stating—"Um neun Uhr ist er gestorben." With no context, the prince can only wait until a letter arrives confirming that his cousin died on that day at that time. Next the Sicilian promises to produce the ghost of the friend, who, on his death bed, had called the prince to him and said: "'I shall not see my fatherland again, and thus you will learn a secret to which no one but I has the key. In a monastery on the Flemish border lives a ——'—here he died. The hand of death cut the thread of his speech; I would like to have him here and to hear the continuation" (NA XVI, 58). The prince wants to know how this story ended, he wants the fragment made whole, and he also wants his wish to see a ghost fulfilled. The Sicilian obliges and conjures up a ghost, which begins the story anew: "'In a monastery on the Flemish border lives ——'" At this moment, however, a second ghost appears and interrupts the scene.

The second ghost finishes the twice-broken story, giving the prince the answers he wants; but he also leaves him with an enigmatic warning, thus beginning the cycle anew.

The prince has longed for knowledge beyond rationality, for certainty beyond the grave (in his desire to see a ghost and to know the conclusion of his dying friend's story), and through their elaborate fiction the Sicilian and the Armenian have heightened his desire and then provided such "knowledge." The entire process is closely tied to storytelling, as the prince's susceptibility to the flow of a story demonstrates. When the Sicilian momentarily breaks off his account, the prince can scarcely contain himself: "a shudder of expectation arrested our breath——" (NA XVI, 87). What the prince wants above all else, is closure, finality, fulfillment, whether rational or irrational, whether true or false, whether moral or immoral.

But all the satisfactions attained in the novel grow out of artificial constructs; all closure is fraudulent. The stories begin within the plot constructed by the Armenian and his friends, and the endings are all part of their scheme. Contrary to that tendency, however, the novel itself "ends" without closure. Its final phrase arouses expectations that are never fulfilled: "At the bed of my friend I finally heard the unprecedented story" (NA XVI, 159).[24]

Surely the Count von O. . is not to blame for the lack of closure here. His strongest desire is to exonerate the prince by disclosing the perfidy of Jesuitical Freemasons. He gains nothing by cutting off his story, and in fact this break causes him to lose power over his reader (the power to influence, the power to uncover the full plot and lead to perfect belief). Just as the prince has only been led part way toward the Armenian's goal (there remain, perhaps, a family murder and the taking of the throne), the reader too must be drawn to the end of the plot. So who cuts off the story here, and why?

I do not intend to suppress evidence that Schiller meant "to continue [the novel] further" (SA II, XXXI), although the reader should be aware by now that my interpretation has its own bias and that evidence is being manipulated to a calculated end. But the internal evidence heretofore cited gives good reason to conclude that Schiller (as opposed to the various narrators) meant, for either artistic or antiartistic reasons, to leave the novel a fragment. He was, as Lotte had prophesied, "besieged for the continuation" ("um die Fortsetzung bestürmt," SA II, XXXVII); even princes(!) pressed him for a

continuation. But after so carefully exposing a fatal desire for closure and so fully undermining those who provide such fulfillment,
how could he seriously consider continuing the story?

A final clue as to Schiller's motivation lies in the original
philosophical conversation between the prince and the Baron von
F. . ., a passage written at a time when Schiller claimed to have lost
interest in the story. The conversation is very long and seems un-
necessarily tedious in its context. Besides that, as others have
pointed out (NA XVI, 394), the ideas of the second half of the conversation are such as to lead the prince out of his spiritual slavery,
not further into it as continuation of the novel would require. Recognizing both of these facts, Schiller severely cut the conversation
in the second book edition (1792) and further cut it for the third
(1798). The following passage, then, originally attributed to the
Prince, was subsequently cut as unnecessary and/or not in character.

The Baron von F. . . has just commented on the utter perfection of God's creation, and the prince answers:

> That upon which *you* and *others* base your hopes, that very thing
> has overthrown my own—this very sensed perfection of things. If
> everything were not so resolved in and of itself, if I could only see
> even a single disfiguring splinter rising out of this beautiful circle,
> that would, for me, prove immortality. But everything, everything
> that I see and take notice of falls back to this *visible* middlepoint,
> and our most noble intellectuality is a so absolutely necessary ma-
> chine to drive this wheel of transitoriness. (NA XVI, 183)

Neither the Armenian nor the Count von O. . has spared any effort
to create a perfectly closed and affective system. But such perfection, the argument goes here, necessarily has an end. Any end can
be *seen*. Closure is effable. Preferable to this finite "perfection" is a
fragment, an unclosed system that allows for progression, that pro-
vokes questions and thoughts and learning. That *The Ghost-Seer*
remains a fragment reflects Schiller's commitment to work against
the grain of the characters and narrator he has created.

This leads finally back to Schiller's decision to feature the
myth of Jesuit infiltration of Masonic lodges. The myth itself grew
out of a desire to explain bewildering political, social, and intellectual changes in the latter part of the eighteenth century, the
"anarchy of the Enlightenment" as Schiller describes it in his discussion of Bode. The most simple explanation of the threatening

changes was that someone had planned them, that a secret society had conspired to radically alter the course of history.[25] This is, of course, precisely what the Count von O. . would have the reader believe about the altered course of the prince's life, and his warnings concerning the Jesuitical and Freemasonic machinations of the Armenian and his friends take the same form as the conspiracy theory. The result is a false sense of knowledge, of closure, of satisfaction of desire.

The Freemasonry Biester and friends defended was a bastion of the Enlightenment, while the new, high-grade, Jesuit-inspired systems were seen as enemies. In Schiller's story the Armenian and his coconspirators indeed use Freemasonry's organization and semiotic system to disabuse the prince of Enlightenment ideals. But Schiller also exposes the conspiracy theory propagated by the narrators (and Biester), a theory that fixes blame on Jesuits and draws attention away from an even more accute problem: the prince's (and more generally, eighteenth-century society's) absolute need for closure, a need easily manipulated by artists and confidence men. Freemasonry may indirectly undermine an absolutist political system; but as Schiller demonstrates here, in its secrecy and gradually unfolding ritual, it also plays on a very human desire for closure. Such closure, politically speaking, is exemplified by the absolutist system the Armenian brilliantly reestablishes.

Setting out to write about an immoral, directly political use of art, Schiller found a perfect vehicle in the Freemasonry attacked in the *Berlinische Monatsschrift*, for it featured a symbolic system employed for political ends. By focusing on the use of such symbols, by identifying his narrators with the Masonic and Jesuitical confidence artists and thus calling art into question, by pointing to conspiracy theories as satisfying but empty solutions, by leaving his own work a fragment, and finally by turning away from "immoral art" for nearly six years to study and write philosophy and history, Schiller proved his dedication to the "republican freedom" of the reading public.

CHAPTER THREE

Ritual Routes in
Wilhelm Meister's Travels

Des Maurers Wandeln / Es gleicht dem Leben.
—Goethe, "Symbolum"

Welch ein schönes Symbol des immerthätigen aber zu-
gleich mit Gefahren umringten Lebens, sind diese Reisen
mit dem auf die Brust gekehrten tödtlichen Stahl.
—Karl Philipp Moritz,
Fragmente aus dem Tagebuche eines Geistersehers

Karl Philipp Moritz published his "Masonic novel" *Andreas Hartknopf* in 1786, the year before Schiller's *Ghost-Seer* began to appear.
Like the other authors who concern us here, Moritz was not primarily interested in holding up a mirror to contemporary Freemasonry,
but found the fraternity a convenient vehicle for expressing other
concerns: "The author of *Andreas Hartknopf* did not merely . . .
choose the form of a novel to clothe certain concepts of Freemasonry, but *the Freemasonic in his book is itself only clothing* by which
he *wanted to disseminate . . . certain, still much misunderstood
truths.*"[1] That precisely describes Schiller's novel, which depicts
high-grade Freemasonry because its paradigmatic ritual, like much
art, denies a democratic arbitrariness and promises mystery and authoritarian closure. *The Ghost-Seer* is not about Freemasons, but
rather the production of signs, and in this it is closely related to *Wilhelm Meister*, both the *Apprenticeship* and the *Travels*, for Goethe's
novels likewise use Freemasonry to examine arbitrary and natural
figures.

59

A poem introducing the 1821 version of *Wilhelm Meister's Travels* describes writing and reading the novel in terms of unearthing treasure, smelting metals, and coining coins:

Und so heb' ich alte Schätze,
Wunderlichst in diesem Falle;
Wenn sie nicht zum Golde setze,
Sind's doch immerfort Metalle.
Man kann schmelzen, man kann scheiden,
Wird gediegen, lässt sich wägen,
Möge mancher Freund mit Freuden
Sich's nach seinem Bilde prägen![2]

And so I raise old treasures,
Most curious in this case;
If [I] do not "count" them gold,
   [settle them out, metallurgically, so that gold
   remains; write or print them so they become gold][3]
They are still metals.
One can smelt, one can separate,
Becomes pure, can be weighed,
May many a friend joyfully
Coin it himself in his own image.

Besides offering a delightful invitation to a plurality of readings, the poem presents a novelist *cum* treasure hunter seemingly untroubled at the thought that his treasure may not prove gold. The unexpected modesty can be tentatively explained by a statement about alchemy and gold in Goethe's *Theory of Colors (Farbenlehre)*. The alchemical search for gold, he writes there, is "the misuse of the genuine and true, a leap from the idea . . . to reality." In Goethe's opinion, there is nothing intrinsically wrong with a desire for gold, unless, that is, one falls prey to the alchemist's promise to spring supernaturally from the idea to reality. To temper such an impatient desire for gold, Goethe suggests "the highest education,"[4] an education thematized on the first pages of the *Travels*.

As the novel opens, Wilhelm's son Felix picks up a stone and turns to ask his father:

"What is this stone called, Father?" the boy said. "I don't know," replied Wilhelm. "Is that gold that gleams in it so?" said the former. "It is not gold!" replied the latter, "and I remember that people call it fool's gold [cat's gold, *Katzengold*]." "Katzengold!" said the boy smiling, "and why?" "Probably because it is deceitful and people believe that cats too are deceitful." (HA, VIII, 7)

The gold of the discussion between Wilhelm and Felix (and of both the poem and the passage on alchemy) is unreal or at least unattainable. Education—analogical education like that given here—is the real treasure. This disclosure leaves Felix holding a worthless stone, but he has had a worthwhile lesson in simile. "I will make a note of that," he says.[5] The exchange contains a second lesson as well, for although the discussion of names and analogy proves more important than the supposed gold, without the "gold" there would have been no analogy. The novel will prove full of similar "old treasures," treasures the reader must simultaneously suspect as fool's gold and use metaphorically.

The poem about the novel as treasure is deleted in the novel's 1829 version. In its stead appear two scenes that similarly feature the novelist as treasure hunter or the novel as treasure. Early in the book, Fitz leads Wilhelm, Felix, and Jarno to a charcoal burner's where "a peculiarly suspicious group" gathers around. The next morning Jarno takes Fitz to task for his acquaintance with one of these men: "'the tall, very last one, the one who kept writing signs in the sand and whom the others treated with some esteem, was certainly a treasure hunter with whom you are conspiring'" (HA, VIII, 41). This last man is the new embodiment of the poem's treasure-hunting novelist. In the poem the metals could be formed (or interpreted) at will; and here the treasure hunter writes his signs in the ever-shifting sand. From the beginning, then, it would seem that this novel thematizes the arbitrariness of language. But there is a second side to the problem as well.

Jarno's further discussion with Fitz reveals that the treasure hunter has bought cross stones (*Kreuzsteine*, chiastolite) to help him find treasure (or, as novelist, to help him find the "old treasures" he needs as building blocks for his novel). Fitz describes the stones as "a precious mineral, without it no treasure can be raised; I get paid very well for a small piece" (HA, VIII, 42). On one level, the cross stones are supposedly efficacious in supernatural undertakings; but on another level they are natural signs the novelist must have to express the concepts he terms "treasures." In a letter to Zauper written while working on the *Travels*, Goethe says that nature can serve as a metaphorical key to self-understanding: "Nature, if we understand how to grasp it correctly, everywhere mirrors itself as an analogue to our mind; and if it only awakens tropes and similes, much is already won."[6] In the novel Jarno speaks of the cross stones as such natural figures: "One is rightly happy when lifeless nature

61

brings forth an image of that which we love and honor" (HA, VIII, 35). Others may use the cross stones to search for gold, but Jarno, understanding their true metaphorical worth, goes so far as to reverse the process and exchange gold for information about the stones: "'Take your gold piece,' replied Montan, 'you have earned it for this discovery'" (HA, VIII, 35). Nature does not produce magical signs that disclose supernatural gold; but it does bring forth signs that are more than arbitrary.

Jarno speaks of his geological studies in terms that link the search for precious metals and reading a text: "'If, however, . . . I were to treat these very crevices and fissures as letters, if I were to try to decipher them, form them into words and learn to read them perfectly, would you have anything against that?" (HA, VIII, 34). He continues his geological lecture much later in the novel and contrasts a fruitless reliance on the supernatural with rational inquiry. Jarno finds the earth's metal (lead and silver, not gold!), he claims, because he has learned the language of the mountains. Although some people suspect that a divining rod (or cross stones or esoteric lore) leads him to the ore, he explains that such superstition keeps them from the very knowledge that would unlock the secrets of geology. There *is* a natural language but not one composed of transcendental signifiers. One *can* uncover the metals of meaning, but the gold of mystery remains beyond language.

This explains why Fitz, a superstitious boy of questionable character, possesses the cross stones and why the novelist appears as a disreputable treasure hunter.[7] For the novel contains "old treasures," natural signs that lend themselves to both metaphor and misuse. On the one hand, without the treasures there is no figure. But on the other hand, failure to recognize the figure as figure results in a fatal jump from idea to reality. In building his novel on an occult symbolic foundation, the novelist works with a slippery medium. He indicates this and points his reader to a figurative reading by questioning his own activity.

Fitz possesses the key to another treasure that likewise weaves together hermetic, tropic, and novelistic motifs. In the Giant's Castle (*Riesenschloss*) which Wilhelm and Felix visit the day after their stay at the charcoal burner's (while Fitz has followed the lure of Jarno's gold), Felix finds a mysterious little box: "the bold one [Felix] raised himself quickly out of the crevice and brought with him a little box, not larger than a small octavo volume, with a splendid, old appearance; it seemed to be of gold, decorated with enamel" (HA, VIII, 44). The apparently gold box thus promises what the young treasure hunter seeks. But this is no normal box: the size of an "octavo volume," it is explicitly called a "splendid little book" (*Prachtbüchlein*). The designations "Prachtbüchlein" and "Oktavband," added in the 1829 version (along with the mysterious treasure hunter), accomplish within the novel what the original poem did outside the narrative: they identify the novel (the 1829 version was indeed an octavo volume) as treasure and the novelist and reader as treasure hunters.

The key to the box/book, found later in Fitz's jacket, is depicted in the novel and has been linked by Wilhelm Emrich to Freemasonry.[8] Friedrich Ohly builds on Emrich's careful speculation while discussing a book Goethe read in July of 1819: August Kestner's *The Agape or the Secret World-League of Christians* (*Die Agape oder der geheime Weltbund der Christen*). Kestner postulates a pseudo-Masonic society of early Christians through which Christianity supposedly achieved the unity and strength to become a major religion. Comparing two esoteric signs depicted in Kestner's book with the key in the *Travels*, Ohly concludes that Emrich was right in seeing in the key a combination of Christian and "Freemasonic" symbols.[9] The key and the box or book have many functions unrelated to Freemasonry, as Emrich points out;[10] but in our context the fictional attempts to get at the secrets of the seemingly golden box are analogous to efforts to understand the "golden" novel through the esoterica of Freemasonry. When, for example, Felix, in a fever to discover the mysteries within, turns the key with Freemasonic markings, the key breaks. The fact that the box ultimately remains closed to Wilhelm and Felix manifests the enigmatic quality of the novel or, more important, the fact that the message lies not in a spurious transcendental signifier, but rather in the figures themselves. The only person to open the box, in the end, is the goldsmith. His daily work with gold teaches him the secrets of the trick key; but he counsels amateurs to leave the contents of the box untouched.

In summary, the poem of the 1821 version compares the novelist and reader to treasure hunters and the novel to a treasure. In the 1829 version that comparison gives way to the writing treasure hunter and to the box/book. The mystery promised is not the gold of supernatural expectations but the more useful metals of allegory and metaphor. The keys to buried treasure and the "splendid little book" are, respectively, the cross stones and the key depicted in the novel, whose form originated in a book on a secret society of early Christians, a supposed forerunner of Freemasonry. Used as occult objects, or viewed as transcendental signifiers, the two keys are of questionable value. But when seen as tropes they may open up new perspectives. Their power to do so, however, comes in part from their origin in the mysterious, secret, irrational, questionable world Fitz knows, a world known also by many eighteenth-century Freemasons.

GOETHE AS FREEMASON

On February 13, 1780, having recently returned from a trip to Switzerland, Goethe explained to the head of the Freemasonic lodge Amalia in Weimar that social inconveniences encountered during his trip had intensified a long-standing wish to become a Freemason.[11] On June 23, 1780, he was taken into the lodge as an apprentice. Exactly one year later he was made a fellow and on March 2, 1782, became a master Mason. Writing to Kayser on June 14, 1782, Goethe enthusiastically claimed that a *sub rosa* tour of lodge rooms hitherto closed to him had given him unbelievable knowledge of the secrets of Freemasonry: "In the order I am a Master, which means little. A good spirit led me, extracurricularly, through the remaining halls and chambers. And I know the incredible."[12] It would seem at this point that the young man believes he has found the gold the older Goethe will disavow. During the next year Goethe also became a member of the Iluminati, recruited along with Karl August and Herder by the publisher and translator Bode. Within months, as the result of increasing quarrels between different Freemasonic systems, the lodge Amalia ceased operation.

In another letter to Kayser, several months after the lodge closed, Goethe showed early signs of distancing himself from Freemasonry:

> The secret sciences have given me neither more nor less than I hoped. I was searching for nothing for myself in them, but I am taught enough as I see what others sought, found, are seeking and hoping for in those sciences. . . . I have also found that in the small world of the brothers everything happens as in the large world, and in this sense, it has been very useful to me to pass through these regions.[13]

Consistent with his later use of Freemasonry, Goethe here views the fraternal world as a kind of microcosm of the larger world. In the *Travels*, the final aphorism "From Makarie's Archive" echoes this earlier concept of education through analogy: "Whoever lives long in significant social circumstances will experience—not everything that can happen to a person—but certainly the analogue, and perhaps something without parallel" (HA, VIII, 486). Although failing to satisfy youthful desires for mystical wisdom ("the incredible"), Freemasonry, like alchemy, provided Goethe with symbols, themes, and structures for his lifelong literary endeavors.

In the following years Goethe expressed himself more and more negatively concerning the Freemasons and secret societies in general, writing, for example, in a letter to Karl August:

> Jena was, as you know, threatened with a lodge . . . the idea of having a lecture given on the mischief of the secret society is excellent. I have also made a suggestion to the directors of the [Jena] Literary Journal, which they have accepted, which will seriously set back all secret societies. You will soon read it in print. It is good to publicly establish enmity between oneself and the fools and scoundrels.[14]

Goethe expressed this antagonistic view of mystical Freemasonry, and especially its notorious proponent Cagliostro, dramatically in *The Grand-Cophta* (*Der Gross-Cophta*, 1791).[15] But even in these years when other men were seeking "gold" in secret societies and he was keeping his distance, Goethe still drew on the symbols of Freemasonry for his work.

Four years after *The Grand-Cophta*'s negative depiction of secret societies, Goethe finished *Wilhelm Meister's Apprenticeship*, a novel whose secret society has a positive, if highly ambivalent, influence on the young hero. In these years Goethe also worked on a sequel to *The Magic Flute* (*Die Zauberflöte*), Mozart's and Schickaneder's Freemasonic opera, to be called *The Magic Flute, Part Two* (*Der Zauberflöte 2. Theil*).

Goethe's shifting association with Freemasonry took yet another turn in 1808, when, with his support, the lodge Amalia began functioning once again under a more rational system created by the Hamburg actor Friedrich Ludwig Schröder. For four years Goethe was again fairly active as a Freemason; but in 1812 he asked to be relieved of all responsibilities vis-à-vis the lodge. Even after this date, however, he wrote occasional poetry for the lodge and participated in special occasions; for example, on February 18, 1813, he gave the speech "Zu brüderlichem Andenken Wielands"; and he wrote the poem "Symbolum" in 1815, first published in *Hymns for Freemasons* (*Gesänge für Freimaurer*, Weimar 1816).[16]

THE RITUAL ROUTE

In "The Architecture of the Lodges: Ritual Form and Associational Life in the Late Enlightenment,"[17] Anthony Vidler discusses the general belief of Enlightenment utopian writers that environmental form shapes the individual. Freemasonry, a kind of "lived utopia," developed an initiation ceremony that gradually included progression along a ritual route from a point of entry into the lodge past various symbolic objects to a final station where the initiate stood before officers of the lodge. At first the routes were traced in chalk on the floor, but as the rituals became more elaborate various floor coverings were used. These coverings primarily represented the type of the Masonic lodge (Solomon's temple) and secondarily Egyptian temples and pyramids. As the actual ritual structures of the Egyptians were studied by Masonic iconographers, they were thought, Vidler writes, to have been "deliberately constructed to affect the succeeding states of mind of the aspirant by providing, as it were, a stage set for the initiation. . . . The spatial organization of the initiatory sequence . . . becomes an agent of mental change" (87). This corresponds closely to the use of architectural and esoteric Masonic symbols to influence the prince in Schiller's *Ghost-Seer*.

As increasingly occult Freemasonry spread through Europe, and as individual patrons of individual mystics emerged, new cultist lodges were established on secluded estates. Cagliostro, for example, built a lodge of "Regeneration" on the estate of the banker Sarasin near Basel in 1781. Such "temples in the garden," as Vidler calls 'them (89), represented an extension of the ritual routes into the landscape of the English garden, as discussed in Chapter 1. A description of an initiatory sequence in such a "lodge," written by the English mystic and novelist William Beckford and quoted by Vidler, provides a good example of the practice.

In a 1784 letter to his sister,[18] Beckford claimed to have been driven in a shuttered carriage by the architect Ledoux, the same man who drew plans for the pyramid in which Terrasson's Sethos is tested, to an estate outside of Paris. Beckford was required to ask no questions concerning what he might see or hear. The two men left the carriage before a stone wall, and, passing through gates, found themselves in a vast space occupied by woodpiles. Walking through a rude door in the largest of the piles, they entered a "gloomy vestibule, more like a barn than a Hall." The next door led them into a "plain room like the chamber of a cottage . . . overlooking a little garden." Passing through an apartment of better proportion and furnishing they then came into a bright, "lofty square room" with marble pilasters and containing a sleeping cockatoo. A grand portal, its tapestry curtains open, invited them into a magnificent salon with a "coved ceiling, richly painted with mythological subjects." In front of a fire sat a "grim-visaged old man" with "most vivid and most piercing eyes." The old man suggested that he examine the works of art in the room, remarking that "'they merit a deliberate survey.'" Obeying, Beckford eventually came to an enormous bronze cistern filled with water in which he saw ghastly shadows. Hearing chanting from an adjoining room, all three men descended a stairway and passed into a tribune room from which they could see a large chapel in which a strange service was taking place. Here, Beckford writes, he faltered, and, in the words of the architect, "lost an opportunity of gaining knowledge which may never return." If he had undergone a slight ceremony he might have asked any question with the certainty of answer. But, the moment gone, Beckford and the architect retraced their steps, guided through the woodpiles by an "impish looking lad with a lanthorn," and found their way home.

Like the men who designed this symbolic route, Goethe subscribed to the Enlightenment belief that environmental form shapes the individual. In fact, he ordered architectural symbols along ritual routes in several of his works "to affect the succeeding states of mind" of a character. Take, for example, "The Secrets" ("Die Geheimnisse," 1784–1785), a fragmentary epic poem in which, at the outset, Brother Markus moves toward the dwelling of a Rosicrucian order by way of marvelous paths. He views mysterious signs and paintings and longs to know their meaning; and then, in the following lines, he is found worthy to know the secrets behind it all:

> Das, was du siehst, will mehr und mehr bedeuten;
> Ein Teppich deckt es bald und bald ein Flor.
> Beliebt es dir, so magst du dich bereiten:

Du kommst, o Freund, nur erst durchs erste Tor;
Im Vorhof bist du freundlich aufgenommen,
Und scheinst mir wert, ins Innerste zu kommen.
    (HA, II, 271–281)

That which you see will mean more and more;
A tapestry covers it sometimes, and at others crepe.
If you desire, you may prepare yourself:
You will come, oh friend, at first only through the first gate;
In the outer court you are hospitably received,
And appear worthy to me to enter into the most inner [place].

The architectural metaphor, this passing through the first gate into the courtyard and finally into the inner sanctum in search of ever greater knowledge, intrigued Goethe. He returned to it often, notably at the beginning of his "Introduction to the Propyläen," the entry gate to the temples of the Acropolis in Athens and now the title of Goethe's journal:

The youth, when drawn by nature and art, feels capable of entering soon, with a lively effort, into the inner sanctum; the man notices, after long travels, that he still finds himself in the outer courtyards.
    Such an observation gave rise to our title. Stair, gate, entrance, vestibule, the space between the inner and outer, between the sacred and profane—only this can be the place in which we and our friends will usually dwell. (HA, XII, 38)

The Propyläen is thus a station on the path of knowledge whose end presumably lies in the temple of Athena. But the mystical end does not interest the man, as opposed to the youth; the man is content to move along the path, to learn in the space between the inner and the outer, between the sacred and the profane.

The youthful impatience depicted here is similar to the definition of alchemy quoted above: "a leap from the idea . . . to reality." Both alchemist and youth draw on true feelings but rush to false conclusions. Wisdom would eschew the mystery, would condemn the jump from idea to reality, for there may be no such reality: no gold, no mystical epiphany, no absolute transcendence of the mediating figure. The "truth" may lie in the sign itself, in that "space between inner and outer," in the Propyläen: "The true is similar to divinity; it does not appear unmediated, we must guess it from its manifestations" ("From Makarie's Archive," HA, VIII, 460). As Neil Flax has recently pointed out in a discussion of Goethe's *Faust*, none of the signs Faust hopes will afford him transcendence actually do so. Behind each sign stands another sign, not the absolute being he seeks.[19] But the sign is not totally arbitrary either: "We have the ineluctable, deeply serious task which must be renewed daily: to grasp, as well as possible, the unmediated meeting of the word with what is felt, seen, thought, experienced, imagined, reasoned" (HA, VIII, 469).

As its title "Symbolum" suggests, Goethe's best known Masonic poem directly addresses the problem of figuration, hinting at the possibility of transcendent meaning, but counseling the initiates to set aside their fascination with transcendence and focus rather on action:

> Des Maurers Wandeln
> Es gleicht dem Leben,
> Und sein Bestreben
> Es gleicht dem Handeln
> Der Menschen auf Erden.
>
> Die Zukunft decket
> Schmerzen und Glücke.
> Schrittweis dem Blicke,
> Doch ungeschrecket
> Dringen wir vorwärts.
>
> Und schwer und schwerer
> Hängt eine Hülle
> Mit Ehrfurcht. Stille
> Ruhn oben die Sterne
> Und unten die Gräber.
>
> Betracht' sie genauer
> Und siehe, so melden
> Im Busen der Helden
> Sich wandelnde Schauer
> Und ernste Gefühle.
>
> Doch rufen von drüben
> Die Stimmen der Geister,
> Die Stimmen der Meister:
> "Versäumt nicht zu üben
> Die Kräfte des Guten.
>
> Hier winden sich Kronen
> In ewiger Stille,
> Die sollen mit Fülle

Die Tätigen lohnen!
Wir heissen euch hoffen."
  (HA, I, 340–341)

The Mason's travels
Resemble life,
And his efforts
Resemble the deeds
Of persons on earth.

The future shrouds
Pains and happinesses.
Step by step to the view,
Yet undismayed
We press forward.

And heavy and heavier
Hangs a veil
With reverence. Still
The stars rest above
And below the graves.

Observe them more exactly
And see, thus enter
Into the breast of the hero
Changing thrills
And serious feelings.

Yet from the other side call
The voices of spirits,
The voices of the masters:
"Do not neglect to exert
The powers of goodness.

Here crowns wind themselves
In eternal stillness,
Which are meant to reward
The active with fullness!
We bid you to hope.

At the outset the poem proclaims a congruence between the development of the Freemason and the life of mankind, between his
efforts and mankind's actions.[20] As the Freemason moves along his
ritual route he symbolically approximates the stages of life. The
covering that hangs "heavy and heavier" with reverence
(*Ehrfurcht*),[21] the veil bearing symbolic stars and graves, is a figure
that, as figure, both veils and discloses. The initiate is asked to ob-

serve it; but, as he begins to be entranced by the symbolic depth, he is exhorted by the spirits, by the masters (those supposedly in possession of the final secret, the absolute significance behind the signifiers) that although transcendence may be possible in another realm, for the present he should engage in good deeds.

These three examples of ritual routes in Goethe's work— "The Secrets," the *Propyläen*, and "Symbolum"—manifest an ongoing concern with esoteric architectural symbolism, ritual education, and figuration itself. These related topics find even broader expression in the two *Wilhelm Meister* novels.

THE RITUAL ROUTE IN THE *APPRENTICESHIP*

In *Wilhelm Meister's Apprenticeship*, which preceded the final version of the *Travels* by more than thirty years, several emissaries from the Society of the Tower direct Wilhelm's education while he simultaneously develops according to internal norms.[22] Schiller immediately saw the need for such emissaries in Goethe's Bildungsroman:

> The forces of the Tower, a higher understanding, working in secret, accompany him [Wilhelm] with their attention and without disturbing nature in its free movement, they observe and lead him from afar, guiding him to an end which he himself does not (and may not) sense. As gentle and light as this influence from outside is, it is still really there, and for the achievement of the poetic aim it was indispensable. An apprenticeship is a relative concept, it demands its correlative . . . mastery, which is only the work of a matured and perfected experience.[23]

It is not surprising that Schiller so aptly characterized this mechanism, for his novel served as a prototype for Goethe's work. A description of Jarno, for instance, one of the Tower Society's emissaries, reveals the flashing eyes of Schiller's Armenian, along with the Armenian's force of character that ambivalently attracts the hero he is sent to influence: "Large, bright blue eyes flashed out from under a high brow. . . . Wilhelm . . . felt a certain inclination toward the stranger, although he simultaneously possessed something cold and repelling" (162).[24] Unlike contemporary popular novelists who reproduced Schiller's Armenian because a powerful emissary was a good catalyst for an exciting story, Goethe, like Schiller, found the

Masonic ritual related to such a figure a key to investigating problems of artistic production.

The Tower Society draws its name from a mysterious tower —part of what is described as an "old irregular castle with several towers and pediments." An entire wing of this "singular building," as it is called, remains closed to Wilhelm until Jarno promises to show him the tower and introduce him to the secrets of its society. Jarno first leads Wilhelm from known parts of the castle to unknown rooms. A large, old door serves both actually and symbolically as an entryway into a new world. Inside a room once used for religious purposes, Wilhelm moves through a curtain from utter darkness to blinding sunlight. In this partially secularized space (a table covered with green cloth stands where an altar once stood), Wilhelm learns that members of the society have carefully directed his education. They introduce him to an extensive archive to which he now, as an initiate, has free access. The Abbé gives him a document of indenture (a *Lehrbrief*) to further instruct him, and the scene ends as Wilhelm's son Felix appears and father and son move about the garden outside; Felix asks for the names of plants they see, and Wilhelm somewhat lamely trys to teach him.

In the irregular castle, in the tower, in the initiatory path (from room to room, through the large door and past the curtain to the brightly lit hall housing the archive, and finally into the garden), Wilhelm is introduced to a symbolic, pedagogic architecture. The Tower Society, he is told, stands on a mystical base (the nonsecularized chapel), the symbols of which still have value even if final assumptions are no longer shared. But as the *Lehrbrief* reiterates (in much the same language quoted earlier from the *Theory of Colors*), impatience leads many to skip the progressive steps of education in an attempt to immediately grasp the mystery—"The pinacle excites us, not the stairs; with the peak in view we like to walk on the level" (HA, VII, 496). Finally, after warning against an exclusive preoccupation with signs ("Whoever works merely with signs is a pedant, a hypocrite, or a dabbler"), the *Lehrbrief* suggests action and describes an education by analogy (exactly the education the *Travels* thematize): "where words are lacking, the deed speaks. The genuine pupil learns to explain the unknown from the known and draws nearer to the master."[25]

The architectural pedagogy of the Tower Society continues as the novel nears its end and Wilhelm travels to the Oheim's estate. Having entered the courtyard, holding his sleeping son in his

72

arms, Wilhelm "found himself in the most earnest, in his mind the most holy place he had ever entered" (HA, VII, 512). The next morning, rising early, Wilhelm looks around the house that has so affected him: "It was the most pure, the most beautiful, the most worthy architecture he had seen. True art, he called out, is like good society: it forces us, in the most pleasant way, to recognize the measure according to which and for which our most inner [self] is formed" (HA, VII, 516). This contrasts with Wilhelm's grandfather's asymmetrical house that originally held the art collection now housed in the Oheim's more symmetrical dwelling place, and also the disordered home of the Tower Society. Later, while walking in the garden, Natalie introduces Wilhelm to the "Hall of the Past," an imposing architectural construction with Egyptian motifs: "All of this splendor and decoration presented itself in pure architectonic relationships, and thus everyone who entered seemed to be raised above himself as he first experienced through the harmonious art what a human was and what one might be" (HA, VII, 539–540). Thus both the house and the "Hall of the Past" are said to represent an architecture so pure that it acts to educate the attentive viewer, heightening the present level of education, teaching of the measure to which the most inner self corresponds.

While undergoing this increasingly orderly architectural education in the company of mentors and friends, Wilhelm witnesses Mignon's death, finds himself torn between Theresia and Natalie, and grows bitter about the way the Tower Society has mechanically structured his life. In a key exchange about ritual and meaning, Jarno tells Wilhelm that "'all the things that you have seen in the tower are actually only relics from a youthfull undertaking.' . . . 'So we are only playing with these worthy signs and words,' Wilhelm exclaimed. 'We are ceremoniously led to a place that inspires us with reverence . . . and we are no wiser than before'" (HA, VII, 548).[26] In answer, Jarno asks for the *Lehrbrief* and comments on various passages from it. He says that secrets, ceremonies, and grand words often attract young people with depth of character. The society has kept its ceremonies, Jarno continues, to provide "'something lawful in our meetings. There were the first mystical impressions on the establishment of the whole, afterward it took on, as if through a simile, the form of a craft which raised itself to an art. Thence came the appelations apprentices, assistants, and masters'" (HA, VII, 549). He continues to describe the archive they developed and finally says that, because not all people are interested in true education, some are deliberately sidetracked through mystification. Exclusively literal understanding caused by the overwhelming desire for actual mysteries makes the symbol opaque for such people. Nonetheless, as represented also by the secularized chapel, the original mystery has continuing value, if only as symbol.

When Jarno describes the transformation of a craft into an art for figurative purposes, he does not mention which craft; but the parallel to Freemasonry, where the skills and tools of masons lose their concrete functions and take on figurative significance, is clear. Such a transformation of craft to art also occurred among the occult, alchemical, Freemasonic *Gold-* and *Rosenkreutzer* of the late eighteenth century. Many of them practiced the actual craft of alchemy ("the first mystical impressions"); but in some cases this craft was raised to an art, and the transformation of metals became a metaphor for education, a set of symbols that educates. Raising the craft to art, then, as the Tower Society has done, does not mean, as Wilhelm first thinks, that he is led into a place which fills him with reverence and then is left with nothing, but rather, that he should come to the education he expects through the symbols he sees, secularized or not. The Egyptian doorways, mysterious towers, and perfectly harmonious buildings are agents of growth. Through the "craft . . . which rased itself to art," through alchemy which becomes Freemasonry, through architecture which becomes symbolic architecture, Wilhelm's education continues.

RITUAL ROUTES IN THE *TRAVELS*

The first paragraphs of the sequel to the *Apprenticeship* immediately sound themes that alert the reader that Wilhelm's travels are meant to provide a figural education and that each stage along his ritual route is important. As one poem preceding the 1821 edition states: "The journeyman years are now begun / And every step of the traveler is critical."[27] The novel's first sentence places Wilhelm in meaningful surroundings: "Wilhelm sat in the shadow of a powerful cliff, an awful, meaningful place." Felix's question, "What is this stone called, Father?" links the novel at its outset with the scene immediately following Wilhelm's initiation into the Tower Society in which Felix asks for the names of plants growing in the garden. Felix's questions and Wilhelm's answers—one explaining the name "Katzengold" by analogy to cats, and a second identifying part of a plant as a fir-cone by comparison of its scales or bracts with those of better known fir-cones—show Wilhelm's ability to think analogically, begin to teach Felix to do the same, and awaken in the reader a sensitivity to figures of all sorts. Wilhelm and the reader are thrust even further into this figurative mode when Joseph appears carrying the planing ax (*Polieraxt*) and square (*Winkelmass*) of a carpenter (cf. the trowel, compass, and square of the mason and Freemason), leading a donkey bearing a woman in red and blue who carries a baby (HA, VIII, 9). Wilhelm is, of course, astonished to find the "Flight to Egypt" become reality in this mountain setting.

Wilhelm sends Felix with this odd family, and, as the day comes to a close, he climbs back up the peak to retrieve his papers and pack. Following a route that resembles the one in "The Secrets," Wilhelm climbs ever higher until he once again sees the sun, "the heavenly star which he had lost more than once" (HA, VIII, 11). In the hut he writes to Natalia that the mountains he is about to leave behind will act as a wall between them. The last sentence of the letter, written just as he leaves the border house high on the mountain, depicts him as a man about to die (thus leaving behind the world of the *Apprenticeship* and undertaking a new life). The next morning he will descend the mountain and find a valley in which lies the monastery of St. Joseph, under whose broken altar the cross stones lie. These motifs—mountain, sun seen setting several times, valley, monastery, and cross—are precisely those encountered in the first stanzas of "The Secrets," where Brother Markus ascends a mountain near the end of day, the sun appears again as he reaches the top, he "is like newborn" when he hears a bell, and he finds a valley in which lies a monastery with a rosy cross on its door. These striking parallels make it clear that the Rosicrucian and Freemasonic substance of "The Secrets" continues here in the *Travels*.[28] These first stages of a ritual route in the *Travels*, recognizable as such in part by the comparison with the poem, expand into a more elaborate route that remarkably resembles the one described by William Beckford.

The half-ruined, secularized monastery of St. Joseph is Wilhelm's first stop after leaving the mountain top. Religious services no longer take place here, but a religious spirit still pervades the atmosphere; depictions of the life of St. Joseph line the walls. Wilhelm voices his surprise at the congruence between the paintings and his host's appearance, and the new St. Joseph replies that the building has made the man:

> Certainly, you marvel at the congruence between this building
> and its inhabitants whom you met yesterday. That congruence is,
> however, perhaps even more singular than one might surmise: the
> building has actually made the inhabitants. For when the lifeless
> is alive, its products can also be lively. (Denn wenn das Leblose
> lebendig ist, so kann es auch wohl Lebendiges hervorbringen).
> (HA, VIII, 15)

Influenced by artistic representations of St. Joseph as a carpenter,
the young man who already bore the saint's name also took on his
craft. Jarno spoke in the *Apprenticeship* about the Tower Society's
initiation rites as a "craft which raised itself to an art," an art which,
through its symbolic architecture and ceremonies, furthered Wilhelm's education. In the case of St. Joseph the Second, the craft
raised to art in the paintings has led him to choose carpentry as his
vocation. Thus the craft has become art, and the art leads back to
the craft. The movement, like that in "Symbolum" and the *Lehrbrief*,
is from action to symbol to action. The cycle continues to art as the
young man uses his carpentry skills to rebuild and restore the
chapel housing the paintings.

After conversing on this subject, Joseph finds Wilhelm worthy of further education: "'It is right . . . that I satisfy your curiosity
. . . I sense that you are capable of taking even the peculiar seriously, if it rests on a serious foundation'" (HA, VIII, 17). The extraordinary appearance of Joseph and Mary rests on the serious
foundation of the reciprocal relationship between craft and art, and
Wilhelm can consider seriously the marvelous family because of his
ability, demonstrated in the *Apprenticeship*, to recognize symbols
where others might find the supernatural.

Wilhelm's experiences at the monastery make him once
again aware of the power of architecture and painting to educate,
and of the productive nature of the progression from craft to art to
craft. The route he has traveled so far has been allegorically rich,
with the details sketched here closely approximating a Freemasonic
ritual route. After Wilhelm and Felix leave St. Joseph's, each step of
their journey continues to be part of a route meant to educate the
young journeyman and his son. They travel from estate to estate,
and each separate stage repeats the basic sequence described by
William Beckford. The journey from St. Joseph's to the Oheim's estate especially is structured as a Masonic ritual route.

First, Fitz leads Wilhelm and Felix to Jarno, and Jarno lectures Wilhelm at length (there are connections here to the *Lehrbrief*)

on the alphabet of nature, on a craft that becomes figurative through art, and on the cross stones as natural figures. As night approaches they all follow Fitz "on wondrous paths" to the charcoal pile in the middle of the woods.

The night passes, and Jarno continues to lecture Wilhelm: "If, however, you cannot let it be, and if you are bent on a perfect education, then I do not understand how you can be so blind, how you are inclined to search forever, how you do not see that you are in the very close proximity of a splendid educational institution" (HA, VIII, 39). Wilhelm does not understand, so Jarno explains; by using the charcoal pile as a metaphor—again raising the craft to art —he describes the confining environment of the charcoal pile in which the wood only partially burns, becoming highly useful as charcoal. The lesson is of the powers of limitation and skill in a single trade. While this pedagogy takes place, a mysterious group of men, including the novelist/treasure hunter, gathers around the charcoal pile; and the next morning Jarno accuses Fitz of being in league with them.[29]

Fitz and Jarno go their own way, and Felix and Wilhelm come to the giant's castle, a natural architectural wonder where Felix finds the box or book already discussed. Fitz returns and leads them from the "straight, broad, beaten path" onto what seems a short-cut. They find themselves traveling rapidly downhill through a wood, "which, becoming ever more transparent, let them finally see, in the most clear sunlight, the most beautiful property which one can imagine" (HA, VIII, 45). But the sudden vision achieved by taking the short-cut suggested by Fitz, the supplier of magic cross stones, proves false, for a deep ditch and a high wall separate them from the uncle's estate (cf. alchemy or transcendental signifiers as similar short-cuts). Fitz has anticipated this and cannot conceal his *Schadenfreude* when Wilhelm recognizes what has happened.

To avoid a long detour, Fitz next suggests that they approach the estate through vaults built to control rain water from the mountains as it enters the estate. Just as Felix insisted, in his youthful enthusiasm, on seeing the giant's castle and entering its caves, he again wants to enter the vaults: "When Felix heard about vaults, his desire drew him irresistibly into this entrance" (HA, VIII, 45). The three enter the vaults, climb down stairs, and find themselves now in the light, now in the dark. Suddenly a shot sounds, and iron grates fall to imprison Wilhelm and Felix. Fritz escapes but leaves his coat caught in the fence.

Men from the estate appear and lead Wilhelm and Felix as prisoners up a circular staircase. At the top they find themselves in a comfortable but barred room. An official enters the room, and after hearing Wilhelm's story and seeing his papers, helps father and son into a beautiful garden room where refreshments await them. Next they walk to a castle fronted by trees, a natural "entry hall of the imposing building." Inside the building, they pass quickly through the vestibule, ascend a stairway, and enter a main hall. Each separate space exhibits its own set of paintings. The master of the house, "a small, lively man advanced in years," welcomes his guests and asks them, pointing to the paintings around the hall, whether Wilhelm knows the cities depicted there. Wilhelm's reply demonstrates a thorough knowledge of several of them. During the next two days Wilhelm finds his way into a gallery where the old man shows him portraits, relics, and manuscripts. "Finally he laid before Wilhelm a white sheet, asking for several lines, but without a signature; then the guest found himself dismissed through a tapestry door into the hall, standing at the side of the archivist" (HA, VIII, 80). Wilhelm and Felix later leave the uncle's to travel to Makarie's castle, and the route they trace plays an important role in a later phase of this discussion; but for now, the route just described bears comparison with William Beckford's ritual route.

Beckford describes (1) his route from Paris, (2) the wall of the estate, (3) the woodpiles, (4) the pyramidal entrance, (5) the "barnish hall," (6) the cottage and garden, (7) the antechamber, (8) the curtain, (9) the main salon with the grim-visaged old man who suggests that Beckford carefully observe the mythological paintings, laver, and fire, and (10) the chapel and tribune. Vidler's schematization appears:

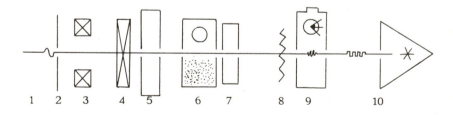

A schematization of Wilhelm's route reveals some remarkable similarities:

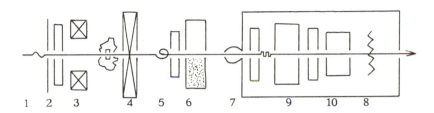

Wilhelm travels (1) the route from the *Apprenticeship* to (2) the mountains that act as a wall; the monastery of St. Joseph reminds him that the building makes the man. (3) The wood pile of the charcoal burner is a natural educational institution, and the giant's castle is nature's ruined temple with a secret at its center. (4) A vault serves as both an entrance and a trap, and from there Wilhelm and Felix walk up a spiral staircase to (5) a prison room. This environment, oppressive to Felix, gives way to (6) a garden room and then to (7) a natural vestibule surrounded by trees. Inside the castle father and son move through (9) a series of rooms with paintings on the walls. In the main hall "a small, lively man of advanced age" meets Wilhelm and asks him about the paintings. Finally Wilhelm moves through the gallery to (10) the inner room with its treasures. He leaves through (8) a curtained doorway.

Beckford's and Wilhelm's routes have in common (1) a path to the estate, (2) a wall, (3) woodpiles, (4) a pyramidal entrace, (5) a barnish hall/prison room, (6) a garden room, (7) a vestibule, (8) a curtain, (9) a hall with paintings and an old man who recommends observing them, and (10) an inner room or chapel in which the final disclosure is or is not made. Despite the remarkable congruence, there seems to be no way that Goethe could have known Beckford's description of his initiatory journey, written as a letter to his sister. Although this specific case may not be the source for Wilhelm's pedagogical journey, it provides information concerning the substance of similar, contemporary ritual routes, transferred from the floor-drawings of Freemasonic lodges into the gardens and buildings of estates. It also provides a context in which the structure of the *Wanderjahre* can be more fully understood.

PARALLEL ROUTES IN THE *TRAVELS*

We began this discussion by pointing out that the esoterica present in the *Travels* must be treated as possible fool's gold. Once that was understood, Freemasonry and alchemy could be mined for metaphoric meaning. After introducing Freemasonic architecture and ritual routes, several works were cited in which Goethe employed a similar architectural and pedagogical strategy. The *Apprenticeship* especially portrays the initiation rites and architectural pedagogy of a pseudo-Masonic secret society and does so, in part, to examine the production of symbols. A reading of early scenes in the *Travels* established that once again Freemasonic architectural symbols play a substantive role in the text and that this novel too self-reflexively deals with transformations of craft to symbol to craft. Finally, a remarkable congruence was found between Beckford's description of an initiatory route and the path Wilhelm follows in the early pages of the novel. This last discovery has value primarily in leading to a close examination of the various routes Wilhelm follows in the course of the *Travels*. If the architectural details are taken seriously, as components of an educational sequence inspired by Freemasonry, there is a new basis on which to compare and contrast different stages in Wilhelm's journey. These stages have been interpreted in various ways in the past. A look at two such interpretations will put what follows in a broader context.

Ohly, for example, draws on the teachings about reverence in the Pedagogical Province to examine the monastery, the giant's castle, the uncle's estate, and Makarie's realm as representative of "reverence for that which is above us," "reverence for that which is under us," "reverence for that which is the same as us," and "reverence for that which is in us" respectively, and then finally the Pedagogical Province as the "the spiritually pure center" (411–433). He is quite convincing, especially in his reading of the successive estates as symbolic regions; but in the end one feels that the complexity of the novel calls for other perspectives as well. Why, for instance, should the Pedagogical Province and its teachings be seen as the center of the novel?[30] And why does the final region Wilhelm enters, that of the Tower Society, not fit into the scheme of things?

Wilhelm Vosskamp likewise considers several regions, this time within the structure of utopias.[31] The uncle's estate, the Pedagogical Province, and the two groups of Tower Society members are convincingly considered as contrasting utopias. Vosskamp supports his argument with solid textual analysis, noting, for example, that Wilhelm enters the uncle's estate and the Province through gates that set the utopias off from the surrounding countryside. He does not, however, mention additional doors and gates that similarly set off the other realms of the novel. And why does he deal with only four regions and leave others undiscussed? Again, the system used to examine the novel proves only partially successful.

What follows builds on Ohly's and Vosskamp's (and others') attempts to analyze the successive regions along Wilhelm's route in his *Travels*. This essay too remains fragmentary, but it begins to approach a more comprehensive interpretation.

Putting aside for the moment the fictional and biographical realms Wilhelm enters through reading and hearing the various stories, the following stages make up his journey: St. Joseph's monastery, Montan's mountain realm (including the charcoal pile and the giant's castle), the uncle's estate, Makarie's house, the Pedagogical Province, the Lago Maggiore, the scene of Wilhelm's medical studies, and finally the estate on which the Tower Society has gathered. Chart 1 makes clear the congruities and incongruities between the various routes Wilhelm takes. The basic pattern consists of (1) a *path* leading to the estate or place of "initiation," (2) an *entrance*, usually a door, gate, or vault, (3) a *guide* figure, (4) a large *hall* with instructive *paintings* on its walls, (5) an assurance that Wilhelm is *worthy to proceed* further, (6) a *veil* or curtain, (7) an *archive* or *treasure room*, (8) and finally a *garden*.

First, in every case the path to the respective estate is described. One region (Montan's) may actually have three parts, for the travelers make their way to the peak where Jarno works, to the charcoal burner's, and then to the giant's castle on another peak. Descriptions of the respective paths to these places are "without path," "wondrous paths," and "difficult path."

Second, most estates are separated from the outside world by at least one wall through which a door leads. The Lago Maggiore seems to be an exception.

Third, a guide (often an old man) leads Wilhelm through the house or countryside to, *fourth*, a hall with paintings or sculptures. In each case Wilhelm studies the paintings. Sometimes he demonstrates his knowledge of the people or places depicted and thus wins the favor of his host, and sometimes the paintings are used explicitly as pedagogical tools. The various collectors are characterized by their collections as well. Wilhelm's journey takes him

Chart 1. Routes of Wilhelm Meister's Journeys

Estate	Path	Entrance	Guide	Hall/Paintings	Worthy to Proceed	Curtain	Archive or Treasure	Garden
WM Lehrjahre	led through galleries 493	old door 493	Jarno 493	hall, chapel, paintings 493	deeper into the secret 493	tapestry opens to reveal light 493	Archive 497	in garden with Felix 498
St. Joseph	from mt. to valley 13	open gate 14	Joseph	hall, chapel, paintings 14	right to answer curiosity 17	—	Kreuzsteine	ruins and garden 16
Montan	"without path" 30, 37, 42	—	Fitz Jarno Messenger	—	refusal! "Give it up!" 33, 36	—	box book 43	takes place in nature
Oheim	broad path or steep shortcut 44	vaulted entrance 45	the "man of years" 49	hall, paintings 49, 64, 79	repeated statements 49–50, 79, 80	tapestry door 80	manuscripts 80	from prison to garden room (not at end) 48
Makarie	through pleasant area 114	gate, door 114	Astronomer 115	hall, paintings 115	we will lead you further 126	green curtain 115	archive 124	from observatory to garden 122
Province	path determined by T. Society 149	gate, door, portal 154–161	"the Three" 154	8-cornered hall paintings 158	counted among the trusted 165	veil over sorrows 164	sanctuary of suffering 164	gallery with garden 158
Lago M.	from mt. to valley 226	—	travel guide 234	island paintings 234	arrow leads to trust 231	—	suffering 239	takes place in nature
Medical Studies	from hall to sculptor's 325	door 325	Sculptor 325	room with figures, busts 326	"Do you want to be my student?" 326	door between two rooms 326	artificial anatomical figs. 326	America as more natural home for pedagogical aids 328–330
Tower Society	map, through countryside 310, 316	castle gate 316	Steward 316	hall, letters 311	accepted 311	—	banquet sorrow 316	into the garden at the end 318

Note: All page numbers refer to volumes VII and VIII of the Hamburger Ausgabe, 6th ed., 1964.

to the paintings of the life of St. Joseph which so affect the modern Joseph and Mary, to Montan's natural signs (the "letters of nature"), to the uncle's geographical representations and portraits (no painting with a religious or mythical theme), to the historical paintings on Makarie's walls, to the eight-sided hall of the Pedagogical Province with its paintings from the Old and New Testaments, to the landscapes of the painter in Italy, to the instructive anatomical sculptures, and finally to the complete absence of paintings in the temporary lodgings of the Tower Society. This sequence of paintings naturally sets up expectations of a meaningful pattern; and although I fail to see the principle behind an overall ordering, let me suggest several possibilities that might bear fruit.

An interesting pattern appears, for instance, when one moves from beginning and end toward a center. Bracketing out, for a moment, the final hall of the Tower Society where there are no paintings (only letters), the first and last works of art (the paintings depicting the life of St. Joseph and the anatomical sculptures) are both examples of the cycle moving from art to craft to art. Moving inward, the second pair consists of the natural settings of Montan and the landscape paintings of the Lago Maggiore. Then, the "nonreligious" paintings at the uncle's find an opposite counterpart in the mythological paintings at the Pedagogical Province. And finally, the historical paintings at Makarie's, along with the marvelous natural signs of the stars, stand at the center of this series of paintings, symmetrically surrounded by nonreligious/religious paintings of the uncle/Province, by the nature/landscapes of Montan/Lago Maggiore, and finally by the paintings/sculpture linking art to craft at St. Joseph's and the medical academy. The centrality of Makarie in this series of paintings focuses attention on her historical paintings (mentioned in only two fleeting phrases) and on the nonhistorical stars (described as ahistorical, as "always the same," yet manifesting day and hour through their "regular course"). Wilhelm argues that the telescope which reveals Jupiter to him disturbs the natural order, jumping from idea to reality in the alchemical sense; but in his dream or vision he finds the pure gold of Makarie's ascension as a star: her chair "gleamed gold, her clothing shone sacerdotally" (HA, VIII, 122). The vision immediately gives way to the real "star" of Venus and quickly to the reality of the morning. The gold of this novel, found in a dream, is carefully preceded and followed by more substantial "metals" and related by the astronomer to the center of Wilhelm's being, recognizable by its working, its effects, its actions.

The scene depicts what one aphorism "From Makarie's Archive" states: "One does not do well to dwell too long in the abstract. The esoteric only harms when it seeks to become exoteric. Life is best taught through the living" (HA, VIII, 477). The green curtain opens for only a minute, then Wilhelm returns willingly, maturely, from the inner sanctum back to the *Propyläen*. The scenes at Makarie's estate are often seen as central to the novel, but as we have seen here, they take on added significance as the sequence of paintings structurally focuses attention on the events there. Finally, in this discussion of paintings, if there are paintings in the other regions, why are there none in the last one? One answer may lie in the pedagogical purpose of the earlier paintings. Wilhelm gains knowledge from the consecutive sets of paintings; and in one sense the education culminates when he learns the trade of surgeon (*Wundarzt*) with the help of the last set of artistic depictions. The absence of paintings thereafter signals that completion. After asking innumerable questions at each previous stage of his *Travels*, Wilhelm now, in the company of active men, of comrades from the Tower Society, is forbidden to ask questions. In place of the paintings, Wilhelm sees a Latin saying in golden letters: "'Ubi homines sunt modi sunt'" (That when people come together in society, the way and manner in which they wish to be and remain together will develop automatically). In each succeeding realm Wilhelm has seen a different way of life, in each case a life strictly ordered and ruled by a specific world view. The paintings, along with various related declarations of values, have given him insight in each case. But now, at the end, no realm is the exclusive, final, highest embodiment of Goethe's thought. The golden letters leave Wilhelm and the Tower Society free to organize themselves as they will. Here are no normative paintings—only various sorts of action. Here too the sign goes over to deed. If the gold of Makarie's chair gave credence to the idea of transcendence, the gold of these letters points directly to this-worldly deeds.

This brief discussion of possibilities revealed by the sequence of paintings is obviously inadequate and remains to be thought out more thoroughly elsewhere. But here it demonstrates how recognizing the various ritual routes can result in productive comparisons between the routes.

Fifth, with regularity Wilhelm gains permission to enter further into the marvelous and secret affairs of the respective hosts: "it would be unjust if we would not lead you deeper into our secrets";

"it is right . . . that I satisfy your curiosity"; "the master of the house, satisfied that the guest knew how to value a so richly evoked past, allowed him to see manuscripts"; "Do you wish to be my pupil? Let the guest be accepted." A notable exception comes when Wilhelm asks Montan for information about the mineral world so he can instruct Felix, and Montan repeatedly turns him down, "give that up" (HA, VIII, 36, 260). Montan gives several reasons for his refusal to initiate Wilhelm into the secrets of nature, but, in the end, the best answer is probably that nature's archive can only be read directly, without mediation; Goethe even rejected the use of many scientific instruments. As Wilhelm approaches Montan's cliff, then, he climbs "without having a path before him" (HA, VIII, 30).

Sixth, several realms have curtains or veils through which Wilhelm receives access to a treasure of some sort. In the *Apprenticeship* he passed through a curtain to the bright light of the secularized chapel, the table (previously an altar) was covered with a green tapestry, and a curtain covered the empty frame. Before Wilhelm sees Makarie, both in reality and in his dream, "a green curtain opened." And in the Pedagogical Province the depictions of Jesus' death are kept veiled: "we draw a veil over these sufferings." One of the more interesting of this series of curtains or veils is the one Wilhelm passes through at the uncle's. Only *after* visiting the inner rooms where the uncle keeps his treasures does Wilhelm go through a tapestry door. This may be a veiled statement about the relative worthlessness of the uncle's highly rational and totally empirical way of life.

Seventh, Wilhelm finds various treasures as he passes into the inner rooms. In the *Apprenticeship* he finds an archive, a *Lehrbrief*, and then, turning from the empty word as the *Lehrbrief* suggests, discovers his son. At St. Joseph's, after being found worthy, Wilhelm is rewarded by Joseph's story of how the building with its paintings made the man and of the fruitful give-and-take between craft and art. The cross stones, natural metaphors once under the altar there, represent another treasure. In the giant's castle the treasure is the box or book. The uncle shows Wilhelm relics and manuscripts. At Makarie's Wilhelm gains access to a very interesting archive—a collection of aphorisms, among other things—and learns the great secret about Makarie's wonderful ties to the cosmos. The sculptor, a man thought by many to be a goldmaker (HA, VIII, 325), leads Wilhelm through rooms usually closed to others and teaches him, not alchemy, but a new approach to anatomy which again involves an exchange between craft and art. The secret of the Province lies in the suffering of Jesus on the cross, a "sanctum of pain" Wilhelm does not enter. Recognition of pain as the "treasure" here leads us to include as "treasures" the pains of two other realms as well. The emotional high point of the Lago Maggiore scene lies in the suffering of the four pilgrims as they contemplate leaving one another's company and remember, all too vividly, Mignon's suffering. And, with the Tower Society, Wilhelm takes part in a banquet, often the end of a traditional ritual route and the culmination of Freemasonic ceremony. Here too the participants suffer deeply at the thought of parting, but like the four sufferers at the Lago Maggiore, they have been "initiated into all the pains of the first grade of the renunciants" and pass through this potentially destructive mode to action. Five, or six, if Montan and his "letters of nature" are included, of the regions have archives at their centers; the sculptor's is an anatomical archive. And three of the last four regions share pains as their secret, pains overcome through renunciation.

Eighth, in all these ritual routes leading to various central places and secrets, a garden regularly appears as the last stage of the journey. After his initiation into the Tower Society Wilhelm takes Felix into a garden where they begin their educations anew. The *Travels* begin with Wilhem and Felix in a natural setting. After observing Joseph's paintings Wilhelm goes out into a garden. Montan's realm is entirely natural. Wilhelm and Felix leave a prison room at the uncle's and enter a garden room. After his miraculous dream on the observatory at Makarie's, Wilhelm goes into a garden. The Lago Maggiore is once again almost totally garden.[32] Pristine America is projected as the best place for the anatomical sculpture. After the banquet with the Tower Society, Wilhelm steps out into the castle gardens and overlooks a broad valley. And as the novel ends, Wilhelm and Felix once again lie in the arms of nature. No matter what secrets each region conceals at its center, it seems, the ultimate treasures lie in nature. The exception to this is again the uncle's estate. There the garden appears early in the sequence that ends with the curtain instead of the archive. The uncle is thus further characterized as having an odd set of priorities.[33]

These eight stages on the ritual route provide eight related opportunities to gauge Wilhelm's progress throughout the novel, opportunities of which we have scarcely been able to avail ourselves as we have rushed to catalogue the routes. And even so, we have ignored large portions of the novel, most notably the novellas, for until now we have traced Wilhelm's various routes exclusively in the frame of the novel. The novel's various novellas, however, provide what Goethe calls "repeated mirrorings" of what takes place in the frame, including Wilhelm's ritual route.

"The Pilgrim Fool," the first novella, is given to Wilhelm to read during his stay at the uncle's. When the young woman in the story is brought to Revanne's castle, she proves her worthiness for such an environment through her reactions to the castle; "she shows herself to be a person who is acquainted with the fashionable world" (HA, VIII, 54). After receiving refreshments she comments on the furniture, the paintings, and the division of the rooms and finally, in the library, shows that she knows good books. This, of course, mirrors almost precisely the process Wilhelm had just gone through with the uncle (cf. HA, VIII, 49–50 and the pages after the story in which Wilhelm sees the uncle's manuscript collection).

In "Who is the Traitor?" Lucidor finds himself at one point in a hermitage with a Chinese roof. There he sees hundreds of paintings that disclose the historical inclinations of the old man who sometimes lives there. Later he is led through "long, extensive passageways of the old castle" to a court room in what was once a chapel. There he finds an archive containing some of his own work. Next he is brought to a large hall where people await a festive announcement of his marriage. He flees into a garden hall where he finally, miraculously, finds the woman he loves. There is considerable congruence between this story and the accounts described above: the hall with historical pictures mirrors several other halls, the movement through the castle hallways to an archive in a secularized chapel mirrors Wilhelm's initiation in the *Apprenticeship*, and the final flight to the garden finds a parallel in the many final garden scenes already discussed.

"The Man of Fifty Years" contains a rather extraordinary ritual initiation. The actor in the story brings with him a "priceless dressing case ('Toilettenkästchen'), which, with its promise of extended youth, mirrors the little box Felix finds with its promise of a great secret. The way to the secret of youth, to the "higher secrets," to the "secrets for the initiated" leads, the man is told, over "levels and degrees." In the course of the story the man of fifty years loses a tooth, and the arcane promise is called into question, just as the gold of the box or book has been questioned here.

"The New Melusine" carries on the box/book/gold metaphor, illustrating the consequences of a passion for the secret (the
box, the gold coins, and the gold ring). The metaphor of a little
world in a box also deftly mirrors the box or book that is the novel.
In the lines immediately following this story, Hersilie writes to Wilhelm about similar temptations she combats in the presence of the
"little treasure box": "like a divining rod my hand reached for it, my
bit of reason held it back" (HA, VIII, 377).

The repeated mirrorings of these novellas, then, give added
cause to consider the novel's symbolic landscape and architecture in
the context of Freemasonic ritual routes. Only a few examples of
such relationships have been provided, and much work remains in
interpreting the various patterns that arise out of this perspective.
We are, however, in a position to summarize our findings.

When Theodor Mundt reviewed *Wilhelm Meister's Travels*
in 1830, he complained that the novel was full of "petty Freemasonic secrecy."[34] Freemasonry does, indeed, strongly influence the
paths Wilhelm and Felix follow, but not esoterically. The remnants
of Freemasonry seen in the novel, primarily the Masonic initiatory
route, lead to a close examination of the routes to and through the
various regions Wilhelm visits. Far from engaging in esoteric or hermetic games, Goethe here raises the craft to art. He builds on the
foundation of Freemasonry a building whose successive rooms
figuratively teach Wilhelm and the reader. With its repeated Masonic images, the novel works within a sign system often read as
transcendentally significant; but it does so with care, with self-
reflexivity, warning constantly that it is not an esoteric text, but
rather a text drawing metaphorically on a rich esoteric tradition.

Schiller's *Ghost-Seer* revealed the power inherent in Masonic symbols and argued against an artistry that would promise
absolute closure. Goethe too is concerned with false closure, but he
also searches for a means to overcome the purely arbitrary. To solve
the problem of arbitrariness he uses the traditional, productive signs
of Freemasonry, and to solve the problem of false or premature closure he undercuts that motivation by delivering self-reflexive tropes
where the reader expects more direct, "golden," disclosures. The
Masons' route may be, as the poem "Symbolum" claims, like life,
but such figuration is not conclusive: "The secrets of life's path may
not and cannot be revealed; there are stumbling-blocks over which
every traveller must stumble. The poet, however, points out the
place" ("From Makarie's Archive," HA, VIII, 460).

CHAPTER FOUR

Knights of Spirit: 1848 and Gutzkow's "Masonic Novel"

Ich sehe keine Möglichkeit, dass die Hebel der
Geschichte, die jetzt im Grossen und Offenen wirken,
das Glück der Erde fördern können.
—Karl Gutzkow, *Die Ritter vom Geiste,*
V:283)

In human society no single injustice, no single violation
of the principle of equality occurs without there being
planted, simultaneously, the seed of a secret society
which seeks to atone for the injustice and to avenge the
offense.
—George Sand,
Le Compagnon du Tour de France
(1850 German translation)

Twenty years after Theodore Mundt complained about the Freemasonic esoterica he thought he recognized in Goethe's last novel, Karl Gutzkow, a leading "Young German" and a friend of Mundt's, published a novel that likewise drew criticism for its use of Freemasonry. As opposed to Goethe, however, Gutzkow's focus was not on Masonic ritual in the interest of investigating natural and arbitrary figuration, but rather on Masonic politics, for *The Knights of Spirit* (*Die Ritter vom Geiste*, 1850–1851) is a response to the failed revolution of 1848 and subsequent reaction.

The plot of the nine-volume political novel turns around a block of apartment buildings once owned by the last member of an order of Knights Templar. For several centuries the city (recognizably Berlin) and state have managed the property and enjoyed the resulting profits. Managerial policies, however, have led to deteriorating buildings and an increasingly bad life for the poor tenants. The reader is clearly meant to see the buildings as the state, the managers as government officials, and the tenants as oppressed victims.

Dankmar and Siegbert Wildungen, young, socially committed descendants of the original Knight Templar owner, find documents that indicate they have more right to these properties than does the government, and they file suit. While the suit goes on, forces of the reaction increase and political oppression grows. Finally frustrated in their attempts to work within the public sphere, the brothers establish a political secret society, the "Knights of Spirit," drawing inspiration from several earlier groups, including the Knights Templar, the Jesuits, and the Freemasons. In the end reactionary forces take control, and the Knights of Spirit face jail or exile. But as the ninth and final volume closes, they look toward the future, even in the face of extensive material losses, with enthusiasm based on their hard-won unity of spirit.

Gutzkow's choice of a secret society to represent his hope for the future would have gone unquestioned at the time of *The Ghost-Seer* or *Wilhelm Meister's Apprenticeship*, if not the later *Travels*. But in 1850 he received immediate criticism on the subject. Julian Schmidt argued, for example, that the correct avenue to political change lay in the existing political parties, not the romantic fantasies and secret societies "of intelligent but confused people."[1] Less than a decade later, another critic, Robert Prutz, also found Gutzkow's use of a secret society untimely:

> The idea of that sort of secret society, of a Freemasonry for the highest and most lofty purposes, was still quite natural to Goethe and Schiller and their humanistic efforts: as indeed Freemasonry itself played its most influential role in that very time and—just think of Lessing and Herder—celebrated its most beautiful triumphs. For our time, however, a time of a most complete and unmitigated public sphere (Öffentlichkeit), these mysteries have lost their attraction and therewith also their importance.[2]

Gutzkow would surely have taken exception to Prutz's assertion that they were living in a time of "a most complete and unmitigated public sphere," for he was subject to continual and intense censorship.[3] And both Schmidt's and Prutz's assertions that post-Enlightenment Freemasonry was literarily passé are at least debatable.[4]

HISTORICAL DEVELOPMENTS

In several senses, however, such critical reactions were predictable, for the century had seen important changes in both Freemasonry and the political situation. The number of Freemasons had increased steadily throughout the nineteenth century;[5] but a list of nineteenth-century literary Masons—Freiligrath, Sealsfield, Zschokke, Rückert, Börne, Auerbach, and Immermann—while impressive, hardly compares to the eighteenth-century brotherhood of Goethe, Lessing, Wieland, Klinger, Klopstock, Lenz, Herder, Claudius, Fichte, Moritz, and Forster. Findel admits in his *History of Freemasonry* (*Geschichte der Freimaurerei*) that the decade from 1814 to 1824 cannot be counted among the finest of German Masonry, and he later states that Freemasonic activity of the 1830s "does not seem to have found itself in a state of great prosperity."[6]

Mundt's deprecation of Freemasonic esoterica in Goethe's novel suggests a possible reason for the decline: a negative reaction to esoteric, mystical, high-grade systems active at the time. Findel, with an alternate explanation, argued that political unrest in the years following the 1830 July revolution in France may have been the cause of decreased Masonic activity. The energies of individual Freemasons, he writes, were so taken up with attempts to change public conditions that they found little time to work to improve themselves in the lodges.[7] Implicit in Findel's assessment is the availability of a public sphere in which Masons and non-Masons can work politically. Depending on just how open that public sphere really was, the politically progressive secret society as described by Koselleck and Habermas might or might not have been relevant.[8] But whatever the cause, increased esotericism, increased opportunities for political action, or something else, Masons themselves felt the need to reform their brotherhood.

One of the most interesting and literarily fruitful developments in early nineteenth-century Freemasonry was the reform attempted by Karl Christian Friedrich Krause, the philosopher whose thoughts on Masonic ritual are discussed in Chapter 1. In Krause's philosophical system humanity is seen as an intimately connected organic whole. To facilitate interaction within that whole, Krause proposes a worldwide league of humanity. He advances his views in several works on Masonry, the most important of which is his two-volume study, *The Three Oldest Documents of the Craft of the Masonic Brotherhood* (*Die drei ältesten Kunsturkunden der Freimaurer-brüderschaft*, 1810 and 1813). To fulfill its promise as a precursor of the league of humanity, Freemasonry required a radical transformation, including dismantling the high-grade, esoteric system and abandoning secrecy in favor of public action. Like others, Krause sensed that a public sphere was now newly available. In the spirit of such openness, he published early Masonic rites in his book, rites he felt were more effective when recognized as arbitrary, as conveying no supernatural truth. Many contemporary Masons, however, still held these rites both sacred and secret; and for his troubles Krause was excommunicated. Later Masons, however, were so taken by the concept of Masonry as a league of humanity that the article on Krause in the *Internationales Freimaurer-Lexikon* goes so far as to suggest that he should be ranked with Lessing as a spiritual father of German Freemasonry.[9] As we will see, Krause's work made him an important model for Gutzkow's Knights of Spirit, he appears as a character in Oppermann's *Hundred Years* (*Hundert Jahre*) as well, and the "Krausissmo" movement in Spain was another surprising witness of his influence.

For the time being, Krause's proposals did little to change the actual Masonic institution. Responses to the proposals, however, reveal two emerging, opposing viewpoints in nineteenth-century Masonry which soon became as disruptive of the system as was the heated eighteenth-century opposition between Enlightenment and mystical Freemasonry. Krause, Findel, and others like them were politically and socially progressive and wanted their brotherhood to play a more open, direct role in developing a democratic and cosmopolitan society. Opposing Freemasons, however, placing heavy emphasis on the nonpolitical clause of Anderson's *Constitutions*, opted for the supposedly nonpolitical positions of nationalism, absolutism, law and order, and exclusion of Jews from their lodges. These political differences were exacerbated by the revolutions of 1848 and 1849, which elicited strong feelings from both sides and which gave rise to Gutzkow's novel. Articles published in two contemporary Freemasonic journals graphically illustrate this split in Freemasonry.

FREEMASONIC JOURNALS: REVOLUTION AND REACTION

The Tyler in the East of Altenburg (Der Ziegeldecker im Osten von Altenburg), a monthly Freemasonic journal published by Bernhard Lützelberger from 1837 to 1847, was typical in its conservative political outlook. The 1845 (no. 2) article by Br.ʼ. Beatus, "May the Freemason be a Worthy Charge of the State," is a good case in point; the author, as the title suggests, investigates various means through which the Masons can insure protection by enlightened German monarchs.[10] During the uncertain events of 1848, the journal, now called *Fraternal Papers for Freemasons (Bruderblätter für Freimaurer)*, makes no direct reference to the revolution. Until a victor appears, it seems, neutrality is the safest policy. But in the first issue of 1849, with the revolution foundering, Br.ʼ. Apel finds it both expedient and necessary to remind his brethren that Masonry and politics do not mix:

> In the Constitution Book of the first grand lodge in London, printed in 1723, the following passage, well worth consideration, appears: "The Mason is a peaceful subject of the civil powers, wherever he dwells and works, *and should never let himself be entangled in plots and conspiracies against the peace and the welfare of the nation*, nor show himself to be disloyal to the authorities."

This is the sort of response to political unrest one might expect from well-to-do and socially prominent Freemasons, even given the potentially explosive moral teachings they espoused in their lodges. But other Masonic writers saw in the changing times outward manifestations of their most cherished principles. The most telling of these is the series of articles published in the influential *Freimaurer-Zeitung (Freemasonic Journal)* in 1847 and 1848.[11]

The lead essay in the first number of the journal (January 1847), "How Do We Stand?"[12] responds to concerns about decreasing Freemasonic influence and references "to the Freemasonic league as an aged, decrepit creation of early times." Such attacks on the brotherhood come, the author argues, from the progressive political party, which sees in Freemasonry a supporter of aristocracy and conservatism, and from the ecclesiastical or reactionary party, which sees in Freemasonry a detestable source of rationalism. The essay then discusses the relationship between Freemasonry and the state: "[The league] does indeed awaken the love of freedom in its members; but besides that, it also nourishes a sense for order and

lawfulness and instructs its members to peacefully subjugate themselves to the existing order until their view proves itself and is taken
up by the majority or by the representatives of that order." The author himself recognizes the tension between "the love of freedom"
the brotherhood awakens in its members and the authoritarian regime they are bound to support. Nonetheless, attacked by the left
and the right, hated by the church, and under suspicion by the
state, Freemasonry is still, the essay concludes somewhat proudly,
"sought by the middle classes and defended by the healthy sense of
the people."

An essay in the second number of the *Freimaurer-Zeitung,*
"That the Human Race May Become a Fraternal Chain!" (January
1847), written by the journal's editor R. R. Fischer, progressively
addresses growing class distinction and economic deprivation
brought on by industrialization and warns of possible revolutionary
consequences.[13] Masons, who in their lodges ritually unify the
classes society divides, must work in their families, among their
employees, in whatever circles they have power, to provide necessi-
ties and ensure opportunity for education and advancement. As
Fischer sees it, many dedicated men can change social conditions;
and they can do so without recourse to direct political action. There
will be no revolution from below, he suggests, if the middle class
reaches down and raises its brothers. The careful yet still progressive statements of Fischer and the author of "How Do We Stand?"
(aimed at balancing the radical content of Freemasonry with the
demands of states that have vested interests in limiting freedom and
equality) give way, a year later, to more fiery rhetoric as the March
revolutions are at their peak.

In late March 1848, the *Freimaurer-Zeitung* announced "The
New World" in its lead article, an excited, optimistic appraisal of the
situations in France and Germany during the ongoing upheavals:

> Round about us there is a powerful impulse stirring and stretching
> and raising, the hour of the spirit has come; it wants to give birth
> to something new and grand, it wants to form the world anew. . . .
> Oh, what sort of people would we be if we were to hide ourselves
> in our circles, as if we had heard and seen nothing, while our
> hearts are so full with what has happened!

Freemasons, the author continues, practice a free self-governance
daily, recognizing no difference in class. Why should they not, then,
rejoice when the French, and now the Germans, attempt to intro-

duce such a condition into the public sphere? Although the article repeatedly points to the *spiritual* role of Freemasonry in the events of the day and states that Masonry has no place in actual politics, the author clearly feels that men trained in the lodges have played important political roles in the movement toward greater freedom, a free press, the right to free association, a German parliament, and equal rights for all religious groups. He goes so far as to claim that the lodges are the "mineshafts . . . out of which the ore is won that now builds a new world." For more than a century Freemasons had claimed they had no need to resort to politics, that the education which took place in the lodges would produce (indirectly and nonviolently) a better world. Now, it seems, years of work in the lodges has born fruit. In a time of reaction such claims will come back to haunt the Masons, whom rumors had already linked to conspiracies behind the American and French revolutions; but for this brief moment it seems that the democracy practiced and modeled in the lodges has become public reality. The author is ecstatic.

One May number of the journal continues this advocacy of revolutionary principles as it prints a call to action by the national lodge of France, claiming once again that the Freemasons, practicing freedom, equality, and brotherhood in their lodges, have prepared the way for the revolution that has reestablished these principles in public life. But as early as June the editor begins to distance his publication from revolutionary events, and by July the journal prints a speech by Br.˙. Muhl of Trier who argues strongly against revolution and in favor of law and order, *inner* freedom, and even unabashedly for reaction. He compares the revolution to a dangerous storm and reprimands those who tend to extremes to satisfy their own passions and selfish desires. The Mason's task is clear, he continues. He must teach the "raw masses" to overcome the chains of sensuality and enter into the kingdom of spiritual freedom. Further essays in October and November continue to solidify this movement away from the revolution. They rail against insecurity, confusion, political agitators, pride, passion, sensuality, rabidity, lawlessness, party struggles, and violence. At the same time they champion law, order, virtue, unity, peace, comfort, and protection of property. Such unmitigated reaction is surely the basis of many negative political evaluations of nineteenth-century Freemasonry. But, as evidenced by the essays of March through April 1848, some Masons, however briefly, openly identified the aims of the revolution as their own.

THE CONSPIRACY THEORY

Whether nineteenth-century Freemasonry was in fact reactionary, revolutionary, or nonpolitical, the eighteenth-century perception of the order as a powerful conspiracy against the established powers of throne and altar lost none of its power as the new century progressed. The 1817 gathering of student fraternities at the Wartburg lent credence to this theory; and in 1819, when a fraternity brother assassinated Kotzebue,[14] governments acted quickly to ban such fraternities.[15] Public perception that secret societies were behind political unrest throughout Europe grew substantially when the Carbonari successfully concluded their 1820 revolution in Italy. After a later, unsuccessful putsch attempt in France, for example, the French attorney general Marchangy explained: "The present revolutions are . . . not innate, but learned, and this same lesson, running from north to south, explains the similarity of the aberrations. . . . The secret societies are the workshops of conspiracy."[16] And Friedrich Schlegel pointed at Freemasonry as the source of revolution in his lectures on the *Philosophy of History* in 1828: "A society from whose bosom, as from the secret laboratory of Revolution, the Illuminés, the Jacobins, and the Carbonari have successfully proceeded, cannot possibly be termed, or be in fact, very beneficial to mankind, politically sound, or truly Christian in its views and tendency" (457).

In one of the most literarily interesting variations on the conspiracy theory, the group of writers identified in the goverment ban of 1835 as "Young Germany" was seen as a potentially dangerous secret society. Eitel Wolf Dobert points out that while the "Young Germans" were certainly not a secret society, some of their assertions could have led governments to think so: Laube wrote of forming a party, Gutzkow suggested combining together in a conspiracy, and Mund wrote to Kühne that he wanted to convene these men who longed for a politically active league.[17] Friedrich Engels wrote that Wuppertal textile merchants saw "Young Germany" as a secret society led by the conspirators Heine, Weinberg, and Gutzkow.[18]

In the eighteenth century, conspiracy theories had led people to link Freemasons, Enlightenment philosophers, and liberal constitutionalists; but in the nineteenth century, such theories began to associate Freemasons with Jews and the democratic-socialist movement.[19] Eduard Emil Eckert, a Catholic lawyer in Prague, published a pamphlet in 1852 arguing that the Constitution of the German Reich of 1848–1849 had been the product of a Masonic league of social democrats.[20] And a "Call of Warning to Princes and Peoples" by a "German Patriot" published a few years later made similar accusations: *Freemasonry and Social Democracy, or, Is Freemasonry, Along with Social Democracy, also Demonstrably Dangerous to Religion, State, and Society?*[21] People ultimately feared that these conspiring societies might be related to the communists, whose manifesto (1848) begins with the famous paragraph about current and widespread rumors that link every opposition party with a shadowy and dangerous conspiracy: "A specter is haunting Europe" ("Ein Gespenst geht um in Europa").

LITERARY FREEMASONRY FROM BÖRNE TO GUTZKOW

Gutzkow knew the general rumors of conspiracy, some of which were aimed at himself as one of the "Young Germans," and he had access to Freemasonry through his mentor Ludwig Börne, whose biography he wrote.[22] Börne, a practicing Freemason and a powerful, political man of letters, felt a tension between his hopes for Freemasonry and actual practices; and in his speech "On Freemasonry" ("Über Freimaurerei," 1811?) given in his lodge "Zur aufgehenden Morgenröte" in Frankfurt, Börne questioned Masonry's secrecy, attacked contention between various lodges and systems, and characterized true Masonry: "It should give order to the entangled rights of life. . . . It destroys the separating wall erected by the prejudice between one person and another. . . . In this manner, my brothers, Masonry should act, thus it should be. But only seldom *was* it so, and it *is* not so."[23] Enlightened practices of Börne's lodge were used by later propagandists as "proof" that Freemasonry was a Jewish front. Börne's Freemasonry surely played a role in Gutzkow's decision to feature a secret society in *The Knights of Spirit*. So too did the Masonic fictions of the years leading up to 1848. Since the late eighteenth century, to which time critics Schmidt and Prutz relegated productive fictional use of Freemasonry, novelists had continually returned to the themes and motifs of the fraternity.

In 1817 Achim von Arnim published the first volume of his *Guardians of the Crown (Kronenwächter),*[24] a novel in which a secret, powerful, and unscrupulous league of aristocratic knights plots to depose Kaiser Maximilian of the Hapsburg monarchy and to reestablish one of the Hohenstaufen family on the throne. Opposing this conspiracy is a forward-looking league of democratic masons (or Freemasons, for they invite nonoperative, or speculative Masons into their lodges) complete with "verbal signs, greetings, and handshakes" (562) and with a sense for the power of solidarity ("Alone we are nothing, we must live in unanimity"). Fourteen years after Arnim's "political" use of Freemasonry, and two years after the final version of *Wilhelm Meister's Travels* appeared, Ludwig Tieck published a story about the deleterious effects of Masonry: "The Miracle Addicts" ("Die Wundersüchtigen," 1831).[25] Despite much praise for a true, enlightened Freemasonry like that in the first half of the eighteenth century, the aristocratic family of this story falls for the tricks of a self-styled emissary from a mystical branch of Masonry, a man with all the talents and attributes of Cagliostro or St. Germain. The novel tempts its characters with the philosopher's stone, spirits, immortality, omniscience, unknown heads of powerful orders, Jesuit takeovers of Freemasonry, conversions of gullible princes to Catholicism through powerful emissaries, lodges of adoption for women, the unmasking of the first magus by a second, and more. It is the much embellished and trivialized story of Schiller's *Ghost-Seer*, a portrait of pitched battle between enlightened and superstitious sects of Freemasonry near the end of the eighteenth century; and it ends triumphantly as all members of the family overcome "this sickness of miracle addiction."[26]

In 1835 Karl Immermann, himself a Mason, finished a more substantial work, *The Epigones* (*Die Epigonen*).[27] Along with a plot and characters drawn in part from *Wilhelm Meister's Apprenticeship* (Mignon = Flämmchen, Natalie = Kornelie) he includes several secret societies as analogues of the Society of the Tower. In fact, the often quoted sentence from the novel, which expresses a generation's frustration at following the literary giants of Weimar—"We are, to state the entire misery in one word, epigones"—is pronounced during an intriguing Masonic initiation ceremony.

Wilhelmi, counselor to the ruler of a tiny principality, feels that fate has dealt him less than his talents deserve and he has developed a sense for "the general inadequacy in the world. . . . Unsatisfied with everything he saw in reality, he built for himself a sort of dream world" (117). One night after several games of chess, Wilhelmi initiates Hermann, the novel's young protagonist, into that dream world: "'Thus I accept you, my brother, into the new degree which I hereby establish'" (123). After they complete the business of setting up a reformed Freemasonry for the salvation of mankind, the two men, "knights of truth" (126), turn to good food and champagne, as is the Masonic custom. Under the influence, Wilhelmi begins to sing student songs, "in which, because they all breathed freedom, fraternity, and justice, Hermann, enflamed by the newly-won honor, joined in enthusiastically" (126). As the night progresses the party grows wilder, and by morning they have wrought havoc in the once perfectly ordered study. Wilhelmi is so hung over that he cannot fulfill his morning duties. Clearly the new order of Knights of Truth set up to renew Freemasonry is an impotent fantasy, another creation of Wilhelmi's dream world.

But the novel, which covers the years 1823–1835, identifies other secret societies as more than laughable relics of the past. Since the book burnings at the Wartburg by student fraternities, radical students have been involved in various political plots; but Hermann, except when drunk, has decided to oppose such youthful fanaticism. At one point he attends a meeting of students who have formed a radical men's league (*Männerbund*). Disgusted by the demagogery, he pulls a pistol and gives the young men a lecture at gunpoint. Unfortunately for him, police arrive on the scene and mistake him for the gun-weilding leader of the demagogues. Only the intervention of Menon, a high government official, effects his release. Menon himself is later arrested as part of "a great conspiracy which was intent on the overthrow of the throne and on regicide. The most important men were supposed to be involved in the plot" (484). As befits such a man, Menon was raised by a former Jesuit and learned early that the end justifies the means (527). He fought for his country "when the great call of freedom rang through Germany" (527–528); and when that battle was lost, he decided that the existing order must be destroyed by an anarchy-sowing conspiracy from within.

Wilhelmi and Menon, then, are two men bitterly disappointed by both society and government. Their responses are antithetical. Wilhelmi is a man of thought, while Menon is a man of forceful action. They are related, however, by a similar reliance on a secret society as the vehicle for their plans. Wilhelmi's inner-directed, nonpolitical Freemasonry corresponds well to the Masonry of his time; even his call to reform Masonry mirrors efforts in the real order. But Menon's Jesuit-inspired conspiracy also reflects current conditions and fears. Assertions like that of Sammons—Menon as a conspirator "is an ideological straw man, not corresponding to anything in social or political reality"[28]—would seem unfounded. Politically subversive secret societies did exist during the mid-nineteenth century, and if they had not, the public's fear of conspiracy was a major factor in both social and political reality.[29]

Georg Büchner's *Woyzeck* (written in 1836, the same year *The Epigones* was published), movingly portrays those contemporary fears:

> Woyzek. Yes, Andres, the place is cursed. Do you see the bright strip over there in the grass where the mushrooms are growing now. In the evening the head rolls there. Someone picked it up once, he thought it was a hedgehog: three days and three nights, and he lay on shavings. *Softly:* Andres, that was the Freemasons! I've got it, the Freemasons! . . . It's happening behind me, under me. *Stamps on the ground:* Hollow, do you hear? everything hollow down there! The Freemasons![30]

Hans Mayer sees in this overwrought fear of a Masonic conspiracy a concrete example of a larger worry "about the independence of human existence from conditions which 'lie outside us.' Büchner sensed the 'monstrous fatalism of history' and its 'destructive' power already in his earliest Giessener time" (339). Freemasonry serves two opposite purposes in the face of such loss of control. On the one hand, as in *The Epigones* or *Woyzek*, secret societies are seen as the insidious cause of chaos, manifestations of external, uncontrollable forces. But on the other hand, as in Krause's and Börne's hopes for Freemasonry, a league of morally determined men lend order to a disintegrating society.[31]

In 1842, the year the radical poet Ferdinand Freiligrath became a Freemason,[32] Gutzkow traveled to Paris; and one of his *Letters from Paris* (*Briefe aus Paris*, March 29, 1842) describes a visit with George Sand, whose calls for women's emancipation from social and religious constraints had helped shape Gutzkow's *Wally, the Doubter* (*Wally, die Zweiflerin*). Sand's novel *Consuelo*, which appeared during that year and the next, and its sequel, *La Comtesse de Rudolstadt* (1843–1844), surely influenced Gutzkow's thinking concerning secret societies.[33] Secret societies were, for Sand, instruments of political and social change. In the preface to an earlier novel, *Le Compagnon du Tour de France* (1840), translated into German as *Isolde* in 1850[34] (that is, just after the failed revolution and as the first volume of Gutzkow's *The Knights of Spirit* appeared), Sand describes secret societies as necessary champions of equality and emphasizes their historical role in bringing down empires.[35]

In Sand's work alone Gutzkow had ample contemporary literary precedent for the politically active secret society he introduced in *The Knights of Spirit*. And in the person of Börne, as well as in works of Tieck, Goethe, Immermann, and Büchner, he had a wide range of political and nonpolitical nineteenth-century examples as well.[36] Add to these literary representations (1) the responses of historical Freemasons to the revolutions of 1848 (both conservative and liberal) and (2) the current conspiracy theories, and it becomes clear that those criticisms of *The Knights of Spirit* which relegate its pseudo-Masonic secret society to the eighteenth century must be seriously reconsidered. To argue, then, as did Schmidt and Prutz, that the subject belonged to Goethe's time and definitely not to the mid-nineteenth century, is to misread the historical and literary trends leading up to 1848. Freemasonry continued to figure prominently in world affairs at least through the end of the twentieth century (cf. the government scandal caused recently by the P 2 lodge in Italy); and Tolstoy and Thomas Mann would be just two of the novelists to make extensive use of Freemasonry in their works during the next century.

It seems clear that Gutzkow cannot be faulted for writing about Freemasonry. But his critics also express concern for *how* he uses secret societies in his novel. Herbert Kaiser, for example, echoes Schmidt's claim that Gutzkow would have done better to oppose the existing system with a political party:

> After a first phase of the development of modern political parties was already almost completed through the revolution and its parliaments, Gutzkow does not only hold fast to the organizational form of pre-March (vormärzlicher) political secret societies, but depoliticises and mystifies it to such a degree that it resembles the pedagogical Society of the Tower in Goethe's *Wilhelm Meister* much more than a republican league of the Metternich era.[37]

And Claus Richter contends that *The Knights of Spirit* are sadly typical of the apolitical liberal intelligentsia, that they substitute myth for political action.[38] It is difficult to argue with either Kaiser or Richter. *The Knights of Spirit* are far from an ideal organization and can easily be faulted for any number of things. In fact, the novel as a whole is unwieldy and betrays the haste in which it was written. But the information just presented about the potent conspiracy theory and contemporary use of Freemasons by French and German novelists gives us ample reason to ask why such a secret society stands at the center of Gutzkow's novel, as opposed to why it should not do so.

KNIGHTS TEMPLAR, JESUITS, FREEMASONS, AND CLUBS OF RIGHT AND LEFT

Five actual historical and contemporary "secret societies" are presented in the novel as precursors of and inspirations for the Knights of Spirit: the Knights Templar, the Jesuits, the Freemasons, the reactionary League of Regret (*Reubund*), and political workers' clubs. Early in the first volume Dankmar characterizes the Knights Templar, whose tradition he hopes to continue, and praises them as the inheritors of a rich tradition leading from India to Solomon's temple and to Jesus Christ's grave. They served an important role, he says, as an independent power between church and state. Armed with a grand, world-historical vision they performed glorious deeds and died as brave martyrs. Unfortunately, they lost their sense of historical purpose and eventually sank into gluttony and banality.

In Dankmar's history, after the decline of Catholic and Protestant Templars, the Jesuit Order arose. The Jesuits' main representative in the novel is Sylvester Rafflard, an egotistical, dangerous man who comes to Berlin from Paris to carry out a series of political schemes. If half of what Rafflard claims to have accomplished is true, and there seems to be no reason to doubt his assertions, then Dankmar's admiration for Jesuit political power derived from a secret, hierarchical organization is fully understandable.[39]

Acting as a foil to the Jesuits and continuing the tradition of the Knights Templar are the Freemasons, an admired but also satirized society. Schlurck, Gelbsattel, and Rafflard, three of the novel's more despicable characters, are all Freemasons, as are the more likeable Harder, Rudhard, and Ackermann/Rodewald. Gutzkow's assessment of contemporary Masonry can be characterized by noting that the first three are active Masons, while the latter three have distanced themselves from the order. Of Harder, for instance, it is said "that he is the head of all Masonic lodges of the country and is considered deeply knowledgeable about Masonic secrets" (II, 326). But the old man has not visited a lodge for ten years. At one point he complains about the development of what was once a vigorous

Enlightenment institution: "But to base this league so entirely on nothing, as it has now been brought low, to so utterly strip it of every connection with great historical ideas, and to transform it only into a kind of finer choral society, who wants to go along with that" (IX, 173–174).

According to Harder, then, Freemasonry has followed the course of the late Knights Templar, forsaking historical purpose for empty sociality and pleasures of the palate. There is also a decided turn to the mystical, as Schlurck describes: "We have two sects in Freemasonry, a rationally enlightened one and a mystical one. I have joined the mystical, dark one. . . . I want to call magicians, treasure hunters, those who conjure up the dead. Perhaps I'll even become a Jesuit" (VIII, 137–138). But while Schlurck is attracted to this sort of Masonry, the more principled Rudhard says that he left the brotherhood specifically because of its growing mysticism (III, 457). Rudhard still defends the original Freemasonry as a highly rational anti-Jesuit institution (VIII, 293), and eighteenth-century Masonry also receives credit for acting charitably, for serving humanitarian causes, for giving impetus to culture, for furthering rationality, for helping men out of the bonds of religion and class, for preparing the "good" results of the French revolution, and for strengthening the sense of community among intellectuals (VIII, 293–296). But elsewhere Dankmar faults as much too general the seemingly uncontroversial goal of educating humanity: "the betterment of the world begins when one betters oneself, . . . such a doctrine necessarily degenerates into lassitude, thoughtlessness, epicureanism, . . . [the] destructive dry-rot on the invisible buildings of the Freemasons" (V, 286).[40] Harder echoes this description of political impotence when he refers to a lost opportunity forty years earlier, a time when Masonry had the chance to affect history meaningfully by setting out to transform itself and the world into a league of humanity, an opportunity raised by publication of Krause's *The Three Oldest Documents of the Craft of the Masonic Brotherhood* (1810).[41] Krause's call for a more public working of Masonry, and especially his teachings about the historical necessity of a league of humanity, far outweighed, in Harder's estimation, any technical mistakes he may have made. The forty intervening years have been politically difficult as absolutist oppressors and angrily partisan groups have fought for political control. Now, after 1848, a league of humanity is more necessary than ever.

Two additional societies have arisen in the wake of the Knights Templar, Jesuits, and Freemasons. Both are more political than the weak Freemasons, but unfortunately, in the narrator's view, both are radical organizations. The first group consists of various workers' clubs with vague ties to Communism (VII, 485). The Knights of Spirit sympathize with them and their democratic principles (VI, 158–159), but find their politics too radical and step in to blunt their calls for revolution (VIII, 377). The second society is the League of Regret (*Reubund*), based on the historical League of Faithfulness (*Treubund*) founded in 1848 as an antidemocratic organization. Early in the novel Schlurck speaks of the *Reubund* as a post-Masonic secret society with facilities for eating well. Dankmar, who places more emphasis on the political leanings of the order than on the quality of its food, blasts the *Reubund* for its servility in the face of growing reaction: "The League of Regret seems to me really one of the most hopeless offspring of a people which is exhibiting its total immaturity for political education" (I, 184). But later, as Dankmar contemplates the conversation he had with Schlurck, he begins to wonder about the *Reubund* as a possible vehicle for his plans. Couldn't he infiltrate it and turn the bastion of absolutism into an antiabsolutist secret society?

A secret society as part of the battle against absolutism—this is a key idea for Dankmar. In this context, each of the five precursors to the Knights of Spirit has something to teach the new society. From the Knights Templar comes the continuity of ages. The Jesuits have an organization that produces political power. The Freemasons are an incipient league of humanity. The workers' clubs promote democracy. And even the *Reubund* is attractive as an organizational means to promote a political agenda.

THE KNIGHTS OF SPIRIT

Dankmar is amazed as he begins to realize how various societies have worked secretly to guide the course of history, or how history has progressed by using secret societies: "thus the secret societies were suddenly for him a secret nightside of society . . . who can follow the paths which the mole of the World-Spirit (der Maulwurf des Weltgeistes) digs for itself deep in the womb of the earth" (I, 205). Given the general political conditions of present and past centuries, Dankmar reasons, given the lack of opportunity for the public to influence government policy, given the immoral absolutism under which most people have suffered, is it any wonder that men would gather together to establish a secret, more moral society, a private sphere in which alternative "levers of history" can be pulled?[42] If the state enforces its power by arms, then several possibilities lie open to the opposition. One option, armed revolution, has just been tried, and it has been defeated, Dankmar feels, because of disunity. But with individual strength magnified by the shared purpose of many and with a secretly wielded moral lever political force may be exerted in a new way. In two long speeches—the first to friends as the new order is being planned, and the second a speech of dedication as the order is founded—Dankmar elaborates on his vision of the Knights of Spirit.

Spirit, he says, is the key. Unfortunately, people of the nineteenth century seem no longer to have a spiritual center for which they live. But there are a few concepts, simple and deeply grounded within each person, that people of all levels of intelligence can embrace. They need no other proof than that they give light and warmth. On the basis of these shared concepts the Knights of Spirit will be founded; and Dankmar predicts that given fifty years to work, his society will unify mankind. When he gathers his friends around him to found the society, each friend speaks of their shared desire for democracy; but as Dankmar points out before he begins his own speech, one has recommended immediate and vigorous action, one has suggested only a tentative experiment, and another wants to work peacefully within the existing system. Dankmar argues that before all else come unity and simplicity; and, he says, "we must forsake bringing forth positive creations and satisfy ourselves with promoting only the spirit in which they might grow up" (VI, 285). Any concrete ideal, Dankmar states, necessarily creates dissonance. But weak generalities are no help either: "And neither will I recommend that one be satisfied with generalities in the mutual exchange of ideas and plans, as are the Freemasons" (VI, 327). So what does Dankmar believe? For what ideas will his Knights of Spirit fight? He is not completely sure. "I want a league of men who relate their life, their nearest and most distant duties only to a single goal, the final victory of truths which are still, unfortunately, in question" (VI, 331). But then again he seems to have the necessary knowledge: "The truths are obvious, but thousands are avoiding them. The pages of history are open. People refuse to read them. We know the goal toward which humanity is steering" (VI, 331–332).

After this positive, if general, declaration of historical purpose, Dankmar waxes eloquent about the battles that could be won by several thousand people united together in the service of these well-known truths. But then he returns to his negative definition of the task: "It lies in the nature of a time which needs to clear away more than to build, that its truths are more negative than positive. The Knights of Spirit will be clearer about that for which they do not let themselves be used than about what they themselves want" (VI, 332–333). Although one cannot exactly describe the perfect temple of mankind, he says, parts of it can be approximated; and these include a free press and the right to work, the "fundamental right of all peoples." Present conditions, Dankmar states, deny those rights, and he swears that his league will "clear things away, and quickly" (VI, 334). But even so, he claims that his ideas will not lead to conspiracy and revolt. As one Knight of Spirit tells a mob of angry workers, they should quit demonstrating and place their trust in the *Weltgeist*, working even then in silent, unknown ways (VIII, 379).

But there is another side to the matter as well. Although the Knights of Spirit eschew material solutions, Dankmar does not want to denigrate his organization "to a mere phantom of inflamed police imagination" (IX, 376). He knows how many people are being influenced by rumors and finds it advantageous during police interrogation to encourage reports about the Knights of Spirit: "He wanted to be the bearer of all the images of terror with which the enemies of freedom frighten themselves" (IX, 377). At least in rumor and for the police, then, the secret society is a revolutionary, even terrorist group. And some actions support such an assumption: Dankmar's forcible rescue from prison; other "friends of the people" who unexpectedly find their ways out of prisons; early warnings of police searches; the monetary and moral support the order gives to those who lose their state jobs because of their insistance on personal autonomy (VIII, 190); and the growing number of deeds done under the neo-Masonic symbol of four dots. A scene late in the novel reinforces this active side of the Knights of Spirit.

With many of its members in exile, with their country ever more fully in control of reactionary leaders, and with the money they have won in court reduced to ashes, the group meets for its second great convocation. A nameless young man speaks of the nonviolent ideals for which they strive: "The league of spirit, I sense it, will be entirely of the spirit. We cannot fight with golden weapons. . . . The kingdom of God is within us" (IX, 533). But such selfless control has its limits, and the young man continues: "The spirit of this age cannot be gentle and still, you brothers! . . . the age of long-suffering brought no fruit for two thousand years . . . the dove may no longer be the symbol of the spirit! . . . Who can sleep? If finite nature wants the spirit too, to sleep, so let it be with a hand on the hilt of the sword. Act!" (IX, 534). He quickly returns to the assertion that ideas alone can change the world, but the threat has been uttered. However metaphorical his use of "sword" may be, political metaphors tend to reification; and the tone of frustration and rebellion struck here at the end of the novel is ominous.

As this speech demonstrates, the Knights of Spirit have created for themselves an ambiguous position. They decry violence yet carry the seeds of violence. They propound positive, progressive changes but refuse to specify their goals. They fault Freemasonry for its weak generality but finally propose only generalities themselves. And they oppose not only the existing system but also the various opposition parties. Along with Gutzkow's critics, one is left wondering just why he set this secret society at the center of his novel.

WHY A SECRET SOCIETY AFTER 1848?

In the reaction following the failed revolutions of 1848, the tension between political reality and desires for democracy was greater than ever before, for Gutzkow and his fellows had briefly tasted the first fruits of *direct* political power. Their dreams of democracy had nearly become reality, only to disappear in a chaos of party strife and an overwhelming reaction. Given the new limitations on public political action (the state had proven its power even under considerable revolutionary pressure), should it be so surprising that Gutzkow, in his novel, turns to secret moral action? Knights of the barricade had failed to change the government, and in the aftermath Knights of Spirit again arise to pursue the same goal indirectly. Tactics developed during the Enlightenment are resorted to once again.[43] Near the end of the novel, a Masonic historian, Dagobert von Harder, is cited concerning the recurring historical need for secret societies: "People have always fled from the ruling facts and their coersive alliances into a free, invisible alliance of higher truths" (IX, 316).

Besides the secrecy and the moral truth of the lodges, the *tradition* of secret societies weighed heavy in Gutzkow's judgment. More than anything else, the Knights of Spirit seek to prove their right to carry on an honorable tradition. During and after the revolution of 1848 there were many accusations of selfishness and anarchy thrown at political parties and "mobs"—most strongly at the disturbing Communists. What right did any one person or party have to overthrow the existing order? What was the sense of exchanging one self-seeking government for another? In short, where was the legitimacy of the new? The secret society formed by the Knights of Spirit answers such criticism through its insistence on *Erbrecht*, the right to inherit.

Nearly all the novel's many plot strands deal with inheritance in some way. Most important is the Wildungen's inheritance from the Knights Templar, the right, in effect, to govern in the place of the caretaker state. At one point Dankmar states the issue forcefully: "now my own and my brother's personal affair is formally a symbol of the question of our century . . . everything is about the right of a person, about the lasting power of the past" (VI, 242). And later he repeats that assertion: "my lawsuit has thus become an image of our age" (VI, 245). Dankmar's suit challenges long-held beliefs and accepted rights on the basis of an alternate and even older tradition. He sets out to prove that he has more historical right to the property in question than does the city or state: "We too appeal to the same seal from which the state and the church, the general populace and the community derive their rights. We are demonstrating by means of a harsh example that laws and rights are inherited like an 'eternal sickness'" (VI, 319). The order is to be a new one, founded "over and beyond the league of Freemasons" (VI, 286); but however new, the order's genealogy, an inheritance proven by "documented historical facts" (II, 58), gives it legitimacy.[44] As quoted earlier, Dankmar is sure his Knights of Spirit are playing a legitimately inherited role in the progressive unfolding of history: "The pages of history are open. . . . We know the goal toward which humanity is steering" (VI, 331). As tools of the *Weltgeist*, the Knights of Spirit insist on the historical validity of their cause and continually emphasize their genealogy of spirit. Accused of radicality, selfishness, and illegitimacy, the proponents of the new order seek historical validity by focusing on their spiritual genealogy and calling attention to the illegitimacy of the present system.[45] Gutzkow thus counters the specter of political arbitrariness in the same way Goethe countered symbolic arbitrariness—by turning to the tradition of Freemasonry and its predecessors.

While his Knights of Spirit try to balance political revolution and tradition, Gutzkow situates his novel on a related border: between *literary* tradition and revolution. Alexander Jung, in his *Letters on Gutzkow's Knights of Spirit* (*Briefe über Gutzkow's Ritter vom Geiste*, 1856),[46] wrote that while critics have singled out Dankmar's secret society as an object of scorn, the same was the case when Goethe published *Wilhelm Meister* (9); and Jung finds *Wilhelm Meister's Travels* and *The Knights of Spirit* remarkably similar, in form as well as content.[47] Gutzkow himself compared his novel to *Wilhelm Meister*: "I wanted, as it were, to write a political Wilhelm Meister, simple, natural, true-to-life."[48] A political *Wilhelm Meister*. Fifty years earlier Novalis found Goethe's novel too prosaic, a *Candide* aimed at true art, and set out to write a more poetic version. But Gutzkow finds that an updated *Meister* needs politics. By writing in and against the tradition of *Wilhelm Meister*, Gutzkow gains the force of a formidable precedent, one against which he can then play off his own ideas for political change.

Finally, and for me most significant, the novel's Masonic secret society, whatever its literary and political tradition, powerfully affects public perception, provoking wild rumors: "The government, Pax said, has uncovered a bunch of dangerous plots. Foreign emissaries have arrived from Paris and America. There are the most exact indications of a developing new revolutionary movement" (VI, 197). The rumors obviously draw on the political phobias of the nineteenth century: "Unsettling enough was the tale of a great, secret league which reached into the furthest branches of all classes and which made the ground on which one daily walked unsafe" (IX, 86);[49] "one spoke generally about a far-reaching league whose head no one knew, whose statutes were still unwritten, which would, however, arise more powerfully" (IX, 143–144).

Foreign emissaries of a new revolutionary movement, a monstrous secret society with tentacles reaching into all levels of society, unknown heads mysteriously leading the powerful society —these are not only the exotic requisites of the league novel but also the nightmares of contemporary political phantasy as well. Dankmar has no compunctions about feeding such perceptions, for they lend power to his order of spiritual Knights. And Gutzkow, despite his many critics on this score, finds in the league novel a ready-made literary genre through which to play on public paranoia so that his own sometimes vague hopes seem more attractive than the alternatives. The carefully established case for political legitimacy (and the illegitimacy of the ruling government), along with the repeatedly stated moderate position of the Knights of Spirit, are calculated to ease fears the novel feeds and to suggest a workable alternative to the various extremes—all while drawing immediacy from the actions of more radical conspiracies, real and supposed.

In the end Gutzkow himself admitted to certain narrative deficiencies in his novel.[50] Nonetheless, there are good historical and literary reasons for Gutzkow to have portrayed such a secret society. Secret societies have traditionally acted as a secret moral (and thus political) force under repressive governments. Their long history lends an aura of legitimacy. And, most significant, a Masonic secret society weds a potent threat of conspiratorial overthrow with a mollifying Enlightenment tradition and thus plays on both sides of the public's perception. In setting up this dual role, Gutzkow approaches politically what authors drawn to the semiotics of Freemasonry also found interesting: that the symbols of an eighteenth-century institution, as arbitrary (revolutionary) as their century demanded that they be, nevertheless had a long esoteric history to motivate (legitimize) them. Freemasonry, politically and semiotically, sits firmly on the border between tradition and revolution, the motivated and the arbitrary, the private and the public, and thus finds its way into a spectrum of German novels broad enough to include both Goethe and Gutzkow.

IN THE TRADITION OF GUTZKOW: OTHER POST-1848 NOVELS

In the decade following publication of *The Knights of Spirit*, two of Gutzkow's "Young German" friends, Gustav Kühne and Theodor Mundt also wrote about Freemasons, as did Joseph von Rathewitz and Eduard Breier. The work of all four was influenced by Gutzkow and clearly mirrors current public interest in Freemasonry; together they provide an informative sequel to *The Knights of Spirit*.[51]

Eduard Breier's *The Rosicrucians in Vienna* (*Die Rosenkreuzer in Wien*, 1852), plays on the conspiracy theory that echoes throughout *The Knights of Spirit*. The Rosicrucians of the novel's title prove bumbling and gullible men eager to follow a Mesmer, Swedenborg, St. Germain, Cagliostro, Schröpfer, or Lavater. An agent of the Illuminati enters this environment of intrigue and intense longing for mysteries; and through the efforts of the hundred Illuminati agents who serve him he appears omniscient and omnipotent. By propagating unrest and discontent he hopes to create political chaos to further the revolution; in this respect he resembles Menon in *The Epigones*, whose conspiratorial aim was likewise to create chaos leading to revolution. Personal greed gradually leads him away from his political goals; and in the end, as his scheme begins to go awry, three mysterious emissaries of the unknown head of the Illuminati arrive to punish him horribly for endangering their great political purpose.

The stated aim of Breier's book is "enlightenment." The narrator attacks, for instance, secret societies that paradoxically combine democratic goals and unknown heads; and superstitions of several sorts are set up for ridicule. But the novel itself feeds the very superstitions it supposedly attacks. A real Rosicrucian is left mysteriously holding the true formula for the philosopher's stone. And when a prophecy "Cagliostro" makes about how three men will fare in the next year is miraculously fulfilled at the end of the novel, the reader is left with a sense for the confidence man's real power. Finally, the reader must deal with the "fact" that unbelievably powerful emissaries of the Illuminati are somewhere out there undermining law-abiding monarchies for their own devious purposes. This theory of conspiracy is surely as destructive as any superstition the novel purports to disclose.[52]

More substantial than Breier's fiction is Gustav Kühne's novel of 1855: *The Freemasons (Die Freimaurer)*. Kühne was a student of Hegel's, a close friend of Theodor Mundt, an acquaintance of Gutzkow, a leading "Young German," the editor of several influential journals (his *Europa* published inflammatory works by several *Vormärz* figures and then ran into trouble with newly repressive authorities after the revolution of 1848), and a prolific, if mediocre author of fiction. He was no more a Freemason than Gutzkow; but like Gutzkow he found in the brotherhood a possible way to realize one of his dreams, at least literarily.

The Freemasons, set in the latter half of the eighteenth century, tells the stories of three men: an autocratic, fiercely orthodox Protestant ruler of a small German principality, his Italian son-in-law (a one-time Jesuit emissary and then Waldensian heretic), and a son of the Italian (who has a Waldensian mother, is raised by Jesuits, and then converts to Protestantism). The novel's title comes from the fact that all these men, despite their marked differences, are Freemasons. And this for a purpose. Kühne's main concern in the novel is the religious strife that separates families and nations. The depictions of cruel Catholic suppression of Waldensians and Jews are stirring, as is the Protestant ruler's heartless treatment of his daughter for having converted to Catholicism. Instances of religious bigotry abound in the novel and establish the need for Freemasonry's palliative influence (or so it would seem). But complications arise as various lodges vie for power, and Freemasonry mirrors, rather than transcends, the sectarian religious strife. In the end, however, the Italian son-in-law, more optimistic than most readers will be, sees Enlightenment Freemasonry as a natural and positive response to the chaotic German political conditions and wishes for a continuation of the order, along with a more open, political institution (597).

The Freemasons follows The Knights of Spirit in depicting religious and political strife. Kühne places more emphasis on the former, Gutzkow on the latter. Both novels present a Masonic secret society that transcends the discord and also depict warring societies. The solution in both cases is a general, utopian, Krausian, Masonic league of humanity.

A third novel about Freemasons, The Three Freemasons (Die drei Freimaurer), published in 1855 and 1856 by Joseph von Rathewitz (an author who, like Breier, has left almost no traces in literary history), directly addresses connections between Freemasonry and revolution, as one can already see from the subtitle: "Revelations from the Life and Deeds of the Same, Since the Year of the Revolution 1848. An Appendage to the Life and Deeds of the Jesuits; From Surviving Papers of a Deceased Freemason."[53]

In this novel Hugo, a young prison escapee originally arrested because of his role in the 1848 revolution, meets a wealthy Freemason, Meerfels, who informs him of Freemasonry's goals. The Masons do not support revolution, he says, but rather the peaceful building of the temple of freedom and humanity. They are secretly at work bringing about what he calls a moral "Masonic-Democracy." In a discussion about the school for artisans the Masons support, Meerfels speaks of revolution: "You know what I think about the revolution. I have always viewed it as a dangerous, epidemic sickness which spread through half of Europe and finally broke out in madness" (163). Once the novel establishes Freemasonry as a democratic but antirevolutionary society, Hugo is asked to join another secret society: the League of the Red Hearts. These men advocate the violent overthrow of the existing government, so Hugo, still impressed by Meerfels's gentle, humanitarian Freemasonry, refuses the offer. Under some pressure he finally attends a meeting; but during the meeting, held underground in the cemetery, he stands up for his new principles and must endure the most vile threats. When he continues to refuse to join, his opponents suddenly burst into cheers and welcome him into their "true Masonic league." Together they sing Mozart's "O Isis and Osiris" and contemplate various Masonic symbols, secure in the knowledge that they are no conspiratorial league against the state, but rather a group of loyally concerned citizens. The plot gradually veers toward Rosicrucian esoterica but finally ends happily for the downtrodden masses.

Like Gutzkow's novel, *The Three Freemasons* combines Freemasonry and postrevolutionary politics. Like the Knights of Spirit, Meerfels's Freemasons advocate movement toward democracy through nonviolent deeds of spirit. But unlike Gutzkow (or Kühne, for that matter) Rathewitz evidences no desire to move beyond Freemasonry to a more openly political group. And like Kühne's and Breier's novels, *The Three Freemasons* is complete with an homage to the occult practices of Masonry's Rosicrucian offshoots.

Although published in 1870, fifteen years after the others, Heinrich Oppermann's *Hundred Years: 1770–1870* (*Hundert Jahre: 1770–1870*) is a good *postscript* to the post-1848 Masonic novel. As a student Oppermann was influenced by Krause, whose philosophy he presented and defended in his *Encyclopedia of Philosophy* (*Encyklopädie der Philosophie*, 1844). Oppermann was politically active, and he contributed to two of Gutzkow's journals. While writing his magnum opus he consulted often with Gutzkow, whose *Knights of Spirit* he saw as a perfect model for broad political fiction.[54] *Hundred Years*, like the *Knights of Spirit*, is a huge novel in nine volumes, originally published serially in a newspaper. In one of the many plot strands an artist named Hellung returns to Dresden from slavery in Tunisia and under the influence of Krause's philosophy becomes a Freemason. In another part of the novel a law student named Gottfried Schulz studies under Krause in Göttingen but has to leave the university because of his political activity. After the failed revolution of 1848, Oskar Schulz (Gottfried's cousin) and Theodor Hellung (son of the artist) emigrate to the United States. Hellung travels on business to California with two of his Freemasonic brethren. Stopping in Salt Lake City, he reports on the Mormons, explaining their borrowings from Freemasonry by pointing out that their "main apostle," W. W. Phelps, was a student of Krause's in Göttingen. While Hellung is in the West, Schulz travels to the South on Masonic business. Pseudo-Masons come into the picture, Schulz must foil a murder attempt on himself, and finally Hellung and Schulz end up in a utopian colony in California. Krause and his league of humanity are even more important for Oppermann's novel than they were in the *Knights of Spirit*. Friesen points out that Krause's address to the combined Dresden lodges comes at the midpoint of *Hundred Years* (183) and that the doctrines taught there are carried to the United States, the land of freedom and promise, where western movement, as the Master of Hellung's Pittsburg lodge says, "makes possible the goal of a world-wide lodge."

Taken as a whole, these post-1848 Masonic novels reveal a common desire for unified political action. Freemasonry offers such unity, especially in the form foreseen by Krause. In addition, at least as late as the revolutions of 1848, Freemasons were still asserting that their principles were changing an absolutist system to bring about a society in which freedom and equality and brotherhood were the rule. And lurking in the background, the ever-powerful conspiracy theory offered a sense of urgency.

Goethe's and Schiller's use of the Freemasonry they found all around them at the end of the eighteenth century can hardly be second-guessed. By mid-nineteenth century, with historical Freemasonry now in a qualitative decline, Gutzkow's (and friends') return to Freemasonry was immediately questioned, not altogether fairly, as I have pointed out. One might expect, then, an end to serious literary portrayals of the brotherhood. Such an assumption could not be further from the truth, for in the semiotic systems and political possibilities explored literarily by Schiller, Goethe, and Gutzkow, Freemasonry embodies concerns that both include and transcend historical reality. Authors of the twentieth century evidence strong, continued interest in the institution raised to literary prominence in the previous two centuries.

Illustrations

Durch Tugend und Fleiß
Erhält man den Preiß.

Abriß
der wahren
Helden=Tugend,
oder
Lebens=Geschichte
des
SETHOS,
Königes in Egypten,
aus
Geheimen Urkunden
des alten Egypten=Landes
gezogen,
und nach
der Frantzösischen Uebersetzung
Eines Griechischen Originals verteutschet
von
C. G. W.
Erster Theil.

HAMBURG,
Gedruckt und verlegt von seel. Thomas von Wierings
Erben, bey der Börse, im güldnen A, B, C. 1732.
Ist auch in Leipzig bey Philip Hertel zu bekommen.

Title page and frontispiece of Terrasson's *Sethos*, first German translation
(1732). Among the most influential of early Masonic fictions.

Masons "working" around a trestleboard. A scene representative of
Enlightenment Freemasonry and its emphasis on allegorical education.
From *The Glorified Freemason* (*Der verklärte Freimaurer*, 1791).

The Raising of a Master Mason. From Erich J. Lindner's *Freemasonic Customs in Pictures 1730–1840* (*Freimaurerisches Brauchtum in Bildern 1730–1840*).

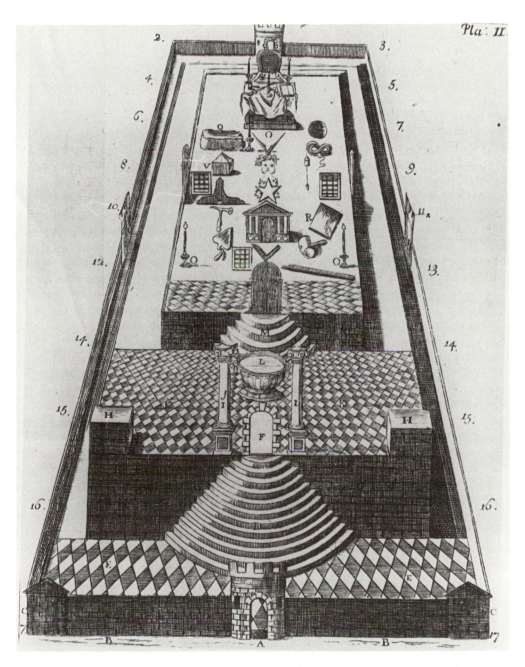

A representation of the symbolic route followed by an initiate in the lodge: successive gates (A, F, *and beneath the square*), stairs (*first 12, then 5*), cistern (L), and then past various masons' tools to the Master's chair. From Abbé Larudan's *Les Francs-Maçon Écrasés* (1747).

Allegorical depiction of the journey of a Freemason in the world (Paris, ca. 1830). From *Das Freimaurermuseum* (1928). *Left* and *right*, the columns "J" and "B" (here wisdom and strength). *Top center*, a column with Venus (beauty). *Center foreground*, a cave with several people in a natural, uncultured state. Minerva helps one of them up a ladder onto the path of culture or Freemasonry. He must pass through trials of air (the head blowing on a figure from behind a pyramid), of fire (the pyramid out of which smoke issues), and water (the river he must swim). He shapes the unhewn stone and then the cut stone. The various monuments bear symbols of grades of the Scottish rite. Finally the Mason comes to the acacia tree on the mountain and passes into the beyond where ancient Masons are assembled. Also represented are Solomon's temple and a Masonic banquet.

Depiction of various Masonic symbols from August Kestner's *Die Agape oder der geheime Weltbund der Christen* (1819), which Goethe read while writing the *Wanderjahre*.

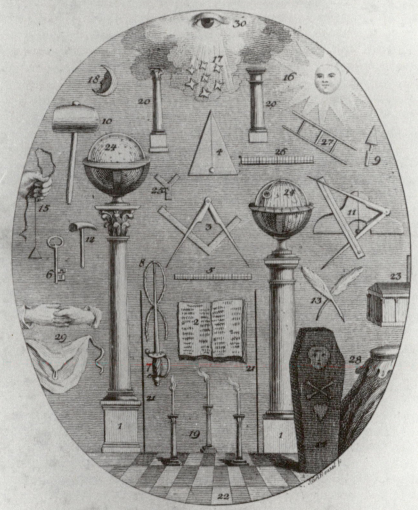

Das Titelkupfer Tafel I. 123

aus

Jachin and *Boaz*

London 1776.

VIDE, AUDE, TACE.

5776.

Published according to Act of Parliament Aug.t 30. 1776, by W. Nicoll.

Herausgegeben, gemäß der Parliaments-Acte, am 30 ten Aug.t 1776, von W. Nicoll.

Frontispiece from *Jachin and Boaz*, London, 1776. Reproduced with a "description of the Regalia and Emblematical Figures used in Masonry" in Krause's *Die drei ältesten Kunsturkunden der Freimaurerbrüderschaft*, 233–236, 252.

"1.   The two Pillars called Jachin and Boaz, the First signifying strength, the Second to establish in the Lord.

2.   The Holy Bible opened, as an Emblem that it should be the rule of our Faith.

3.   The Compass and Square, to square our Actions, and keep them within Bounds, the Master's Emblem or Jewel, which is suspended with a Ribbon round the Neck, and always worn when the Lodge is opened, and on public Days of Meeting, Funerals, etc.

4.   The Level, the Senior Warden's Emblem or Jewel.

5.   The 24 Inch Gauge, to measure Mason's Work.

6.   The Key, the Treasurer's Emblem.

7.   The Sword, presented to the naked left Breast of the Apprentice.

8.   The Cable, or Rope, put round the Neck of every new-made Mason at the Time of Making.

9.   The Trowel, an Instrument of great Use among Masons.

10.   The Gavel, or setting Maul, used in building Solomon's Temple, the first Grand Work of Masonry.

11.   The Plum Level, Compass, and Plum Rule, the Junior Warden's Emblem.

12.   The small Hammer, to knock off superfluous Pieces.

13.   The Cross Penns, the Secretary's Emblem.

14.   A Coffin, with a Figure of the maimed Body of Hiram (the first Grand Master) painted on it. He was murdered by three Fellow-Crafts, for refusing to reveal the Secret.

15.   The Hand Plummet, for taking perpendiculars.

16.   The Sun rising in the East, emblematical of the Master-Mason, standing in the East, and setting the Men to Work.

17.   The Seven Stars, an Astronomical Emblem, frequently engraved on the Medals worn by Masons.

18.   The Moon, that rules the Night.

19.   The Candlesticks, placed in a triangular form.

20.   The Columns, used by the Senior and Junior Wardens in the Lodge.

21.   Two black Rods, carried by the Senior and Junior Deacons.

22.   The Three Steps and Pavement.

23.   Entrance or Porch to Solomon's Temple.

24.   The Terrestrial and Celestial Globes, representing the Works of Creation.

25.   A Machine used by Masons for forming Triangles.

26.   The large Rule for measuring the Work.

27.   The three Step Ladder used in Masonry.

28.   Hiram's Tent.

29.   The White Aprons and Gloves, Emblems of Innocence.

30.   Eye of Providence, the Great Superintendant of all the Works of the Universe, and Masonry represented as under its immediate Influence."

"For Freedom, Equality, Fraternity, but against Violence. Freemasons on the Barricades." From *Humanität*, April 1985.

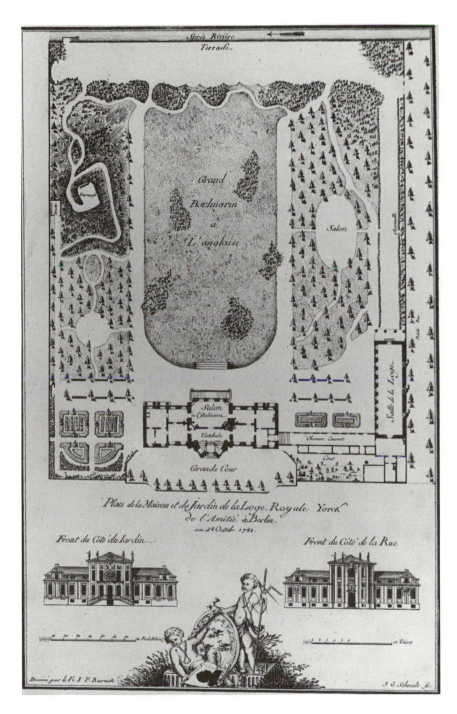

Plan of the Building and the Garden of the Lodge Royale York de l'Amitié in Berlin. From *Tableau général des Frères Francs-Maçons* (Berlin, 1782). Note the democratic English garden (as opposed to the authoritarian French garden).

CHAPTER FIVE

Politics, Semiotics, and Freemasonry in the Early Twentieth Century

A great part of Europe—the whole of Italy and France and a great portion of Germany, to say nothing of other countries, are covered with a network of these secret societies, just as the superficies of the earth is now being covered with railroads. And what are their objects? . . . they want to change the tenure of the land, to drive out the present owners of the soil, and to put an end to ecclesiastical establishments. Some of them may go further.
—Disraeli, 1856 in the House of Commons[1]

Diese Symbolform ist die der jeweiligen Kapazität des Geistes angepasste Erkenntnisform—nicht dass etwa irgendein mysteriöses Ahnen, eine prophetische Sehergabe angenommen werden müsste. Der Umstand, dass der Mensch seinen Symbolen immer tiefere Bedeutung abgewinnen kann, verleiht ihnen den Anschein, als wären sie himmlische Vorboten gewesen der letzten Idee, die sie ausdrücken. In einem gewissen Sinn steckte aber die letzte Bedeutung schon im ersten Auftreten des typischen Symbols.
—Herbert Silberer,
Probleme der Mystik und ihrer Symbolik

CONTINUED PUBLIC INTEREST: ANTIMASONRY AND NEW SECRET SOCIETIES

As the nineteenth century waned, the fear of conspiracy

expressed so forcefully by Disraeli in the first epigraph to this chapter was reinforced by prominent Jesuits who waged a vicious campaign against Freemasonry. They accused the order and its "Jewish allies," among other things, of giving rise to communism, anarchism, the Social Democratic Party, and of being archenemies of the church.[2] As a result, Pope Leo XIII renewed the church ban on Freemasons in his 1884 encyclical "Humanum genus," warning against the forces of Satan embodied in Freemasonry. In this environment arose a fiction about Freemasonry rivaling the best stories of the eighteenth century.

The author (or perpetrator), Leo Taxil (Gabriel Jogand-Pages), was Jesuit educated. He developed into a vocal freethinker, and in 1881 joined the Freemasons. Because of conduct "unbecoming of a Mason" he was soon dropped from the lodge. Taxil began to edit an anticlerical yearbook; but then, in a sudden turnabout, he publically converted to the Catholic church. The new Catholic turned his pen against Freemasonry and won such favor with the anti-Masonic church hierarchy that Pope Leo XIII gave him an audience in Rome. Taxil printed secret Masonic rites and accused Freemasons of being a Satanist cult engaged in sexual orgies and ritual murders. At the height of his deception Taxil wrote of a "Palladinian" lodge whose members included a daughter of the devil Bitru—a woman named Dianna Vaughan. Through Taxil, the fictitious Miss Vaughan made further sensational anti-Masonic disclosures that finally earned her an apostolic blessing from the church. In 1897, after more than fifteen years of posturing, Taxil finally revealed his fraud to the world. The allegations against Freemasonry, he declared, had been created to expose the superstitions of leading Catholic officials.[3]

Despite his final disclosures, Taxil's fictional charges against Freemasonry continued to inspire belief; and soon they were joined by *The Protocols of the Elders of Zion*. This incredible fiction, commissioned by Russian secret police and based in part on a nineteenth-century novel,[4] depicts a diabolical Jewish and Masonic conspiracy to rule the world. First published in 1903 in St. Petersburg, the *Protocols* gained special prominence in the years following the First World War when they were published in France and Germany.[5] As the next chapters relate, they then formed part of a widespread conspiracy theory that influenced both Thomas Mann's *Magic Mountain* and Nazi theoreticians.

Freemasonry attracted other sorts of attention at the turn of the century as well. Leo Trotsky, for instance, spent an entire year studying and writing about Freemasonry while in an Odessa prison. The prison library's holdings were largely of conservative historical and religious journals; and in them Trotsky found frequent discussions of Freemasonry. He wondered where and when and why the movement had begun, and he asked himself how Marxism would explain such a movement. He was surprised to find that the fraternity included revolutionary as well as reactionary branches.[6] Over the course of a year Trotsky filled a notebook of one thousand pages with thoughts on Freemasonry.[7]

Trotsky's Marxist interpretation of Freemasonry is a good example of new historical interest in the brotherhood, although in perspective it is quite different from that of the literary critics and "new romantic" historians who would most strongly influence the turn-of-the-century novelists with whose work we are concerned here. The vicious lies of *The Protocols of the Elders of Zion*, Taxil's fraud which damaged both Catholics and Freemasons, and the Jesuits' anti-Masonic campaign are representative of the waves of anti-Masonic sentiment washing across Europe at the beginning of the new century. In a time of sweeping changes, threatened by modernism, positivistic science, political liberalism, and economic hardship, many Europeans found Jews and Freemasons likely sources of their unease and accused them of conspiracies of every kind. But if secret societies could be seen as the cause of the new malaise, they could also represent a cure.

The *Wandervögel*, a youth movement founded by Karl Fischer, is probably the best known of the antimodernist, nationalistic, protoromantic leagues that grew out of the early twentieth-century fascination with secret societies. On the literary scene, the circle gathered around Stefan George, writes Hansjürgen Linke, "exhibits all the features of a league of men formed in analogy to or even according to the historical example of the Templar Order."[8] Fritz Stern has argued that the *Wandervögel*, the George Circle, and in general Germany's turn-of-the-century predilection for myths, Germanic roots, neoromanticism, the occult, and secret societies are reactions against all the perceived ills, the "cultural despair," of the new century.[9] Parallels can be drawn between this time and the end of the eighteenth century when the anti-Enlightenment *Gold- und Rosenkreuzer* became an influential branch of Freemasonry and when romanticism became an important ideological force. Rather

128

than repeating the work of Stern, Linke, and others, a delightful, but little known parody of the time will here provide insight into the prevailing cultural climate, as will two contemporary books about Freemasonry and its symbolism.

LITERARY FREEMASONRY AND THE OCCULT

The Novel of the XII (*Der Roman der XII*, 1909),[10] the brain-child of publisher Konrad Mecklenburg, has twelve chapters, each written by a well-known author: Felix Hollaender, Ernst von Wolzogen, Hermann Bahr, Georg Hirschfeld, Gustav Falke, Otto Ernst, Gabrielle Reuter, Herbert Eulenberg, Hanns Heinz Ewers, Otto Julius Bierbaum, Olga Wohlbrück, and Gustav Meyrink.[11] Hollaender's first chapter sets the tone for the parody of both *Bildungsroman* and league novel when Gaston Dülfert draws simple-minded parallels between his pedagogical utopia and the pedagogical province in Goethe's *Wilhelm Meister's Travels*. Each succeeding author carries Gaston's plans and education to further extremes. A daemon or "Piefke" tries to guide him. He meets a mystical confidence man every inch a Cagliostro figure. And his father, a member of a brotherhood of alchemists and a Freemason, observes his son through several emissaries and steps in to rescue Gaston's children from their oppressive mother. After Gaston has repeated several developmental steps his father took before becoming a member of the alchemical secret society, the senior Dülfert asks him if he would like to "die," to leave the world in order to join the brotherhood. Although the novel directs Gaston in another direction, the theme of alchemical death and rebirth drawn from early twentieth-century books about eighteenth-century Freemasons and Rosicrucians subsequently draws the attention of both Hofmannsthal and Thomas Mann.

In a twist reminiscent of the several narrators of *The Ghost-Seer*, the twelve (conspiratorial) authors of *The Novel of the XII* themselves have an extensive influence on Gaston's life. Various references link them and the brotherhood of alchemists, they appear fleetingly in the novel, and they are said to be directing Gaston toward a strange telos: not to greater harmony within himself but rather to a loss of his true self:

Foreign powers had reached right into his life, clumsy forces had agitated and swirled his fate in an inept creative mood so that it seemed like half-baked apfelstrudel dough. And with all that he had lost himself, had let himself be pulled back and forth by competing feelings, had become sentimental, almost bourgeois and narrow-minded. Oh, it was high time that he once again found himself. (258)

The light-hearted satire of Freemasonry found in the novel is not appreciated by the compilers of the *Internationales Frei-maurer-Lexikon*. In their entry for Otto Julius Bierbaum they write: "In the novel he instigated, *The Novel of the XII*, a Freemason appears in the 12th chapter in circumstances which indicate that none of the twelve authors has any connection with Freemasonry" (183). The novel was, of course, not instigated by Bierbaum, and in an earlier *Lexikon* entry for Hermann Bahr, the assertion is made that Bahr was indeed a Freemason in his younger years. But even if mainstream Freemasonry was again a staid, Enlightenment institution that worshiped Lessing and abhorred the alchemical excesses of the late eighteenth century, *The Novel of the XII* accurately reflects a strong public interest in Rosicrucian Freemasonry, mysticism, and ideas loosely gathered under the rubric "romanticism."

At least three of the twelve authors of *Der Roman der XII* had written or would write romantic league novels of their own. Felix Hollaender's novel *The Path of Thomas Truck* (*Der Weg des Thomas Truck*, 1902)[12] describes the calculated education of young, idealistic, and enthusiastic Thomas Truck through the efforts of several quite traditional, mystical emissaries. Twenty years after the publication of Hollaender's novel, Hanns Heinz Ewers republished Schiller's *Ghost-Seer* along with his own three-hundred-page continuation of the fragment.[13] In the afterword Ewers compares Schiller's century with his own:

One more word: it is astonishing how modern this Schiller is! . . . The same abracadabra knights then as now, the same miracle workers and saviours in all colors, the same fantastic societies and orders fighting furiously among themselves. Whether the leaders are honest or frauds—or even, as most are, both in one person—whether they are named Schröpfer and Stark, Cagliostro, Dr. Mesmer, Gassner, whether they call themselves Illuminati or Rosicrucians, or, today, occultists, spiritualists, Christian Scientists, Theosophists, Anthroposophists, or whatever: then as now ghost-seers of all sorts were swarming in all cities and countries. Of course one will not everywhere meet such a congenial fellow as Schiller created in his 'Armenian'! (529–530)

Certainly there is no character of that quality in Ewers's continuation or in his other novels (*The Apprentice Magician, Horst Wessel,* etc.); but like Hollaender, Ewers was a popular writer who found in the eighteenth-century league novel an appropriate form for his twentieth-century interests. A third member of *The Novel of the XII's* authorial conspiracy, Gustav Meyrink,[14] was personally involved with Freemasons, Rosicrucians, and several less-known societies with self-satirizing names like the "Brotherhood of the Ancient Rites of the Holy Grail in the Grand Orient of Patmos."[15] He also studied Madame Blavatsky's theosophy, corresponded with her follower Annie Besant, and briefly proselytized for their occult society in Prague.

Meyrink's reputation as an author and scholar of the occult led him to involvement in an anti-Masonic conspiracy during the First World War. Pastor Carl Vogl reports in his book *Notes and Confessions of a Pastor (Aufzeichnungen und Bekenntnisse eines Pfarrers)*[16] that while visiting Meyrink in July 1917 he found the writer busy with a whole pile of books by and about Freemasons. Meyrink said that he had been summoned to the foreign office in Berlin and had been asked to write a novel proving that the Freemasons were to blame for the war. The novel was to be immediately translated into English and Swedish in huge editions. Meyrink had agreed to the project, Vogel says, and was at work on materials supplied him by the foreign office when Vogl visited him. Meyrink soon quit his work on the novel, however, and Vogl reports that subsequently Friedrich Wichtl was given the Freemasonic material and entrusted with the task. Wichtl published his *World-Freemasonry, World-Revolution, World-Republic. An Investigation into the Origin and Final Goals of the World War (Weltfreimaurerei, Weltrevolution, Weltrepublik. Eine Untersuchung über Ursprung und Endziele des Weltkrieges)* in 1919.[17] The ominous cover illustration of the first edition shows a group of stern-looking Freemasons in aprons ready to plunge their swords into coffins bearing the names "Wittelsbach," "Hohenzollern," and "Habsburg."

Meyrink wrote several novels and shorter works that manifest his continued interest both in the occult and secret societies,[18] including *The Angel of the Western Window (Der Engel vom westlichen Fenster)*,[19] which incorporates several themes and motifs of

131

the league novel.[20] After reading *The Novel of the XII* it is difficult to take Myrink's alchemy and mysticism seriously. But the novel demonstrates once again how well the requisites of the league novel meet the needs of an occult novelist. Meyrink also planned a novel to be called *The Guiltless One* (*Der Schuldlose*) in which he lists political Freemasonry among problems to be dealt with: "Connected therewith the exposing of 1) the decline of the German 2) his 'Freemasonic' baseness." The same novel was meant to trace the inner development of a person through stages of Eastern mysticism and to include a "System of Allomatism."[21] The reference to "Allomatism" links Meyrink to a book about alchemy, Rosicrucianism, and Freemasonry that provided Hofmannsthal with an important metaphor for his novel fragment *Andreas*.

The concept of the allomatic evidently comes from Ferdinand Maack's *Twice Dead! The Story of a Rosicrucian from the XVIIIth Century* (*Zweimal gestorben! Die Geschichte eines Rosenkreuzers aus dem XVIII. Jahrhundert*, 1912).[22] Drawing largely on eighteenth-century texts, Maack discusses several Rosicrucian ideas—including periodicity, polarity, duality, transformation, the unity of everything in the universe, and the *aurea catena Homeri*—and he posits the allomatic principle, the "Philosophy of the Other," in which the self always depends on the other for transformation. He traces the history of Rosicrucianism through Johann Valentin Andreae and into Freemasonic lodges.[23] And finally, in the form of a novella but with strong assertions about its truth, Maack tells the story of a certain Court Councillor (Hofrat) Schmidt, an eighteenth-century Rosicrucian who died and was alchemically reborn. This generally resembles the story told with tongue-in-cheek in *The Novel of the XII* three years earlier, in which Dülfert senior died and was reborn through the alchemical elixer.

Two years after Maack's Rosicrucian apologia appeared, Herbert Silberer published his *Problems of Mysticism and Its Symbolism* (*Probleme der Mystik und Ihrer Symbolik*, 1914),[24] a book that provides some key insights into contemporary interest in Freemasonry, Rosicrucianism, and Hofmannsthal's novel. First, like Maack's book, Silberer's draws heavily on the late eighteenth century. Near the beginning he prints a long parable published in 1788: "Secret Figures of the Rosicrucians from the 16th and 17th Centuries." Unlike Maack, Silberer is not interested in propagating Rosicrucian beliefs but rather in psychologically interpreting the Rosicrucian story and, more specifically, symbol formation. Higher alchemy is a symbolic activity, he states, related to practical chemistry as little as Freemasonry is related to practical bricklaying. In his discussion of symbols Silberer covers some of the same ground I have covered while interpreting *Wilhelm Meister's Travels*. Taking the sexual figures and gold making of Rosicrucian texts literally, he writes, has often detracted from serious attempts at personal ethical development. He focuses on the alchemical process of introversion, of mystical turning inward; and sees in Rosicrucian symbols of introversion (death, climbing down into caves, vaults, and dark temples) not only mystical symbols but also psychologically important figures. He cites three possible outcomes of falling under the power of symbols of introversion. The first, a positive outcome, involves either mystical growth or development of the self. The other two, both negative, involve loss of the self: either a passive fall into schizophrenia or an active turn to magic, an attempt materially to actualize what is really a psychological or religious process, as discussed at length by Goethe. Finally, for our purposes, Silberer writes about the production of symbols. Founders of religions are not alone in this crucial task, he points out, but are joined by artists. And in fact, "the absorption in a work of art [by both the artist and the observer or reader] seems to me closely related to both introversion and to the unio mystica" (235).

With new, psychoanalytical tools for investigating the symbols of Freemasons and Rosicrucians, Silberer works scientifically through problems of formation of symbols and their affect on the psyche. Theodor Wieser comments on the book's special attraction for Hofmannsthal, who quotes from it in his notes to *Andreas*: "The psychoanalytic researcher Silberer undertakes in his book to clarify the problem of multiple interpretation using an allegorical story of the Rosicrucians. In the process he makes thorough use of and discusses the symbolism of alchemy and secret societies. The many-sidedly open, so malleable plasticity of the mystical and alchemical tradition must have inspired the poet, reinforced his own best ideas, and challenged him."[25]

HOFMANNSTHAL'S *ANDREAS*

"Das Symbolische an den Rosencreuzern ist ihm sympathisch."
—Hofmannsthal, *Andreas*

One way to describe *Andreas*, written between 1907 and 1927, is as a second *Ghost-Seer*.[26] Like Schiller's novel fragment, Hofmannsthal's novel, also a fragment, portrays the education of a young foreigner at the hands of several powerful men and women. Once again Venice is the setting, for its place between East and West, its intrigues, and its mystery make the city an ideal setting for a story of transformation.[27] As in Schiller's novel there is a mysterious confrontation with a beautiful woman in a church; and both Schiller's prince and Hofmannsthal's Andreas are besieged by theater people artistically well equipped to influence the rather naive young men. Like Schiller's prince, Andreas often finds himself caught in the complexities of language while the people around him speak easily. And finally, Sacramozo plays the pedagogical role of Schiller's Armenian, with the difference that he has Andreas's good at heart. In this he is closer to the emissaries of *Wilhelm Meister* than to the Armenian; and several notes to the novel make this second comparison explicit.[28]

From his first meeting with Sacramozo it is clear that Andreas is to be guided by another in the long list of Masonic mentors inspired by the Armenian and the Abbé:

> He [Sacramozo] is a Maltese Knight, he then continued, but as you see he does not wear the cross on his clothing which he is not only entitled, but also required to wear. He has made a great trip, it is said that he was in the most central part of East India or even at the Great Wall of China; according to one report he is supposed to be in the service of the Jesuits, and according to another he is no less than a Freemason. (83)

Sacramozo's pedagogic influence on Andreas is strong, as befits a Masonic mentor.[29] To guide the education of a young man as traditional Masonic emissaries do, the mentor must have extraordinary knowledge of his charge and the world; and Sacramozo clearly fits that bill. But the novel does not simply reproduce a stock figure in a stock situation. It portrays a second, weak side of Sacramozo's personality: "His confession of the inhibitions, the fate that binds him. He calls himself a wreck, a charlatan" (164). He is left, surprisingly, with a deep sense of loneliness:

> Maltese Knight. The total breakdown of the man of forty years. He can no longer expect that additional enlightenment, rescuing revelations will come—he can not suspect resources, withheld from himself, in those older than he is—he may not imploringly ap-

proach anyone like a trusting pupil—he himself is the last resort. (146)[30]

Here the league novel takes on a new dimension, for the emissary's vulnerability relativizes the absolute outside standard represented by the traditional emissary. The questions raised by the new relationship beteen mentor and pupil are personal, but they also have political implications:

> What fascinates Andreas above all is this: to establish how efficacious a man of action really is (Sagredo [Sacramozo], Napoleon, or Metternich), where the border is drawn between guiding and being given over to fate—in short, how much a man is a tool of fate or a director of fate—further: in which way the recognizable weaknesses of the individual play into the grand action. (203)

Is one a tool of fate or the director of fate? Does one control oneself or is one controlled by outside forces? These questions, made political by reference to Napoleon and Metternich, are, in the larger context of the novel, also questions about language. Sacramozo, as Freemasonic and Rosicrucian mentor, works to aid a young man more formed by language than in control of it; and Sacramozo himself vacillates between controlling and being controlled by the words he uses.

In 1902, five years before he began writing *Andreas*, Hofmannsthal published his fictional letter from Lord Chandos to Francis Bacon in which Chandos describes a severe crisis with language. Chandos writes of his early facility with language, of his plans to use language to penetrate to the center of things, and of his intention to interpret fables and myths as the hieroglyphs of a secret, inexhaustible wisdom. He felt that all existence was a great unity, that he was in the middle of it, and that every creature was a key to all the others. But then he discovered that language is arbitrary, unconnected to any supposed secret center. Both the secrets of religious faith and "earthly concepts" became an allegory "which stands over the fields of my life like a glowing rainbow, at a constant distance, always ready to fall back if I take it into my head to rush toward it and want to wrap myself in the hem of its coat."[31] He no longer found truth in abstract words, and speaking itself became difficult: "I have completely lost the ability to think or speak coherently about anything" (465). Everything seemed to him "so incapable of proof, so mendacious, so full of holes," and the great unity he once sensed now fell apart: "Everything fell into parts for me, and the parts into further parts, and nothing more could be encompassed by a concept. The separate words swam about me; they congealed into eyes which stared at me" (466). This language crisis is repeated in *Andreas* as a major theme of the novel.

Arriving in Venice, Andreas's first thoughts are of his inability to communicate, although he speaks the language: "I know the language, so what, because of that they do with me what they want! How does one speak to total strangers" (40). The first person he sees is a masked man, "who looked trustworthy and who, according to his movements and manners, belonged to the best classes" (40). Impressed and intimidated by these signs of class and power, Andreas speaks, and in so doing reveals his own contingency: "he said quickly that he was a stranger . . . immediately it seemed verbose and awkward that he had named the stations, he became embarrassed and confused himself as he spoke Italian" (41). The masked man's cloak falls open to reveal underclothing in total contrast to the outer, the first of many indications that Andreas should seriously question the veracity of signs. But Andreas wants to believe in what others express with language. When the masked man, whom he already has reason to mistrust, mentions the names of Austrian royalty, Andreas responds positively: "These well known names, spoken here so intimately by the stranger, imbued Andreas with great trust" (41). Andreas plans an optimistic letter to his parents which will replicate the lies and half-lies told him by the man with the mask; but memories of his many humiliations during the trip to Venice make him as unable to write as he is to speak.

While traveling, Andreas had reluctantly taken on a servant, Gotthelf, whose purported linguistic abilities match those of the prince's servant Biondello in *The Ghost-Seer*: "How he spoke Slovenian, Romansch, Ladin and naturally Italian with great facility. . . . He understood stalking and hunting, correspondence, filing, reading aloud, and letter writing in four languages and could serve as interpreter, or, as one says in Turkish, as dragoman" (47). Andreas does not want to employ a servant, but his own inability to control his words ("but Andres again said one word too many" [48]) gives the fluent Gotthelf the opening he needs. Dishonest, lascivious, and brutal, Gotthelf repeatedly enrages Andreas. At one point a speech that "bubbled . . . through his pouting lips" impugns the chastity of Romana, the young woman with whom Andreas has just fallen in love, and Andreas tries to respond: "a burning was in Andres's[32] breast which forcefully rose up his throat, but no speech passed from his tongue, he would have liked to smash him in the mouth with his fist" (60). The result of this confrontation or nonconfrontation is the kind of shattering of a comforting whole spoken of in the Chandos letter: "During the evening meal Andres felt as never before in his life, everything as if cut up into little pieces, the dark and the light, the faces and the hands" (60). Later that night he fantasizes about writing a compensatorily eloquent letter to his parents: "Thoughts came in streams, everything that occurred to him was uncontestable" (63). In his thoughts he describes the joy he will bring his parents by his marriage with the wealthy Romana; and contrary to his normal experience, "The nimble words came to him unsought; the beautiful phrases formed chains by themselves" (63). Drowsiness causes the beautiful chains of phrases to dissolve, and an evil deed by Gotthelf destroys his hopes with Romana; but Andreas has two subsequent experiences that give him a renewed sense for meaning behind the senseless chaos of signs with which Gotthelf and others surround him.

The first comes on the grave of a dog that Gotthelf has poisoned, where Andreas remembers an ugly incident in his twelfth year when he broke the back of his own dog. The memory helps him sense connections between the dog in the grave, Gotthelf, and himself; and out of these meaningful connections "a world spun itself which was behind the real one, and not so empty and bleak" (72). As powerful as this vision appears, however, Andreas is immediately barred from the transcendent world: "Then he was astonished by himself: Where do I come from? and it seemed to him that someone else was lying there into whom he must go, but he had lost the word" (72). The second experience of meaning beyond language comes in the mountains after he has left Romana behind. Watching an eagle soar over him, he envisions the broad expanses of landscape the eagle can see. Such a view would unify all divided things; and this thought gives him the feeling that "His soul had a center" (76). Looking into himself he sees Romana kneeling like a deer, and that "gesture was ineffable to him. . . . An ineffable certainty assailed him: it was the happiest moment of his life" (76).

This security found in nature and in Romana's gesture has a counterpart in the second half of the Chandos letter. Chandos reports that even while surrounded by empty signs, which he likens to eyeless statues, he has joyful moments, moments specifically beyond language: "the words leave me once again helpless. For it is something completely unnamed, and indeed scarcely nameable"

(467). Ordinary things become the vessels of his revelation, filling him with a rising flood of divine feeling. "I feel then," he writes, "as if my body consisted only of ciphers which unlock everything for me. Or as if we could enter into a new, prescient relationship with all of existence, if we were to begin to think with our hearts" (469). Andreas's experiences with the dog and the eagle produce exactly this sort of harmonizing, centering feeling; but the assurance does not last. On reaching Venice, Andreas is as unsure of himself as ever; and his inability as yet to find lasting meaning through language is well portrayed in the memory of a childhood dream: "he had crept hungrily into the pantry to cut a piece of bread for himself, he had held the loaf of bread tightly, but the knife in his hand cut repeatedly past the bread into emptiness" (96).

Andreas's longing for a clear, harmonious center in place of this emptiness relates directly to Sacramozo's role as Masonic or Rosicrucian mentor. When first seen, Sacramozo is at a café writing a letter (Andreas has twice found himself unable actually to write one), exhibiting a relationship to things in strong contrast to Andreas's alienation. Uncomfortably seated and with a wind pulling at his papers, "he should have been impatient, and yet there was control in all his limbs, an—as strange as the word may sound—an obligation (Verbindlichkeit) to the dead objects" (83). Andreas's companion explains the man's extraordinary presence by repeating rumors that he has traveled in India and China and that he may be a Jesuit or a Freemason. Andreas is completely captivated by Sacramozo's grace, and when he hands him a paper he thinks he has dropped, "Andreas thought he had never perceived a more wonderful harmony between the bearing of a person and the sound of his voice. The words: you are very kind, sir, came in German and in the best pronunciation from his lips" (84). In contrast, Andreas's response is confused, and he twitches with embarrassment at his own awkward gestures and broken speech.

The contrast is so great that Andreas is brought to speculate on just what gives Sacramozo the power he so sorely lacks: "Does he belong to a secret society? Andres feels certain: the Jesuits— then: the lodge. Finally: an even more secret league: are there Templars? Rosicrucians!—But he seems beyond all of this, by a spiral turn.—Temple and School-League-Hetaeria: has taken all this into himself" (160). Another note suggests that Sacramozo combines his own incredible sense of personal power with secret missions to change the world: "His foundation: a powerful faith in himself.

Faith of a Messiah. Thus: undertake every mission (Catholic, Freemasonic: Templar): amor fati in the most extreme sense. Grandiose view of his own situation and of the possibility of enhancement of the function of the individual: who can simply change everything" (164).

In secret societies, especially in the Rosicrucians, Sacramozo finds the transcendental signifiers that allow him to live beyond Andreas's sorry semiotic condition:

> Sacramozo What appeals to him about the Rosicrucians is the symbolic—the absolutely symbolic, the use of words transcending the world. For in the soul, he says, is everything: everything that conjures, also everything that can be conjured. Every word is a conjuration: that spirit that calls determines which spirit appears. ... He is intent on the incantation. (106–107)

At times Sacramozo is sure he has the key to the world: "in hours of exaltation he is sure that only he has the true key to the world, everyone else slips past the secret lock" (98); but that key, based on Rosicrucian symbols, based on "true poetry," is itself a signifier, and as such it is hardly the absolute answer he desires. The same note that refers to Sacramozo's possession of the true key states that his fate is "the key of Solomon in Hebbel's epigram" (98). That epigram firmly locates "transcendence" in nontranscendent language: "You think you grasp Salomon's key and can open up / Heaven and earth, and then it dissolves into figures, / And you watch, horrified, as the alphabet renews itself, / But find comfort, in the meantime it has enhanced itself."[33] Hebbel's epigram clearly gives *some* language a privileged place in expressing truth, as does the statement quoted earlier placing Sacramozo a "spiral turn" higher than Freemasons and Rosicrucians; but at the same time it severely limits symbolic access to any truth beyond the sign. Poetry both unifies and separates: "True poetry is the arcanum which unites us with life, which separates us from life" (107). Both poetry and a mentor like Sacramozo achieve a totality, but a totality only in the eyes of others:

> Totality. In life everything is separated—only in writing poetry, in depicting, are things together—in a figure like the Maltese Knight everything seems to indeed be together. Only he himself, such a man, can know what he himself lacks. To compensate heroically for this lack, he dreams of leading himself over into Andreas. (189)

139

Andreas believes in Sacramozo's authority: "Andres—faith in authority through and through, branching into the extremities of peripheral being" (144); while for Sacramozo, even in his most unified moments, "everything remained partial (where, in contrast, Andres has a sense for how everything conjoins, only not: The grasp, to get it); The Maltese Knight knows: my command is a command, my smile has, in general, an attractive power—but what use is it en somme—" (144). Sacramozo is necessary for Andreas, but Andreas is just as necessary for Sacramozo: "Maltese Knight: to kneel down? —as one kneels to receive council from a teacher worshipped as godlike—this gesture—I will have died without having found it on my life's pilgrimage—Will this youth [Andreas] be the one who may kneel? . . . And will I find the way to be him?" (185).

The allomatic principle, or dependence of the self on the other for transformation, that Hofmannsthal borrowed from Maack's "Story of a Rosicrucian from the Eighteenth Century" works both ways in Andreas. Andreas finds the authority, the semiotic assurance, the center he lacks in Sacramozo. Sacramozo can act as that center because of his personal power and the authority he draws from Masonic symbols. The novel keeps from falling into Maack's esotericism, however, as Sacramozo realizes that the symbols, which are enough for Andreas, give way to ever new symbols; they never reveal absolute truth. Sacramozo turns from this epistemological abyss to find meaning in Andreas's belief in wholeness, in the gesture of kneeling before a divine teacher. Romana's kneeling like a deer (within Andreas) brought the young man an ineffable security; and Sacramozo's final assurance, as questionable as it may be, also arises from his vision of Andreas kneeling. That too, of course, is a sign; but the gesture is, in the context of the novel, a spiral turn higher than previous signs.

Schiller's Armenian used Masonic symbols and linguistic facility to awaken a desire in the prince for closure. The emissaries of the Tower Society in *Wilhelm Meister* use the same symbols but take care to move back and forth from craft to art so as to guard against the destructive jump from symbol to the gold of desired transcendent reality. Hofmannsthal's novel continues this semiotic theme, relativizing Andreas's belief in the higher reality behind Masonic signs with Sacramozo's insight into the eternal regress of such signs. Sacramozo's relative position is also called into question, however, by the faithful gesture of Andreas. The sign both unifies and separates.

Hofmannsthal was not alone among twentieth-century authors to find ready-made metaphors for investigating language and politics in the Freemasonry of Schiller's and Goethe's novels (and in contemporary works like those of Maack and Silberer), for, as we shall see in the next chapter, Thomas Mann likewise drew on both eighteenth-century precedents and twentieth-century critical interpretations of those sources to create *The Magic Mountain*, his own novel within the Masonic literary tradition.

CHAPTER SIX

In Two Minds about Freemasonry: *The Magic Mountain* and the German Romantic Novel

Bei den verdorbensten Völkern oder doch den verwild-
ertsten hatten *geheime Gesellschaften* ihren Spielraum.
—Friedrich Schlegel

In allen Zeitaltern finden sich die weisesten, redlichsten,
durch Talent, Kenntnisse, und Charakter ehrwürdigsten
Männer in Orden.
—Johann Gottlob Fichte

Debates about Freemasonry have often been carried on in superla-
tives like those employed by Schlegel and Fichte to describe the
brotherhood as the worst and best of human institutions. Thomas
and Heinrich Mann were on opposing sides in such a debate which
began before the onset of the First World War and continued for
several years after the war ended.[1] One way of describing their
differences would be to categorize Heinrich as political and Thomas
as nonpolitical; and in fact, Thomas spent the war years drawing
that very distinction in his *Reflections of a Non-Political Man (Betrachtungen eines Unpolitischen*, 1918). From another perspective,
however, the difference lay in *kinds* of politics, for Thomas's neoromantic attraction to myth, beauty, psychology, and *Geist* struck
Heinrich as highly (and dangerously) political, and Heinrich's cosmopolitan, antiwar ideas seemed shallow, cowardly, and un-Ger-

man to Thomas. One major blow struck in this battle was Heinrich's novel *The Subject* (*Der Untertan*, largely written between 1912 and 1914).[2]

The novel, a brilliant satire of boot-licking subjects of Kaiser Wilhelm, depicts a most unsavory character who succeeds in business and politics by mixing an absurd romantic mysticism with a brutal will to power. The satire was especially suited to irritate Thomas, placing characters and scenes from his "romantic" *Buddenbrooks* into a political setting in which they seem ridiculous and/or dangerous. One scene in particular, a politicization of the *Lohengrin* scene in *Buddenbrooks*, drew Thomas's wrathful response:

> If one wants to clarify . . . Wagner's relation to politics in general and to the year 48 in particular, one only need remember that he had, at that time, just finished "Lohengrin" and had crowned it with the overture, that romantically most gracefull of all existing pieces of music. "Lohengrin" and the year 48—those are two worlds, connected at most by one thing: the national pathos. And the Zivilisationsliterat is led by a true instinct when he ridicules "Lohengrin" in satirical social novels (Gesellschaftsromanen) by translating it into the political.[3]

As Thomas defines it, then, the battle between the brothers was a conflict between "high" romantic art and "low" political satire. Thomas was so affected by Heinrich's allegations that he spent the next decade writing "anti-Heinrich," both in the *Reflections* and in the first half of *The Magic Mountain*. There were many points of disagreement, but the most interesting for us involves a scene in *The Subject* in which liberal Freemasons and self-serving subjects of the Kaiser respond quite differently to a tense situation.

FREEMASONRY IN HEINRICH'S *THE SUBJECT*

Heinrich first published "The Lück Case" ("Der Fall Lück") in the Munich weekly *März* in April 1913, just as Thomas began writing *The Magic Mountain*. The passage begins with Diederich Hessling and two cronies gossiping about several of the town's more liberal citizens whom they see entering the Masonic lodge. Their conversation echoes many of the rumors about Freemasonry that had grown up over two centuries.[4] They call Freemasonry nonsense and relegate it to the past. They deem it a bothersome sect.

They identify Freemasonry with socialism, a commonplace since the mid-nineteenth century, as is their companion epithet "Jew-Club" ("Judengesellschaft"). In addition to the socialism, they assert jealously and contradictorily that the Masons aid one another in their capitalist enterprises. They are also supposed to celebrate orgies in their lodge; again the lascivious rumormongers are jealous. And finally, Kaiser Wilhelm is evoked as an authority for these anti-Masonic sentiments, for his slightest imagined opinions rule these men's lives; by the end of the First World War the Kaiser will, in fact, be blaming Masons for starting the war and for aiding in Germany's defeat. The events about to take place, however, show the Masons Diederich has just vilified in a different light. Moments after the Masons enter their lodge, a soldier shoots a young worker on the street outside. While Diederich voices his inane worries about imminent revolution, two Freemasons cross the street to support the murdered worker and his distraught lover. One of them, a doctor, refuses to allow the authorities to arrest the woman, stating that her condition will not permit it. The other, a liberal industrialist, immediately offers her a job in his factory and verbally attacks Diederich, who has been moralizing pompously.

Heinrich thus makes the most rational and humane characters of this novel Freemasons. They are outspoken liberals, mildly socialist, and religiously tolerant. They are not, as opposed to Diederich Hessling, exploitative employers, moral degenerates, or obsequious subjects of an oppressive Kaiser.[5]

THOMAS AND THE MASONIC CONSPIRACY

But while Heinrich praised Freemasonry for its rational humanism, Thomas saw quite another side of the brotherhood. In his *Reflections of a Non-Political Man* he repeatedly refers to Freemasons and what he calls *Zivilisationsliteraten* (like Heinrich) in the most negative of terms:

> Historical scholarship will teach which role international Illuminatism, the Freemasonic World-Lodge, naturally excluding the unsuspecting Germans, played in the spiritual preparation and actual unleashing of the World War, of the war of "civilisation" *against Germany*.
>
> We had not sensed that, in God's wide world, under the cover of peaceful international commerce, hate, the unquenchable,

deadly hate of political democracy, of the Freemasonic-republican rhetor-bourgeois of 1789 was accursedly working against us, against our national establishment, our spiritual militarism, the spirit of order, authority, and duty. (XII, 32, 36)

And a final example of angry rhetoric: "the ineffable anti-German declamations of our Franco-Italian Freemasons, epigonal revolutionaries, and opera singers of progress" (119).

Furthermore, the *Reflections* make the neoromantic ideology of Thomas's earlier work explicit by championing romanticism against the modern outrages of Freemasonic, democratic, rational, cosmopolitan, progressive *Zivilisationsliteraten*. With reference to Goethe, Jakob Grimm, Uhland, and Eichendorff, Thomas argues for "the 'feudal principle,' every kind of conservatism, religious, monarchical, national, moral, economic, every opposition against progressive degeneration and decay" (434), for everything, in short, which "is thoroughly rooted" (434). In *The Magic Mountain*, the writing of which was interrupted by the *Reflections*, Thomas planned to continue the neoromantic position,[6] one aspect of which was a pointed anti-Masonry.

The polemic against Freemasonry was not simply a case of acute individual paranoia but an opinion he had seen in print. In a 1918 letter to Paul Nikolaus Cossman, Thomas asked for information concerning an article in the *Süddeutsche Monatshefte* that he had read but lost track of.[7] The article in question, Hofmiller's "Combinazioné,"[8] along with the preceding article by M. Rennert, "The Freemasons in Italy" (459–470), and another article Thomas says he read and enjoyed, Heinz Brauweiler's "Vatican and Lodge in the World War,"[9] all promote a theory of Freemasonic, especially Italian Freemasonic political conspiracy against Germany.[10] In this form Freemasonry was originally to function in the novel. In 1920, for instance, Thomas characterized his character Settembrini as a Freemasonic *Zivilisationsliterat*: "The Civilisationsliterat appears personally in the novel in the form of an Italian Freemason."[11] Early descriptions of Naphta,[12] while setting him at odds with Settembrini, say nothing about the opposing views on Freemasonry he would take later in the novel; nor could they, for Thomas still knew Freemasonry only in nonromantic terms.

Compare the early, anti-Masonic view, however, with Thomas's later statement about Freemasonry and *The Magic Mountain*: "Not for nothing do Freemasonry and its rites play a role in *The*

Magic Mountain, for Freemasonry is the direct descendant of initiatory rites. In a word, the magic mountain is a variant of the shrine of the initiatory rites, a place of adventurous investigation into the mystery of life."[13] Clearly, a change took place between the first half of the novel, in which Italian Freemasonry plays a purely negative role, and the second half, where the descriptions of Freemasonry that constitute a large part of the subchapter "A Soldier, and Brave" ("Als Soldat und brav") present a rich metaphor for Hans's entire stay on the magic mountain.

A NEW VIEW OF FREEMASONRY

The new Freemasonry enters the novel through Naphta's discourses on Freemasonry. He characterizes Settembrini's Freemasonry as a colorless, bourgeois shadow of what was once a carrier of deep mystery. Beginning with the Jesuits and Rosicrucians who drastically changed the eighteenth-century order, Naphta says, Freemasonry took on a ritual depth and absolutist, antiliberal commitment that gave it great power. Settembrini, he surmises, would call this a time of decay, but he, Naphta, finds the "invasion of irrational yeast into an intellectual world of rational, utilitarian social improvement" (704) a welcome antidote. Naphta also discusses alchemy as it found its way into the lodges, speaks of "magical pedagogy," describes the Masons' ritual route, and elaborates on the grave as an important initiatory symbol. He tells Hans about the progressive Catholicization of Freemasonry, about symbols of night and death and transformation and resurrection. He gleefully speaks of festivals that included women and tended to the bacchanalian. But then came the reforms, Naphta says. Freemasonry humanized and modernized itself and became "bourgeois misery in the form of a club" (708).

Hans hears the other side of the story from Settembrini. The Italian Mason begins by noting that there are approximately twenty thousand lodges in the world. He mentions the names of earlier, mostly revolutionary Masons—"Voltaire, Lafayette, and Napoleon, Franklin and Washington, Mazzini and Garibaldi" (710) —and strongly emphasizes Freemasonry's political role: "We profess politics unreservedly, openly . . . for the idea of Masonry was never unpolitical, at no time, it could not be so, and when it thought it was so, it deceived itself about its essence" (711). And finally, he speaks with warmth about the thought of a world league, a legacy of Krause.

146

Settembrini's Masonry, then, is basically that of the political *Zivilisationsliterat*, the role Mann had already envisioned before the war. But Naphta's ritualistic, darker version of the brotherhood brings Freemasonry into play in a radically new way. The event that figured most prominently in the genesis of Naphta's and Settembrini's lectures on Freemasonry was the arrival of a book.

ROMANTIC FREEMASONRY IN *THE MAGIC MOUNTAIN*: THE SOURCE

Mann wrote about the origins of this section in a letter to Joseph Angell: "I remember exactly that at that time, from an unknown source, a text about Freemasonry arrived which I used for the Masonic dialogues between Naphta and Settembrini."[14] For years there has been speculation about what the source might have been, some of the most interesting by Freemasons themselves. In 1930 the Masonic *Eklektisches Bundesblatt* published Fritz Ballin's short essay on "Thomas Mann and Freemasonry" along with a very respectful letter by Mann in reply. Ballin was troubled by the extreme positions taken by Settembrini and Naphta regarding Freemasonry and asked if Mann was simply not aware of the "genuine," humanitarian Masonry (nonpolitical and nonmystical) which had attracted the likes of Goethe, Herder, Fichte, and Mozart.[15] Mann wrote that of course he was acquainted with that sort of Masonry but that he had been interested in the extremes. And in fact, he wrote, in certain of Settembrini's statements one can detect indirect references to the unpolitical, pure character of German Freemasonry.

A later Masonic scholar found those supposed indirect references unconvincing and angrily denounced Mann's sources: "It is clear to see that Thomas Mann used only Romance sources. He did not know English and German Freemasonry."[16] But Mann's source was neither Italian nor French. The book sent to him by an unknown person, the book that helped him drastically revise his plans for the role of Freemasonry in the novel, the book that heavily influenced the subchapter "A Soldier, and Brave," the Peeperkorn character, and much of the final five subchapters, was a book of German literary criticism focusing on the late eighteenth-century league novel.

The work whose name Mann no longer remembered was Marianne Thalmann's *The Popular Novel of the 18th Century and the*

Romantic Novel: A Contribution to the History of the Development of Secret-Society Mysticism (Der Trivialroman des 18. Jahrhunderts und der romantische Roman: Ein Beitrag zur Entwicklungsgeschichte der Geheimbundmystik), which appeared in 1923 in Berlin. Mann finished the "Snow" subchapter of his novel—where Hans Castorp overcomes death and promises never again to feel sympathy with death—in June of that same year,[17] and in the next months worked on the subchapter "A Soldier, and Brave." He must have received Thalmann's work in June or July and immediately incorporated it in his novel. A few representative passages from *The Magic Mountain* and Thalmann's book demonstrate Mann's extensive reliance on her descriptions:

> *Thalmann*: "Der Bund ist nie etwas Beschauliches, sondern immer etwas stark Organisatorisches." (78)
> *Mann*: "Ein Bund ist niemals etwas Beschauliches, sondern immer und seinem Wesen nach etwas in absolutem Geist Organisatorisches." (III, 703)

> *Thalmann*: "Die Kunst des freien Maurers war Regierungskunst." (77)
> *Mann*: "er versteht, dass die Kunst des freien Maurers Regierungskunst ist." (III, 712)

> *Thalmann*: "In einzelnen Ritualen maurerischer Systeme finden sich nach Schauburg nicht undeutliche Spuren, dass der Bruderbund einst symbolisch mit Blut besiegelt wurde." (80)
> *Mann*: "Man hat Anhaltspunkte, dass auch in Maurerlogen ehemals der Bruderbund symbolisch mit Blut besiegelt wurde." (III, 703)

> *Thalmann*: "Wir stehn hier auf dem Boden der Ueberlieferung alter Mysterien, die berichtet, dass die eleusischen Mysterien, sowie die der Isis bei Nacht, gelegentlich überdies in finsteren Höhlen gefeiert wurden." (78-79)
> *Mann*: "Sie erinnern sich, dass die Mysterien der Isis sowohl wie die von Eleusis bei Nacht und in finsteren Höhlen begangen wurden." (III, 708)

> *Thalmann*: "Der Geselle—der Bruder—wird der Vermummte, der Vermittler mit der Maske vor den Augen, der Schatten des Geheimnisses, das hinter ihm steht." (122)
> *Mann*: "Geführt von Vermummten, die nur Schatten des Geheimnisses sind." (III, 707)[18]

Of course, it is possible that Mann and Thalmann are quoting from a common source; but in light of the fact that Thalmann's book was published in the months before Mann wrote "A Soldier, and Brave" and considering the number of direct quotations and close parallels, it is more probable that Thalmann's work is the "text about Freemasonry" Mann received "from an unknown source" and subsequently used "for the Masonic dialogues between Naphta and Settembrini."[19]

It is not surprising that Mann would rely heavily on such a source, for he was always the *poeta doctus*. Heinz Saueressig writes that Mann's propensity to draw on material close at hand was especially strong during the writing of the second half of *The Magic Mountain*.[20] But just what is this little-known book that along with Spengler's *Decline of the Occident* (*Untergang des Abendlandes*) and other influential sources found its way into one of the most important novels of the twentieth century?[21]

Marianne Thalmann's book discusses popular novels of the second half of the eighteenth century and the themes, motifs, figures, and conventions they prepare for the romantic novels that follow. After documenting the rise of Freemasonry in England and its spread to Germany early in the century, she writes at length about the changes Freemasonry underwent as it was influenced by alchemy, Rosicrucians, and the Jesuits. Thalmann gives copious examples from a huge number of novels[22]—the popular novels that exploit a set of sensational motifs including séances, ghosts, graves, alchemy, elixirs, hypnotists, charlatans, secret societies, Jesuits, and guardian spirits. Many of the novels, she points out, feature emissaries from a secret society who guide a young hero along a predetermined educational path. Supplementing her work on these popular novels, Thalmann discusses a group of mainstream romantic novels that uses the requisites of popular literature to express romantic ideas. The book contains such a plethora of quotations grouped around the various themes and motifs that one loses sight of individual novels. But for a reader like Thomas Mann, the extraordinary condensation and thematic grouping provides a unique look at the shared material of hundreds of novels. Preromantic generic tradition and Freemasonic history are brought together in a way Mann could have found nowhere else.

It is astounding how well Thalmann's book describes parts of *The Magic Mountain* written before 1923. The following passage from her book, published over a year before *The Magic Mountain* was printed, could well pass as a section from a review of the novel:

> Overshadowed everywhere by fears of death, these heroes pass
> along the eternal path of the mysteries and experience a hundred
> times the initiation of the master: the rebirth from life through
> death to new life. And here begins the transubstantiation of the
> motifs, their alchemical purification. Death is the gate into infinity,
> into absolute life. Love is thus related to death. Love is the divine.
> Sexuality becomes corporeal spirituality, unio mystica. Music and
> the appearance of ghosts, the palpable sound of instruments be-
> comes music of the spheres, tones of the miraculous in the uni-
> verse, dance becomes a rhythm of death and rebirth. (318)

In the first six chapters of *The Magic Mountain* Mann had already
led his hero to a place overshadowed by the fear of death; and be-
witched by the close ties between love and death, Castorp (in the
snow scene) had experienced "the rebirth from life through death to
new life."

After reading the work on the romantic league novel Mann
immediately expanded the role of Naphta as Freemasonic and Jesuit
emissary intent on indoctrinating Hans Castorp. In the process
Freemasonry lost its exclusive identification with the political *Zivilisationsliterat* and became a symbolic means for an "investigation
into the mystery of life." Freemasonic history, with the continuing
conflict between the rational and irrational, between Enlightenment
and romanticism, between the political and apolitical, and between
arbitrary and natural sign systems, fit the scheme of *The Magic
Mountain* perfectly. In Thalmann's book Mann further found many
of Mynheer Peeperkorn's character traits and the important alchemical metaphors for Hans Castorp's education. He also added the
"music and appearance of ghosts" Thalmann describes and ended
the novel with a reflection on the war as the dance of death and rebirth to which she refers. Indeed little in Mann's seventh chapter
does not figure in Thalmann's book.

ALCHEMY AND EDUCATION

Mann's source for the alchemical metaphors for education
used in *The Magic Mountain*'s final chapter has hitherto been unknown. Commenting on an assertion made by Lothar Fietz, Herbert
Lehnert writes: "According to all our experience with sources of
Thomas Mann, it is to be doubted that he had an 'intimate knowledge' of medieval alchemical theories."[23] Comparison of but a few
passages from Thalmann's book leaves no question but that she is

Mann's source. And in fact, *all* the information about alchemy appearing in *The Magic Mountain* is given by Thalmann.

For example, while explaining his view of Freemasonry to Hans Castorp, Naphta says that for a time the masters of the high degrees were great alchemists. He describes alchemy:

> "Purification, transformation and refinement of matter, transubstantiation, and indeed to the more elevated, thus enhancement, —the lapis philosophorum, the male-female product of sulphur and mercury, the res bina, the dual-sexed prima materia was nothing more, nothing less than the principle of enhancement, of elevation through exterior forces—magical pedagogy, if you will." (III, 705)

Thalmann discusses purification (131), transubstantiation (156), transformation of matter (317), and refinement of matter (318), and then writes about androgyny in terms Mann obviously borrowed: "And from the dual-sexed philosopher's stone, the philosophical product of the female principle of mercury and the male principle of sulphur the romantic rises to spiritual hermaphrodism" (319). This is just one example of several that could show Thalmann as the source for Naphta's lectures on alchemy.[24] Later in the novel Hans Castorp gives his own version of Naphta's lecture on alchemy as magical pedagogy: "But then by accident—call it accident—I was driven up so high into these congenial places. . . . In one word, you do not know that there is such a thing as an alchemical-hermetic pedagogy, transubstantiation, and indeed to the elevated, thus enhancement, if you understand me correctly" (III, 827). This broad paraphrase of Thalmann's "romantic fate is material transformation of the everyday into the infinite" ("Das romantische Schicksal ist Stoffverwandlung des Philisteriums in das Unendliche" [320]) could well serve as an epigraph for *The Magic Mountain*. Hans Castorp's "romantic fate" is indeed dominated by a kind of personal transubstantiation; and Mann was fortunate to find powerful metaphors for that in Thalmann's discussions of alchemy.

MYNHERR PEEPERKORN: GENIUS, MAGUS, EMISSARY

Chapter Six of *The Magic Mountain* ends with the Freemasonic, alchemical lessons of the subchapter "A Soldier, and Brave" drawn from Thalmann's book. Following a brief introduction

("Walk on the Beach"), the first half of Chapter Seven portrays Mynherr Peeperkorn's visit on the magic mountain. The Peeperkorn episode is a late addition to the novel, and as Mann reported in a letter to Ernst Bertram, something of a surprise: "the fates of the Magic Mountain, which, near the end, took a marvelously surprising (surprising to me) turn."[25]

Peeperkorn has always been a controversial character, as T. J. Reed writes: "[Peeperkorn] remains the most enigmatic character in the book and the most controversial, eliciting flatly contradictory judgements."[26] It may bring some order to that confusion to point out that the Peeperkorn figure is the latest in a long series of romantic figures Thalmann calls genii, magicians, or emissaries.[27]

She gives as examples the supernatural genius in Grosse's *The Guardian Angel* (*Der Genius*), the Armenian in Schiller's *Ghost-Seer*, the emissaries of the Society of the Tower in Goethe's *Wilhelm Meister*, and similar genii or emissaries in the popular and serious fiction of the late eighteenth century. She points out that certain characters in league novels share physical and psychological traits that set them apart from the other characters:

> And so those lodges which added the higher rites of the Scottish high-grade system to the ancient Freemasonic degrees and which raised the rational world-reformer to a creative magus have left behind especially visible signs in the popular novel. In any case, here . . . the magician, the powerful, daemonic, solitary figure appears. This magician is another version of the emissary. He is the speaker of the mysteries, the mediating priest between the initiate and the final secrets of nature. The magus is always old. He is the honorable old man with the long, white beard and the flowing gown. One of the aspects of the protean nature of the genius has been isolated and retained and this majestic type rigidifies into a figure commanding reverence, transcending both humanity and time. (125)

Thalmann refers here to a "rational world-reformer" who is then replaced in the popular novel by the "creative magus"—the first figure being drawn from Enlightenment Freemasonry and the second from the later Strict Observance. Settembrini can clearly be seen as a representative of the former and Naphta of the latter. And the "powerful, daemonic, solitary figure" can only be Mynheer Peeperkorn. Like the figure Thalmann describes, Peeperkorn has a long beard, a priestly aura, and the requisite age.[28] Peeperkorn is literally, as Thalmann says of the magus, "a figure . . . commanding reverence" ("[eine] ehrfurchtgebietende Erscheinung" [III, 783]). He also embodies the "protean nature of the genius"; indeed, Peeperkorn's essence shifts constantly: in the same moment he is Christ and Bacchus, "robust and meager," "a singular, personally important, if also unclear man," "ambiguous . . . in a positive manner."

Thalmann further portrays the genius/emissary as a disharmonious figure torn by passion: "They are faces ravaged by all passions—the features of a disharmonious person. . . . The effect is also dual: reverence and repulsion" (100). In his description of Peeperkorn as suffering Christ and sybaritic Bacchus, Mann portrays this duality.[29] Thalmann also points out the hypnotic powers of the genius figure: "the ruling glance of the magician, the consciously fascinating aspect of the contemporary hypnotist (Magnetiseurs)" (101). Mann plays with this aspect of the genius/emissary when Frau Stöhr calls Peeperkorn "a 'money-magnet'" ("einen 'Geld-Magneten'"), and Hans Castorp replies, "But magnet was not bad either, for evidently Peeperkorn exerts a strong attraction" (III, 765).[30] Not only is the genius figure magnetic, hypnotic, torn by passion, highly mutable, old, white-haired, priestly, and daemonic, but he is a ruler whose power comes in part from his knowledge of the natural and artificial worlds, as Thalmann points out: "In him is depicted the physicist, the doctor of natural philosophy, ordained as their master by his knowledge of the forces of nature, that romantic physicist for whom mathematics is magic" (123). Peeperkorn is, like the genius figure, "a doctor of natural philosophy," possessing extensive knowledge about medicine and various poisons. He gives Hans Castorp a long lecture about quinine, a chemical whose properties (in his description) parallel those of the magical elixirs Thalmann discusses. He calls his medicine "a genuine cordial, a magnificent agent for strengthening, resuscitating, and animating, —also an addictive drug, by the way" (III, 800). He talks about quinine not only as a medicine but as a "healing poison," and in an excursus he points out that natives use another chemical taken from the bark of a tree to prepare a "love-potion." Thalmann writes similarly about elixirs prepared by magi and genii: "The elixir of life is the healing salve, the stimulating love-potion, the practical sleeping medicine, the effective antidote" (136–137). Peeperkorn demonstrates related technical and chemical skills while preparing the poison and the bizarre instrument (patterned after the fangs of a cobra) with which he commits suicide. And Thalmann suggests that even this act of suicide is part of the romantic figure's role: "Not only the desire to be dead awakens, but also the desire for suicide. It characterizes the romantic hero that not only his passivity directs him to death but also his activity. His desire for life is in great part a desire for extinction, for the extinction of his disharmonies, and it takes the form of a carefully considered death" (Thalmann, 213).

And finally, when Hans Castorp explains his views on why Peeperkorn exerts such a powerful influence on them, he says the key is "personality": "if you want values, then personality is, in the end, also a positive value, I should think,—more positive than stupidity and intelligence, positive to the greatest degree, *absolutely positive, like life*" (III, 809). Personality, which supposedly overcomes all dualities, is also a trait of the romantic genius, as Thalmann points out: "Only struggling and painfully do they achieve the highest potency, synthetic personality, as Novalis redescribes genius, the product of gravity and light, of male and female" (321).

Peeperkorn, then, is clearly a descendant of the romantic genius, emissary, and magus. But just what does this mean for the novel? Just how does Hans Castorp respond to the many romantic attractions of Naphta's Jesuitical Freemasonry and Peeperkorn's suicidal vision?

AN ANTIROMANTIC CONCLUSION

From the moment Hans Castorp comes down from his vision in the snow, directly following his burst of clarity concerning the seductive power of death (*"One should, for the sake of goodness and love, allow death no mastery over one's thoughts"*), he begins to regress. Naphta lures him with symbols of high-grade Freemasonry, transubstantiation, magical pedagogy, and alchemy. And Mynheer Peeperkorn arrives to exert an overpowering romantic influence, drawing Hans with him into the dark romantic vortex of death.[31] There is good evidence that Hans follows Peeperkorn. After his mentor's suicide Hans becomes more and more like the old man as he grows a sparse beard and takes his place at "the good Russian table." Hans's final approach to death takes him through the supernatural experiences Thalmann describes as "music and appearances of ghosts . . . dance becomes a rhythm of death and rebirth" (318). The subchapter "Fullness of Harmony" ("Fülle des Wohllauts") depicts Hans's increasing obsession with music and death. In the next subchapter, "Highly Questionable" ("Fragwürdigstes"), Hans is able, through music, to cause his cousin Joachim's spirit to appear from the dead, a moment of long-desired yet very troubling transcendence. And in the final paragraph of the novel Hans stumbles across a battlefield in an awkward dance of death (and, the last few lines question, moving perhaps to a rebirth of love?).

In a letter to Arthur Schnitzler, Mann argued that his novel "wanted" to be "a ridicule of death . . . an anti-romantic disillusionment and a European call to life. It is often read wrongly."[32] If the novel is indeed antiromantic, if Hans Castorp's romantic obsessions (fed by figures from the league novel) are questioned, then a rather remarkable transformation has taken place. Begun as an archromantic attack on rational, liberal, Freemasonic *Zivilizationsliteraten* like Heinrich, the novel could have used the romantic view of Freemasonry found in Thalmann's book as a new weapon. The ritual depth, the promise of transcendence inherent in the symbolic system, and the absolutist, antiliberal character of high-grade Freemasonry coincided perfectly with the program Mann had set forth in his *Reflections*; and he now had in his hands a powerful Masonic antidote to the Enlightenment Freemasonry he had set out to discredit. Instead, however, the novel uses that material to depict and question an increasing obsession, a fatal romantic longing for transcendence that can be fulfilled only in death.

Once again, as did Schiller, Goethe, and Hofmannsthal, Mann uses Freemasonry to hold out the promise of absolute closure; and like the other novelists, he finds that Freemasonry and the emissaries of the league novel carry with them the seeds of disillusionment. In this disillusionment, in discrediting Naphta and Peeperkorn and the romantic world they represent, Thomas's original anti-Heinrich feelings have been considerably tempered, and Settembrini's Enlightenment Freemasonry is no longer simply a scapegoat for a lost war. But in the tradition of Goethe (and Hofmannsthal), even while transcendence of an absolute sort is made questionable, the symbols of Freemasonry remain in *The Magic Mountain* to lure the reader on.

CHAPTER SEVEN

Neo- and Anti-Romanticism: Freemasonry from Hesse to Grass

ROMANTIC ILLUSIONS

If Thomas Mann's *Magic Mountain* is, in Mann's words, "an anti-romantic disillusionment," then Hermann Hesse's novels might be called the work of a "romantic illusionist." To the delight of his millions of readers, Hesse had a lifelong affinity for secret societies and for the secrecy and mystery of the league novel. Hesse was well acquainted with German literature of the the late eighteenth and early nineteenth centuries when the league novel enjoyed its first popularity; in fact, he counted several league novels among his favorite works of fiction.[1] As he points out in an autobiographical essay, "Childhood of the Magician" ("Kindheit des Zauberers"),[2] he saw in these romantic novels expressions of the same magical world where he had been at home since early childhood: "I was not raised by parents and teachers alone, but also by higher, more hidden, and more secret powers." One of these was his grandfather: "He was also a magician, a cognoscente, a wise man. . . . This man, the father of my mother, lived in a forest of secrets. . . . People from many countries honored and visited him . . . and after long conversations again travelled away without a sign, perhaps his friends, perhaps his emissaries, perhaps his servants and agents" (*Eigensinn*, 39).

Near the beginning of *The Journey to the East* (*Die Morgenlandfahrt*, 1932) the narrator describes the mood in Germany immediately after the First World War:

> At the time when I had the good fortune to be permitted to join the league, namely directly after the end of the great war, our country was full of saviours, prophets, and discipleships, of presentiments of the end of the world or hopes for the beginning of a Third Reich. . . . There were bacchantic dance communities and rebaptising battle groups, there was much that seemed to beckon to a transcendent world and to miracles; there was also a widespread tendency to Indian, old-Persian, and other eastern secrets and cults at that time.[3]

Theodore Ziolkowski has pointed out that this not only describes contemporary conditions but also catalogues Hesse's earlier works: the bacchanalian dancing of *Steppenwolf* (1927), the Eastern mysteries of *Siddhartha* (1922), and the discipleship of *Demian* (1919).[4] *Demian*, the story of a young man led into an elite group by a powerful mentor, was enormously successful, reflecting the concerns and interests of many youthful Germans. The readers were members of the *Wandervögel* and similar leagues, advocates of Langbehn and Lagarde, disciples of Nietzsche and George, readers of Hollaender, Löns, Ewers, and Meyrink, and fanatic admirers of Hesse.[5] A decade later, in *The Journey to the East*, H. H. theorizes about the effect of these popular tendencies on the league of pilgrims to the East: "all of this led to the fact that even our league, the ancient one, seemed to most people to be one of the fashionable plants that had blossomed so rapidly, and after a few years it fell with them into forgetfulness, in part, and in part into contempt and ill repute" (13). Clearly aware of the potential for triviality and even scurrilousness in secret societies like the one in his novel,[6] Hesse still chooses to pattern his story after the league novel,[7] needing, as the narrator explains, a center to which the events relate, a unifying factor that allows a sense for meaning and causality (35).

André Gide, who wrote a preface to one edition of *The Journey to the East*, found German predilection for secret societies telling:

> For something primitive lingers in the Germanic soul when not ameliorated by culture . . . a somewhat gregarious need to group themselves, to form *Bund*, a more or less secret society, and to wend their way in company toward an end often ill-defined, in appearance all the more noble because it is colored by mysticism and remains rather mysterious. That is, strictly speaking, the subject even of this book; and so it seems to me, in spite of its specious form, strangely revealing.[8]

157

Hesse's beliefs indeed lent themselves to the form and content of the romantic league novel, and his novels are deeply rooted in that tradition, with few traces of the antiromantic side of Hans Castorp's adventures.[9] As Gide suggests, Hesse's novel mirrors a general contemporary tendency to find answers to political, social, and religious problems in secret societies,[10] answers that could be comforting, but that could also lead to disaster.

ANTI-MASONRY IN THE WEIMAR AND NAZI PERIODS

While Hofmannsthal, Thomas Mann, and Hesse were finding the symbolism and history of Freemasonry a rich source of metaphor, less imaginative writers were spreading the old rumors about threatening Freemasonic conspiracies. Helmut Neuberger's recent two-volume study of *Freemasonry and National Socialism: The Persecution of German Freemasonry by the Völkisch Movement and National Socialism, 1918–1945 (Freimaurerei und National-sozialis-mus: Die Verfolgung der deutschen Freimaurerei durch völkische Bewegung und Nationalsozialismus 1918–1945)* gives an excellent account of anti-Masonic movements culminating in the virtual destruction of the order by the Nazis.[11] Several examples demonstrate the extent and kind of anti-Masonry active in the Weimar Republic.

Wichtl's *World-Freemasonry, World-Revolution, World-Republic (Weltfreimaurerei, Weltrevolution, Weltrepublik,* 1919) was a particularly grotesque foray against Masonry, blaming the brotherhood for Germany's "shameful" defeat in the war. But even more paranoid were the anti-Masonic publications of Erich and Mathilde Ludendorff. Erich Ludendorff, proud head of the German armed forces during the war, explained his and Germany's defeat with the "knife-in-the-back" theory; and Freemasons became convenient wielders of the knife. In 1927 Ludendorff published his pamphlet *Destruction of Freemasonry Through the Disclosure of Its Secrets (Vernichtung der Freimaurerei durch Enthüllung ihrer Geheimnisse),* a supposedly new exposé of Masonic secrets, but in reality simply a reprinting of rituals published over the last century and a half. It worked like new, however, and sold 182,000 copies, making it the best-selling anti-Masonic work in history.[12] A sympathetic newspaper summarized Ludendorff's views: "The secret of Freemasonry is everywhere the Jew. There is only one World-Lodge. The goal of Freemasonry is to make peoples Jewish and to establish a Jewish-

and-Jehova government with the help of all peoples. . . . The leagues of Freemasons are dangerous to the state, perhaps even treasonable."[13] As insane as such assertions were, they were matched a year later by Mathilde Ludendorff's *The Unatoned Sacrilege Against Luther, Lessing, Mozart, and Schiller* (*Der ungesühnte Frevel an Luther, Lessing, Mozart und Schiller*).[14] The book uncovers new "facts" concerning the deaths of these august Germans—naturally at the hands of Freemasons revenging secrets disclosed in *The Ghost-Seer, The Magic Flute*, and *Ernst and Falk*. Goethe is said to have listened sorrowfully and helplessly while fellow lodge members planned to murder his friend Schiller. And so on.

Other right-wing politicians were likewise using Freemasons as scapegoats. In Rosenberg's *Freemasonic World-Politics in the Light of Critical Research* (*Freimaurerische Weltpolitik im Lichte der kritischen Forschung*, 1929) and in his *Myth of the 20th Century* (*Mythos des 20. Jahrhunderts*, 1930), the Nazi theoretician attacked Freemasonry and Christianity for transcending the national and racial borders he found organic and necessary. Sentiments like Rosenberg's led to related "scholarly" essays on the "Freemasonic Problem." Adolf Bartels, a Ludendorff follower, wrote *Freemasonry and Literature: Facts and Suspicions* (*Freimaurerei und Literatur: Feststellungen und Vermutungen*, 1929).[15] Bartels's first paragraph is programatic: "As a result of Ludendorff's publications . . . something like a Freemasonic question has arisen. . . . As a German literary historian I want to try here to establish exactly which German poets were Freemasons and to what degree they were active as Freemasons. . . . If one ignores Freemasonry in the life of a poet, the biography becomes incomplete." In the almost hundred pages that follow, Bartels names names, insinuates, states flatly that this and that "Germanic" poet could not have been a Freemason, or that this "non-Germanic" poet was both a Freemason and a Jew. He must admit some Freemasonry in Weimar, but he recommends that its influence not be overestimated. He mentions the rumor about Schiller's death at the hand of Freemasons and relegates it to the literary rubbish heap: "That is mostly nonsense" (42); but then he goes back to his painful discriminations between Freemasonic and non-Freemasonic writers.

Naturally, such anti-Masonic tracts drew satirical attention, of which these lines from Tucholsky's 1928 poem "Ludendorff or Illusions of Persecution" ("Ludendorff oder der Verfolgungswahn") are a good example:

Hast du Angst, Erich? Bist du bange, Erich?
Klopft dein Herz, Erich? Läufst du weg?
Wolln die Maurer, Erich—und die Jesuiten, Erich,
dich erdolchen, Erich—welch ein Schreck!
     Diese Juden werden immer rüder.
     Alles Unheil ist das Werk der .·. .·. Brüder.

Denn die Jesuiten, Erich—und die Maurer, Erich—
und die Radfahrer—die sind schuld
an der Marne, Erich—und am Dolchstoss, Erich—
ohne die gäbs keinen Welttumult.[16]

Are you afraid, Erich? Are you alarmed, Erich?
Is your heart beating, Erich? Are you running away?
Do the Masons, Erich—and the Jesuits, Erich,
want to stab you, Erich—what a shock!
     These Jews are getting ruder and ruder.
     All disasters are the work of the .·. .·. brothers.

For the Jesuits, Erich—and the Masons, Erich—
and the bicycle riders—they are to blame
for the Marne, Erich—and for the stab in the back, Erich—
without them there would be no tumult in the world.

The sort of right-wing anti-Masonry Tucholsky and others satirize was rooted in more than fear of conspiracy.[17] The Nazis actively persecuted Freemasonry as a competing system, demanding exclusive rights to the secret, symbolic, potentially political realm occupied by the Masons.

Early Nazis were members of the Thule Bund (the occult, racist, nationalistic secret society from which many Nazi myths and symbols were drawn); and some organizations within the Nazi party were themselves patterned after secret societies.[18] Alfred Rosenberg, in *The German League-State* (*Der Deutsche Ordenstaat*), a speech published in 1934, compares the Nazi state to a cultic order: "We know—and this is decisive—that a genuine Weltanschauung will not creatively express itself in theoretical principles alone nor in spiritual confessions, but that it must take on cultic form."[19] With Rosenberg's help the Nazi state did express its Weltanschauung and impress its populace with symbols and myths cultivated in secret societies. It was the same confidence game practiced by ambitious high-grade Freemasons at the end of the eighteenth century. It was a blatant exploitation of a national desire for fulfillment. It was everything Schiller and Goethe and Thomas Mann warn against.

And there were, as Arno Schmidt points out, interesting connections between the eighteenth-century league novel and the Nazi state.

ARNO SCHMIDT ON THE LEAGUE NOVEL AND THE NAZI STATE

In a provocative essay ("Dya Na Sore: Blondeste der Bestien"), Schmidt compares National Socialism with the secret society in Wilhelm Friedrich von Meyern's league novel *Dya Na Sore* (1787–1791).[20] The book is first introduced as "a 2500-page prophetic description of a Super=Third=Reich" (19). The two discussants in Schmidt's "Dialogue in a Library" find it necessary because of extraordinary parallels to point out that the novel is not a cheap parody of Nazi practices but rather a forgotten book from the eighteenth century. Common to both the novel and the Nazi state are the cult of genealogy, the universal militarism taught to all levels and ages of society, unmitigated love for the Fatherland, a fanatical youth group, the education of officers in *Ordensburgen* (castles of knightly orders), the secret, hierarchical structuring of knowledge, the use of highly symbolic, even magical words to rule the mystified, the organizational hierarchy through which unknown heads can inspire fear and obedience, elaborate pedagogical institutes beginning and ending with strategy and gymnastics, and the use of great operatic festivals to inspire the people. After disclosing these striking parallels between Meyern's early league novel and the Nazi state (and, we might add, the Armenian's conspiracy in Schiller's *Ghost-Seer*), one speaker expresses disgust at how literary historians have treated the novel:

> And there were literary historians, who—just imagine!—wanted to be done with this Dya Na Sore by referring to the Bildungsroman so popular at that time; who thought of the words "Rosicrucians" or even "Freemasons" in that context. Wachler, famous in his own time, suggests in his history of German literature that "Meyern undertakes morally deep reflections on humanity; and politicizes and humanizes in an original way. . . ." The newest accomplishment in this area are the three-and-a-half lines of the Würzburger professor Dr. Wolfdietrich Rasch, who, in 1952, explained the "doctrines" of Dya thus: "here an ideal state of true humanity is being founded"—in truth, these scholars have been separated from real life by a crust of tradition and methodolgy. (45)

161

Despite the decided and understandable bias of his two discussants against Meyern's novel, and despite the insights their discussion affords as to possible ideological use of symbols and structures of the league novel, Schmidt has nothing against the genre per se. His title essay in another volume, "The Knight of Spirit" ("Der Ritter vom Geist")[21] introduces Karl Gutzkow as an unjustly forgotten writer and praises the political and economic vision of a league like the one in the novel:

> the "salvation of a nation"—that is, the economic, social, political; finally also the aesthetic and scientific salvation—can not come from "above," for example from a ruling noble priesthood, and even less can it come from *below*, from the people. But only from an "organization of the elite," as Gutzkow wrote to his friend Levin Schücking, a "brain-trust of intellectuals"—for which, since then, the German formulation is: "*The Knights of Spirit.*" (39–40)

Schmidt's elitist view of national salvation is shared by few of his contemporaries; but two of postwar Germany's most prominent authors, Martin Walser and Günter Grass, fully agree with Schmidt's negative assessment of ideologies, the rituals of secret societies, and their literary use in *Dya Na Sore*.

MARTIN WALSER: THE MASONRY OF CAPITALISM

"die bourgeoise Misere in Klubgestalt"
—Naphta, in *Der Zauberberg*

Martin Walser's first novel, an important event for postwar literature, was *Marriages in Philippsburg* (*Ehen in Philippsburg*, 1957).[22] The first of the novel's four parts describes Hans Beumann's initial contacts with Philippsburg society. Opportunistically dropping his youthful leftist leanings, Hans finds work with an industrialist, the father of a former student friend, Anne Volkmann. After career worries lead Hans to insist that Anne abort their child, the second and third parts show Hans working his way into the heart of Philippsburg society through one sordid incident after another (a suicide, a vehicular homicide, and another suicide). One powerful man Hans comes to know is the politician Dr. Alwin, who frequents the Sebastian, a nightclub "where he was a regular guest and a keyholder (for the Sebastian was a key club, exclusive in the

strictest sense of the word, and the keyholders were almost an order)" (249). At the beginning of the fourth part, Hans enjoys the
fruits of his efforts. He is engaged to Anne, successful in his profession, acquainted with the powerful and important citizens of Philippsburg, and invited to undergo initiation into the Sebastian club.

One member leads Hans through a heavy door, through a
winding staircase that seems to be in a tower, through a heavy curtain, into the dimly lit and strangely decorated nightclub, a "Temple
of Sociability." After some drinks and a risqué floor show, Hans
finds that he is to be made a Knight of the Order of Sebastian.
Friends lead him before the statue of Sebastian, the Sebastians form
a circle around him, and two candles, glasses, a giant chain, an arrow, and a black box are brought. Maids of Honor are called to
stand by Hans. He must take the arrow in his hand and let the chain
be hung around his neck. The black box is held "as pillows of an order are carried at burials." Two men pull out parchments and begin
to read, and Hans must swear to stand by his new brothers and to
come often to the club. They take a key from the black box and give
it to Hans, telling him: "Arrow and key are the signs of his new
worthiness, as long as he carries them he may call himself a Knight
of the Order of Sebastian." Finally he is given a certificate and a
glass of champagne.

Immediately after Hans's initiation, an unwelcome guest,
the winner of a soccer lottery, demands to be taken in. Despite the
kinship Hans feels with the man, whose dialect is that of his home
town, he pushes him (accidentally?) down some steps to his death.
His fellow club members immediately treat him like a hero, for the
newest member of the order of Sebastian, valiant in his defence of
the capitalist temple, has murdered a man representing the proletariat.[23] The man is one more victim—after Hans's unborn child, the
suicide Birga Benrath, the motorcycle driver, and suicide Bertold
Klaff—of Philippsburg society. With this murder Hans proves that
he belongs.

Walser thus draws familiar motifs from the league novel to
portray an exclusive, ruthless, immoral, capitalist society. The ideals
central to the order—exclusiveness, pleasure, and profit—are expressed in the initiation ceremony. The trial Hans undergoes includes killing his own unborn child; and his task as a member is to
oppress the proletariat, represented by the lottery winner. One
symbol of the order is the heavy chain, the chain of capitalism,
hung around Hans's neck. Using virtually the same structure that

elsewhere depicts alchemical transformations, magical pedagogy, progressive and regressive politics, and semiotic concerns, Walser is able to portray a compromised, capitalist society that, through its elite emissaries and a set of trivial yet powerful symbols, directs the thinking and actions of a passive young man until he has become one of the decadent few.[24] The postwar society whose attraction to esoteric symbols and exclusive secret societies was virtually unchanged despite recent Nazi manipulation of symbols in the service of a murderous totalitarian ideology found Walser's novel disconcerting. Equally provocative were the novels of Günter Grass.

GÜNTER GRASS: MYTHS, FREEMASONRY, AND THE PATTERNING OF HISTORY

The Tin Drum (*Die Blechtrommel*, 1959), Grass's first novel, is an autobiographical account written by thirty-year-old Oskar Matzerath from his asylum bed. The story takes in the people and environs of Danzig and postwar Düsseldorf as seen from Oskar's perspective, that of a bizarrely talented dwarf. The reader sees him performing artistic miracles, is given intimate (often uncomfortably intimate) views of the petty bourgeois society surrounding him, sees the Nazis and Oskar come of age, and watches Germany and Oskar rebuild after the war. Most interesting for our purposes, the novel is an account by an artist of his own artistry, of his own use and misuse (most often the latter) of symbols.

When Oskar decides to provide his neighborhood with mystical closure, to become Christ's successor, he finds his first disciples in the *Stäuberbande*, a kind of hybrid secret society/sect/anarchist group ripe for his kind of leadership. The Stäuberbande's rituals include a secret language ("[they] used a jargon which I did not try to understand"), new names ("remarkable names like Ritschhase, Kohlenklau, Mister, Löwenherz, Blaubart, Störtebeker"), an oath of loyalty ("the Stäuber Formula . . . a text which was so absurd and full of hocuspocus that I can no longer remember it") which they must swear holding the left hand on Oskar's drum ("which the boys viewed . . . as a kind of symbol"), and a cellar meeting place decorated with religious ritual articles.[25] Such hocuspocus was the rule in Nazi Germany, the novel asserts, and the end of the war brings no change. Secret rites also prevail in a postwar bohemian nightclub in Düsseldorf's old town: "Not everyone was permitted in the Onion Cellar," but those who do find their way into the exclusive club climb down five steps to a small landing, and then descend four further steps to the check-room.[26] There the owner welcomes each guest, "as if it were necessary to conduct an initiatory game with every new guest." Finally, guests in the Onion Cellar are given onions they ritually cut up to elicit tears, hoping to thereby release long repressed emotions. These cathartic rites performed in postwar Germany to overcome the effects of the war are a clear satire of real but ineffectual attempts at overcoming the past (*Vergangenheitsbewältigung*). A past based on ritual, the novel suggests, is hardly overcome by instituting new ritual.

At the end of *The Tin Drum*, facing imminent expulsion from the asylum at the age of thirty, Oskar ponders the possibility of forming another ritually cathartic group: "Or, I shall give in, shall let myself be nailed down, shall go out, just because I am thirty, and mime for them the Messiah which they see in me, shall, against better judgment, make more of my drum than it can well represent, let the drum become a symbol, found a sect, party, or even a lodge" (490). Despite lessons of the Nazi time, Oskar cannot rid himself of the need to manipulate others through symbols and secret rites. He is well trained to so act, for he has himself been educated by a mentor patterned on the traditional emissary of the league novel. Like Wilhelm Meister, Oskar unfolds from within: "I educated myself and formed my own judgment." And like Wilhelm, he too is guided by an emissary: "It was left to him to open the world for Oskar and to make of him what he is today, a person whom I, for lack of a better word, shall give the inadequate title of cosmopolitan" (252–253).[27] Bebra is this mentor's name, and he and Oskar, true to the tradition of Masonic mentor and pupil, recognize one another as fellows by their eyes; Bebra's are described as "intelligent, light-brown, ageless eyes" (264). Oskar immediately accepts Bebra as his master and receives guidance through him as the novel progresses. The next time they meet, Bebra has with him the beautiful and somnambulic dwarf Roswitha Raguna, who, like Schiller's beautiful Greek, uses her charms to lead Oskar along the predetermined path.

At this point Bebra has accepted Goebbels as his own master and tells Oskar: "I have failed . . . how could I continue to be your teacher? Oh, dirty politics!" (140). Thus the master of Oskar's education, the fellow dwarf and artist Oskar almost deifies,[28] is a politically suspect artist who is close to the Reich's propaganda minister and who excuses his actions with reference to the court fools of the Middle Ages. Although Oskar rejects this viewpoint for the time being, there are, as he says, "slight, but not inconsequential political differences" (253), and they are indeed overcome in short order. At their next meeting, Bebra offers Oskar a position in his troupe which entertains German soldiers. Although "Bebra alone could not have talked me into the trip," Oskar writes, the great somnambulist Roswitha helps convince him to join them in spreading Goebbels's gospel through art.

After the war Bebra becomes the powerful and rich head of a concert agency; and Oskar begins to do concerts for the agency as a magician, healer, and messiah (464). Shortly after Bebra dies, Oskar enters the asylum where he writes his memoirs, ordering his past with lies and omissions and clever additions in a final self-reflective act of education. Oskar thus completes his training as artist, taught by emissaries from the society of those who have ceased growing—dwarfs who are artists, artists who are dwarfs. And now Oskar plans to go out, against his own better judgment, to pass on the word, to establish a sect, a party, or a lodge. He will continue Bebra's work, promoting mysticism and absolutist political ideologies through art and will once again establish the guild of artistic dwarfs who serve the often evoked "Black Cook" (violent mysticism). This will be an easy task, for the children of this generation, when they sing, "no longer sing: / Is the Black Cook there? Yes—Yes—Yes!" The artists who should guard against superstition and brutality are themselves purveyors of these evils. As it states in Grass's second novel, Dog Years: "In the worm is the worm."

Dog Years (Hundejahre, 1963), begins with the phrases: "You tell. No, you tell! Or you tell,"[29] an exchange that would remind a Freemason of the passage in Masonic ritual—"you begin. No, begin you. You begin."[30] The novel ends with the pointedly Freemasonic initiation of Walter Matern into the mysteries of Brauxel's underground factory, each detail of which has its direct counterpart in Masonic initiation rites. Matern, referred to again and again as a stranger to the mine, and thus in need of initiation, is led past a doorkeeper, receives instruction, signs a statement affirming his intention to go into the mine, must take off his clothing and exchange it for "zünftige Kluft" (clothing appropriate for a guild or craft), and descends in an elevator hung by a mystical cable while a bell is rung three and then five times. During the descent Brauxel instructs Matern as to the makeup, care, and importance of the cable. And the lesson ends with "light" as the elevator arrives and Matern is led into the mine. Between the Freemasonic beginning and ending, very near the mathematical center of the novel, the reader is told that Oswald Brunies, the teacher of the novel's three narrators, was a Freemason (337).

Roughly parallel to this Freemasonic structure is a numerological pattern: the novel begins with a thirty-two-chapter section, ends with a visit to the thirty-two rooms of Brauxel's mine, and has its high point when Amsel's thirty-two teeth are knocked out as he is brutally "transformed" in the snow scene. And between these Masonic and numerological beginnings and endings, surrounding their centers, are hundreds of related references to astrology, myth, superstition, magical transformation, and divination of the future.

Given this profusion of related motifs in *Hundejahre*, the modes of interpretation most often resorted to are naturally theological, mythical, or numerological.[31] Readers conditioned by the most common, mythical readings of Thomas Mann's *Magic Mountain*, which likewise extensively uses symbolic numbers, contains lengthy descriptions of Freemasonic ritual and features a mythical revelation in the snow, are especially apt to rummage through *Dog Years* with delight. But as we have argued, Mann's novel, as mythical as it is, calls its own romantic center into question; and further, Nazi use of symbols and myths has intervened, requiring a new sort of reading (and writing). In a speech given in West Berlin at the opening of the exhibition "People in Auschwitz" ("Menschen in Auschwitz"), a speech he called "A Father's Difficulties in Explaining Auschwitz to His Children" ("Schwierigkeiten eines Vaters, seinen Kindern Auschwitz zu erklären"), Grass commented on the history intervening between art of the Weimar period and his own: "Adorno's statement that after Auschwitz no more poems could be written has provoked so many misunderstandings that an interpretation must be added or at least attempted: poems which have been written since Auschwitz will have to submit to the measure of Auschwitz."[32] But just what is the new perspective from which one must view Grass's postwar *Magic Mountain*?

Grass's statements about myth and history are a good place to begin. When asked about his Flounder as a personification of Hegel's *Weltgeist*, Grass answered: "Yes, I was considering a satire on the German preoccupation with assigning hidden meanings to history. History to me is chaos, plain and simple."[33] In a letter published in *Der Spiegel* Grass addressed another facet of the same problem. After referring to "Idealism" as Germany's basic problem, whether used to support rightist or leftist absolute claims, he writes: "it is always idealistic difficulties which make it impossible for the apostles of salvation to withstand the contradictions of reality and to continually confront their own impotence."[34] In other words, Grass is concerned with the fact that people, faced by the contradictions of reality and conditioned by "Idealism," turn all too quickly to an ideology, to a mythic history promising a millennium, or to a heroic leader. Grass is not alone in seeing in myth an attempt to reconcile historical contradictions. Two of the twentieth-century's leading theoreticians of myth—Claude Lévi-Strauss and Ernst Cassirer—touch on this very point.

In his *Structural Anthropology*, after suggesting that "myths are still widely interpreted in conflicting ways: as collective dreams, as the outcome of a kind of aesthetic play, or as the basis of ritual," Lévi-Strauss defines myth: "the purpose of myth is to provide a logical model capable of overcoming a contradiction (an impossible achievement if, as it happens, the contradiction is real)."[35] Although the attempt to overcome a contradiction with such a logical model is, in Lévi-Strauss's view, a more positive activity than in Grass's view, the basic concept is the same; and indeed, the parenthetical comment on a "real" contradiction seems very close to Grass's own position. In addition, Lévi-Strauss compares "myth and what appears to have largely replaced it in modern societies, namely, politics."[36] Here he contrasts the historian's view of the French Revolution—"a sequence of past happenings, a non-reversible series of events the remote consequences of which may still be felt at present"—with that of a politician, who sees in the same events a pattern from which he can infer future developments. This is the very patterning of history that Grass fears.[37]

A complementary view of myth comes from Ernst Cassirer, who, in Volume II of *The Philosophy of Symbolic Forms*, defines myth positively as "a unitary energy of the human spirit: as a self-contained form of interpretation which asserts itself amid all the diversity of the objective material it presents."[38] But having witnessed the political manipulation of myths described in *Hundejahre*, Cassirer writes of another aspect of myth in *The Myth of the State*:

> In the times of inflation and unemployment Germany's whole social and economic system was threatened with a complete collapse. The normal resources seemed to have been exhausted. This was the natural soil upon which the political myths could grow up

and in which they found ample nourishment. . . . Myth reaches its full force when man has to face an unusual and dangerous situation.[39]

Both Lévi-Strauss and Cassirer, then, see in myth an attempt to overcome a contradiction or dangerous situation, often political, and Cassirer specifically refers to the political myths of Nazi Germany as natural attempts to establish order in a chaotic environment.[40] This is the tendency of which Grass would warn.

> Only ideologists need symbols to manifest themselves. Nazis with their swastikas, Communists with their hammers and sickles, the Roman Catholics with their arsenals full of images, the capitalists with their trademarks. I am even afraid of turning anti-ideology into an ideology. I just know what I want and don't want—the danger is when these things become a system.[41]

Grass's position is quite different from Thomas Mann's, whose work is, among other things, a magnificent *system* of symbols and myths. In the subchapter "Snow," for example, confronting the contradictions between Naphta's radical irrationalism and Settembrini's enlightened rationalism, Hans Castorp achieves a synthesis through the mediation of myth. Of course, the undercutting irony of *The Magic Mountain* must be taken into account as must Castorp's subsequent fascination with romantic Freemasonry, spiritualism, and death. But if, as opposed to Mann, Grass thoroughly distrusts ideologies, symbols, and mythical histories, how is one to interpret *Dog Years*, an extraordinarily complex novel bristling with Freemasonic ritual, astrology, numerology, symbols, myths, and ideologies?

Dog Years is named after a family of German shepherds. They are all black and fatefully attach themselves to anyone who espouses the kind of mystical, mythical, barbaric thought that helped the Nazis come to power and that, according to Grass, still flourishes in the postwar world. The novel is a collection of three accounts of life in a small suburb of Danzig. Eddi Amsel (also known as Brauxel) describes prewar Danzig in his "Morning Shifts," Harry Liebenau tells of the war years in his "Love-Letters," and Walter Matern reports on postwar Germany in his "Materniads." Amsel, a half-Jew, is an artist whose medium is scarecrows, creations that most often depict mythological figures. Matern is Amsel's friend and protector who turns against him in the Nazi years and knocks out his teeth in the bloody attack in the snow. And Harry

Liebenau, a younger acquaintance of the other two narrators, in a bizarre public discussion, brings Matern to trial for his misdeeds as a Nazi. From the very beginning Grass focuses on these three narrators as narrators.

Even the ritual, Masonic, opening sentences of the novel— "You tell. No, you tell! Or you tell"—leave no question as to the primacy of the problem of narration. In the first paragraphs the narrator repeatedly emphasizes the fact that he is the narrator: "He who wields the pen here is, for the time being, called Brauxel. . . . The pen-wielder usually writes Brauksel like Castrop-Rauxel. . . . He who wields the pen here"—all on the first page! This is definitely a narrated text, and the emphasis leads the reader to examine the narrators more closely. Who are these three men through whose eyes a crucial era in Germany's history is seen? How were they educated? And what was the result of that education?

Eddi Amsel, Harry Liebenau, and Walter Matern grow up in Danzig in an atmosphere saturated with myth. In their accounts they refer to three men who exert powerful pedagogical influences on them. Mr. Olschewski, a "reform-addicted young teacher in elementary school," teaches social studies (*Heimatkunde*); but when Eddi asks him about the origin of the name Pluto he lectures for weeks on mythology—Germanic, Greek, and especially Polish myths—about "the gods which existed earlier, still exist today, already existed back then." Since that school experience, Brauxel reports, "Amsel has become devoted to mythology" (68). A second teacher, Oswald Brunies, is a grand old humanist who refuses to have anything to do with the Nazis. But he is also an absurd rooster, scratching in the schoolyard for rare pebbles: "Nothing happened naturally in his case, everywhere he sensed hidden powers. . . . He pretended to be an ancient Celtic druid, or a Prussian oak-tree god, or Zoroaster—he is thought to be a Freemason" (144). This pedagogue, charged with teaching history and German, is addicted to romanticism and to its metaphor in the novel: sweets. His students learn neither spelling nor history; but they do know some Eichendorff, they come to see ballet shoes as magical objects, they can write essays in which they fantasize about marriage customs of the Zulus, they get a large dose of the mystical, romantic geology found in Schubert's *Views of the Night-Side of Natural Science* (*Ansichten von der Nachtseite der Naturwissenschaft*), and there are indications that they adopt Brunies's Freemasonry. They certainly do not learn his aversion to the Nazis. In *The Magic Mountain*, when

Naphta explains Freemasonry to Hans, he depicts an institution with a rational, enlightened beginning and a subsequent turn to an irrational romanticism. Brunies embodies both sides of Freemasonry, but the synthesis of the two, as might be expected here, tips heavily toward the irrational.

Oskar Matzerath, the hero of Grass's first novel, is referred to as a third teacher: "Brauxel and his co-authors were taught by someone who was busy his life long on enamelled tin" (117). This is no recommendation, as we have seen, for Oskar has been guilty of making his drum into a symbol, of using art to promote mythical thinking, of setting himself up as a messiah. The narrators of *Dog Years* learn his skills well.

Walter Matern, for example, is described by Grass as an addicted disciple of ideologies: "In the novel *Dog Years* I have, I feel, successfully created in the figure of Matern a German-Idealist bearer of ideas who, in the shortest time, finds the doctrine of salvation in Communism, National Socialism, Catholicism, and finally in ideological anti-Fascism."[42] While living with his father, who can hear flour worms predicting Germany's economic future, Walter Matern develops his own economic and historical theories and speaks "of history as a dialectical worm-process . . . [Matern] disseminates Marx-nourished worm-myths which are made to support the theory of the necessity of all development" (507–508). This is clearly the ideological patterning of history or the combination of myth and history Grass so vocally opposes.[43] And Matern is not alone in his beliefs.

Harry Liebenau is in love with barbarous Tulla, and, like Matern, also demonstrates a strong interest in mythical history. Liebenau is "a knowledgeable person who read historical and philosophical books indiscriminately." He is "melancholic," a category Grass describes along with "utopian" in *From the Diary of a Snail* (*Aus dem Tagebuch einer Schnecke*, 1972) as being opposed to the rational attitude of doubt. In addition, Liebenau is "a dreamer who lied a lot, spoke softly, became red when, believed this and that, and viewed the continuing war as an extension of the school curriculum." His list of heroes includes Hitler, whose mythical history brought the Nazis to power, and the historian Heinrich von Treitschke, whose ideologically slanted and anti-Semitic history of the early nineteenth century powerfully affected the historical consciousness of Germany. "With the help of these models," it is said, "he was successful in covering over an actual mountain of human bones with medieval allegories" (375).

171

Liebenau reduces the tensions of history with allegory and myth and Matern too seeks salvation through myth; but what about Eddi Amsel, who, as Brauxel, heads the authors' collective?

Amsel has often been seen as the quintessential postwar writer, vigorously struggling to overcome Germany's past. John Reddick, for example, writes that where Matern attempts to mask reality, Amsel always sees clearly. Reddick even identifies Amsel at times with Grass himself.[44] But if one looks at Amsel from the same perspective from which Matern and Liebenau have just been observed, a different figure emerges.

In the account of Olschewski's teaching and Amsel's turn to mythology, mythical thinking is identified with a series of violent and mystical figures, including a black and pregnant German shepherd. Following this terrifying series comes the phrase "but also Eddi Amsel" (68). Later in the book, when Walter Matern is asked in the public discussion to name several "important, influential childhood experiences," he begins with the names of three gods of Prussian mythology; then he lists the same violent and mystical figures seen before; and finally he ends with "but also Eddi Amsel" (604). Eddi Amsel, the artist whose work could teach a rational acceptance of historical contradictions, instead intensifies Matern's mythical thinking. Amsel's mythical scarecrows do frighten away birds; but some are birds themselves and strengthen the superstition of the villagers. During the Nazi period his mechanical figures reinterpret history on the basis of Nazi myths and romantic heroes. Eddi also sponsors miller Matern in his economic divination. As Brauxel, he predicts the end of the world astrologically, dabbles in numerology, and weaves Masonic patterns into his narrative. And most telling of all, he takes over the care of Pluto in the end, leaving the black dog ("SS schwarz, priesterschwarz, Amselschwarz") to guard his factory. Amsel is clearly as guilty as the rest.

Eddi Amsel, Harry Liebenau, Walter Matern, the narrators of *Dog Years*, are not only victimized by but also responsible for those years. The relation of these three would-be overcomers of the past to their past is manifest by the *Erkenntnisbrille* (perception glasses) they use during the public discussion of Matern's guilt. The glasses, a ubiquitous postwar symbol for overcoming the past, are produced in *Dog Years* by Brauxel and company; and "qualified opticians, trained in Jena" (548) act as consultants for the glasses. Jena is not only famous for lenses, of course, but for German romanticism. The glasses' secret ingredient is mica, collected by "romantic" Oswald Brunies. Looking through the glasses one can indeed see the horrors of the past; but the romantic lenses distort the view, and the viewers demonize Hitler and Matern, having no insight into their own guilt. Thus, the glasses made to overcome the past are themselves products of the past. Postwar writers (or at least *Dog Years'* postwar narrators), seeking to overcome romantic thinking, use tools forged by the romantics. Mythical histories are replaced by more mythical histories. Eddi Amsel is a black bird attempting to scare off black birds. Walter Matern attacks fascism with fascist methods. And Harry Liebenau tries and convicts Matern as a Nazi while himself praying to the black German shepherd.

Dog Years, then, is not a romantic/mythical/occult novel; it is a realistic novel *about* romanticism, myth, and the supernatural. The "Morning Shifts," "Love-Letters," and "Materniads" written by Amsel, Liebenau, and Matern are mythical interpretations of segments of twentieth-century history, interpretations of a sequence of events in which all three narrators have vested interests. And the three accounts, beyond any nominal overcoming of the past, admittedly attempt to establish a monument to neoromantic Oswald Brunies.[45] *Dog Years* is about its narrators, and readers must resist the tendency to think in their categories. Their accounts of German history are "confessions" of misled, devious, defensive, and representative minds. After recognizing the myths, the Freemasonry, and the numerology, the reader must step back from the seemingly systematic but ultimately chaotic mass of supernatural and suprahistorical phenomena depicted and read the novel as a realistic account of a common and dangerous flight into the reassuring world of symbol and myth. Fredric Jameson argues that Walter Benjamin read Goethe's *Elective Affinities* (*Wahlverwandtschaften*) in this way, interpreting "symbolic objects to the second power":

> It is the originality of Benjamin to have cut across the sterile opposition between the arbitrary interpretations of the symbol on the one hand, and the blank failure to see what it means on the other: *Elective Affinities* is to be read not as a novel by a symbolic writer, but as a novel *about* symbolism. If objects of a symbolic nature loom large in this work, it is not because they were chosen to underline the theme of adultery in some decorative manner, but rather because the real underlying subject is precisely the surrender to the power of symbols of people who have lost their autonomy as human beings. "When people sink to this level, even the life of apparently lifeless things grows strong. Gundolf quite

rightly underlined the crucial role of objects in this story. Yet the intrusion of the thinglike into human life is precisely a criterion of the mythical universe." We are required to read these symbolic objects to the second power: not so much directly to decipher in them a one-to-one meaning, as to sense that of which the very fact of symbolism is itself symptomatic.[46]

It is Grass's genius to recognize in both Nazi and postwar society the natural and potentially destructive human addiction to symbols and to further recognize his own (and other artists') production of symbols as feeding and perpetuating that desire. League-novel emissaries and a romantic Freemason join proponents of numerology, astrology, mythology, pseudo-Catholic idolatry, and ideologies of various sorts to make Grass's novellic paeans to scepticism necessary.

This chapter began with a discussion of Hesse, whose *Demian* and *Journey to the East*, with themes and figures drawn from romantic league novels, appealed strongly to a population suffering from intense destabilization (of many sorts) following Germany's defeat in the World War. People had lost their faith, as a line from *Journey to the East* suggests: "everything now seemed to become unreliable and doubtful, everything threatened to lose its worth, its sense" (30). In compensation, the country was "full of saviours, prophets, and discipleships, of presentiments of the end of the world or hopes for the beginning of a Third Reich" (13). Hesse's earlier works, like *Demian*, were part of this movement, providing the fulfillment and the closure so lacking in contemporary Germany. By 1932, when *Journey to the East* was published, the desire for a political (or economic or spiritual) center was no less great; but the novel, while thematizing the familiar desires and romantic league-novel solutions, also questions the general enterprise. Discussing difficulties with writing history or telling stories, the narrator asks the same questions that would, after the Third Reich, guide Schmidt's, Walser's, and Grass's thinking concerning the transcendence promised in a secret society:

> Where is a center of the events, something in common, something to which they relate and which holds them together? For something like connection, like causality, like meaning to arise, so that, in fact, anything on earth can become narratable, the historian must invent unities: a hero, a people, an idea; and what really

happened namelessly must be said to have happened to this invented unity.

But if even this is so difficult, to coherently narrate a number of actual, documented events, then in my case it is much more difficult, for everything becomes uncertain as soon as I want to observe it exactly, everything slips and dissolves. . . . Nowhere is there a unity, a center, around which the wheel turns. (35)

After the Nazis' success in providing a center around which the wheel could turn—a success based as much on eradicating Freemasons, Jews, and others whose centers challenged that of the Nazis as on providing a center of their own—postwar authors naturally became suspicious of the desire for power and certainty that makes secret societies (or Nazi ideology) so attractive.

Arno Schmidt found strong parallels between the early league novel *Dya Na Sore* and the Nazi state and excoriated a postwar critic who failed to see the similarities. Martin Walser found the center of a corrupt capitalist society in a secret, exclusive club, implying that while the Nazis' defeat may have brought about some changes, at the heart of things lay the same corruption, nurtured by a secret society. And Günter Grass has dealt with the issue of human attraction to figures and symbols promising transcendence. Although Freemasonry itself plays a rather minor explicit role in *The Tin Drum* and *Dog Years*, the issues repeated in more than two centuries of varied league novels are at the center of Grass's novels, and Freemasonry and the league novel provide access to Grass's most important themes. Where Hesse's narrator in *Journey to the East* finds that "behind the intention and hope, behind my entire, irrepressible desire to tell our story, is a fatal doubt" (36), Oskar Matzerath and the three narrators of *Hundejahre* express no such doubts. They are intent on writing a monument to their romantic, Masonic mentor Oswald Brunies, on founding a sect, or party, or lodge, on gaining power by providing the sweet, transcendent symbols to which their fellow citizens have long been addicted.

Afterword: "So we will get, in any case, profound and religious philosophy and Freemasonry"

Ludwig Tieck's play *Der gestiefelte Kater* (1797), a complex romantic *Puss-in-Boots*, begins with a discussion among several audience members as to what sort of play the strange title suggests. One of them shows himself a true son of his age when he claims that the booted cat can only be a trick—the play is surely about revolution and Freemasonry: "See if I am not right. A revolutionary play, as far as I can tell, with abominable princes and ministers, and then a highly mysterious man who meets with a secret society deep, deep down in a basement where he, as president, is disguised to make the common crowd think he is a cat. So we will get, in any case, profound and religious philosophy and Freemasonry."[1]

Like the audience in Tieck's play, the non-Masonic public has been fascinated by the secret brotherhood for three centuries. In the public's mind Freemasonry has represented both the admirable and the ridiculous, what we at once both fear and long for.[2] Conspiracies against "throne and altar" can be supposed to originate in secretive lodges. Cities and countries, economies and justice systems are all conceivably manipulated by conspiring brothers. But Masons exhibit remarkable charity and intellect and take productive part in community and national events, leading some to envision the lodge as a place of moral education, a school of humanity. Others suppose it to be a repository for grand esoteric truths. Contemporary Freemasonry is a rather conservative social organization with charitable and educational goals; but there remain, somewhere in Masonry's colorful past, historical precedents for even the wildest suppositions. It requires only a single incident like the conspiracy recently uncovered in Italy's P-2 lodge to revive intense public conjecture.

By virtue of its origins at the beginning of the modern period, Freemasonry has a distinctly dual nature, both semiotically and politically. It expresses Enlightenment ideals but does so through symbols and rituals developed in what Frances Yates calls the Rosicrucian Enlightenment. It has roots in the "sacred" seventeenth century, takes part in the desacralizing movement of the Enlightenment, and then plays a strong role in romantic resacralizing. Further, it is among the most influential nonpolitical, yet political, institutions of the century, helping to affect early transitions from authoritarian to democratic governments and figuring, at least in theory, in American, French, Italian, and German revolutions.

The mania for closure Schiller saw in contemporary high-grade Masonic orders figures large in *The Ghost-Seer*, written just as he left off writing poetry and drama to study Kant and write philosophy and history. The novel depicts semiotic manipulation of a prince starving for transcendence, while itself refusing the saccharine pleasures of closure. Concurrently, it unmasks the "enlightened" narrators who find their own false closure in placing complete blame for the "anarchy of the Enlightenment" on an evil Masonic/ Jesuitical conspiracy.

Like Schiller, Goethe warns in *Wilhelm Meister's Apprenticeship* and *Travels* against addiction to transcendence, against attempted leaps from idea through symbol to transcendent actuality (as in alchemy). But even while drawing attention to the arbitrary nature of symbols, Goethe motivates the symbols with reference to their long traditions. The chapel on the Masonic ritual route is indeed a *secularized* chapel; but it is also a *chapel* secularized. The esoteric is bracketed out as actuality and simultaneously drawn in as possibility. As an institution balanced between the sacred and secular, Freemasonry supplies potent figures for a novel self-reflexively concerned with its own figuration.

Karl Gutzkow's "political *Wilhelm Meister*" also makes use of Freemasonry's dualities. After the disappointments of 1848, the neo-Masonic Knights of Spirit represent an opposition party under an absolutist government, as did Freemasons during the eighteenth century. But Gutzkow, neither willing to settle for indirect political activity nor ready to advocate violent overthrow of the government, depicts both an Enlightenment secret society, only indirectly political and utterly rational, and a radical conspiracy that frightened authorities connect with communism. Memories of the Illuminati and Carbonari make the conspiracy theory a potent force in the novel;

and the moderate Knights of Spirit are meant as an attractive alternative. In addition, Gutzkow establishes political legitimacy for his Knights of Spirit by pitting the (semi-) historical chain from Knights Templar through Freemasonry against the inherited right of kings, a move that bears some resemblance to Goethe's motivation of otherwise arbitrary signs with reference to Masonic and Rosicrucian tradition. Finally, Gutzkow endows his secret society with rituals and symbols endemic to such societies, aware that they will enhance the political impact, evidently unconcerned that political use of symbols preys on what Schiller called the "republican freedom" of the public.

Unwilling totally to concede to the apparent arbitrariness of language and drawing on the Rosicrucian and Freemasonic metaphors he found in works by Schiller and Goethe and in twentieth-century accounts of eighteenth-century secret societies, Hofmannsthal, like Goethe, finds qualified motivation in the eighteenth-century Masonic symbols situated between motivated and arbitrary language. He finds meaning in a movement from mentor to disciple to mentor, from the disciple who believes in a transcendence behind the mentor's signs to the mentor who finds meaning in the disciple's gestures of faith.

Thomas Mann learned about the mystical, high-grade side of Freemasonry from a contemporary work of literary criticism about the league novel; and he opposed the romantic alchemy of the newly revealed Masonry to the politically liberal Masonry he had so hated in his brother Heinrich's novel. Then, however, he recognized in the romantic quest for transcendence through Masonic symbols an obsession fulfillable only through death; and the novel became "eine antiromantische Desillusionierung." As earlier for Goethe, Hofmannsthal, and even Gutzkow, Freemasonry's position between the mundane and the transcendent makes it attractive to a writer working on that boundary himself.

After Nazi manipulation of similar rituals and symbols in the service of absolutist power, postwar authors like Walser and Grass are seriously concerned with the immoral molding of political will through Masonic (or religious or capitalist) symbols. In the tradition of Schiller, Grass's novels are narrated by men anxious for closure, men who achieve power through their brilliant use of symbols. Even after their moral bankruptcy has been demonstrated, they turn once more to the same symbols to escape guilt, to "overcome the past," and to build a new base of power.[3]

In "The Entered Apprentice's Lecture" the Mason swears, in reference to the "secret Mysteries," that he will

> not write it, print it, cut it, paint it, or stint it, mark it, stain or engrave it, or cause it so to be done, upon any thing moveable or immoveable, under the Canopy of Heaven, whereby it may become legible or intelligible, or the least Appearance of the Character of a Letter, whereby the secret Art may be unlawfully obtained ... under no less Penalty than to have my Throat cut across, my Tongue torn out by the Root, and that to be buried in the Sands of the Sea, at Low-Water Mark, a Cable's Length from the Shore, where the Tide ebbs and flows twice in twenty-four Hours.

Schiller, Goethe, Gutzkow, Hofmannsthal, Thomas Mann, and Grass, along with many other novelists, have indeed written it and printed it "whereby it may become legible or intelligible," and have done so in part because of the threat the violent oath expresses, because of the potent merging of word and deed in what claims to be a totally natural language, and because of the constant tension between politics and nonpolitics in Masonic ritual. That Freemasonry has been and remains a force in the Western world is due as much to their fictions as to the nonliterary history of the secret society.

Appendix:
The Entered Apprentice's Lecture

At the center of Masonry, guarded by solemn oath, is a fascinating ritual. Exposés of Masonry uniformly print parts of the ritual under the assumption that the various words and actions *are* the secret. Publication, on this view, would destroy the fraternity. But after centuries of such disclosure, Freemasonry continues to flourish. Obviously the assumption is false. The ritual, like rituals of other cultures, is allegorical in nature, simultaneously veiling and disclosing its meaning. For the "profane" it may be a veil. For the Mason in a community of Masons it may prove revelatory.

Karl Christian Friedrich Krause, whom German Freemasons rank with Lessing as a "father of humanitarian Masonry," recognized this as he worked in his lodge in the early nineteenth century. He took strong exception to other branches of Freemasonry that routinely promised extraordinary concrete (nonallegorical) revelations as their initiates advanced from one high grade to another. Such false promises can be devalued by publication; and to this end Krause published several Masonic rites. His stated wish was to further the most worthy aims of his fraternity.

I reprint part of one of these rituals here, the "Entered Apprentice's Lecture," and do so in Krause's spirit and from Krause's book: *Die drei ältesten Kunsturkunden der Freimaurerbruderschaft* (Dresden: Arnoldische Kunst- und Buchhandlung, 1810), 146–181. Grammar sometimes betrays the German printing.

> *Master.* Brother, is there any Thing between you and I?
> *Answer.* There is, Worshipful.
> *Mas.* What is it, Brother?

Ans. A Secret.

Mas. What is that Secret, Brother?

Ans. Masonry.

Mas. Then I presume, you are a Mason?

Ans. I am so taken and accepted amongst Brothers and Fellows.

Mas. Pray, what Sort of Man ought a Mason to be?

Ans. A Man that is born of a Free Woman.

Mas. Where was you first prepared to be made a Mason?

Ans. In my Heart.

Mas. Where was you next prepared?

Ans. In a Room adjoining to the Lodge.

Mas. How was you prepared, Brother?

Ans. I was neither naked nor cloathed; barefoot nor shod, deprived of all Metal; hood-winked, with a Cable Tow about my Neck, where I was led to the Door of the Lodge, in a halting moving Posture, by the Hand of a Friend, whom I afterwards found to be a Brother.

Mas. How did you know it to be a Door, you being blinded?

Ans. By finding a Stoppage, and afterwards an Entrance or Admittance.

Mas. How got you Admittance?

Ans. By three distinct Knocks.

Mas. What was said to you within?

Ans. Who comes there?

Mas. Your Answer, Brother?

Ans. One who begs to have and receive Part of the Benefit of this Right Worshipful Lodge, dedicated to St. John, as many Brothers and Fellows have done before me.

Mas. How do you expect to obtain it?

Ans. By being free born, and well reported.

Mas. What was said to you then?

Ans. Enter.

Mas. How did you enter, and upon what?

Ans. Upon the Point of a Sword or Spear, or some warlike instrument presented to my naked Left Breast.

Mas. What was said to you then?

Ans. I was asked if I felt any thing.

Mas. What was your Answer?

Ans. I did, but I could see nothing.

Mas. You have told me how you was received, pray who received you?

Ans. The Junior Warden.

Mas. How did he dispose of you?

Ans. He delivered me to the Master, who ordered me to kneel down and receive the Benefit of a Prayer. Brethren, let us pray!

O Lord God, thou great and universal Mason of the World, and first Builder of Man, as it were a Temple; be with us, o Lord, as thou hast promised, when two or three are gathered together in thy Name, thou wilt be in the Midst of them: Be with us, o Lord, and bless all our Undertakings, and grant that this our Friend may become a faithful Brother. Let Grace and Peace be multiplied unto him, through the Knowledge of our Lord Jesus Christ: And grant, O Lord, as he putteth forth his Hand to thy Holy Word, that he may also put forth his Hand to serve a Brother, [but not to hurt himself or his Family]; that whereby may be given to us great and precious Promises, that by this we may be Partakers of Thy Divine Nature, having escaped the Corruption that is in the World through Lust.

O Lord God, add to our Faith Virtue, and to Virtue Knowledge, and to Knowledge Temperance, and to Temperance Prudence, and to Prudence Patience, and to Patience Godliness, and to Godliness Brotherly Love, and to Brotherly Love Charity; and grant, o Lord, that Masonry may be blest throughout the World, and thy Peace be upon us, o Lord: and grant that we may be all united as one, through our Lord Jesus Christ, who liveth and reigneth for ever and ever. Amen.

Mas. After you had received this Prayer, what was said to you?

Ans. I was asked who I put my Trust in?

Mas. Your Answer, Brother?

Ans. In God.

Mas. What was the next Thing said to you?

Ans. I was taken by the Right Hand, and a Brother said, Rise up, and follow your Leader, and fear no Danger.

Mas. After all this, how was you disposed of?

Ans. I was led Three Times round the Lodge.

Mas. Where did you meet with the first Opposition?

Ans. At the Back of the Junior Warden in the South, where I gave the same three Knocks as at the Door.

Mas. What Answer did he give you?

Ans. He said, Who comes there?

Mas. Your Answer?

Ans. The same as at the Door, One who begs to have and receive Part of the Benefit of this Right Worshipful Lodge, dedicated to St. John, as many Brothers and Fellows have done before me.

Mas. Where did you meet with the second Opposition?

Ans. At the Back of the Senior Warden in the West, where I made the same Repetition as at the Door. He said, Who comes there? One who begs to have and receive Part of the Benefit of this Right Worshipful Lodge, dedicated to St. John, as many Brothers and Fellows have done before me.

Mas. Where did you meet with the third Opposition?

Ans. At the Back of the Master in the East, where I made the Repetition as before.

Mas. What did the Master do with you?

Ans. He ordered me back to the Senior Warden in the West to receive Instructions.

Mas. What were the Instructions he gave you?

Ans. He taught me to take one Step upon the first Step of a right Angle oblong Square, with my Left Knee bare bent, my Body upright, my Right Foot forming a Square, my naked Right Hand upon the Holy Bible, with the Square and Compass thereon, my Left Hand supporting the same; where I took that solemn Obligation or Oath of a Mason.

Mas. Brother, can you repeat that Obligation?

Ans. I will do my Endeavour, with your Assistance, Worshipful.

Mas. Stand up, and begin.

Ans. I—A.B. of my own Free Will and Accord, and in the Presence of Almighty God, and this Right Worshipful Lodge, dedicated to St. John, do hereby and hereon most solemnly and sincerely swear, that I will always hale, conceal, and never will reveal any of the secret Mysteries of Free Masonry, that shall be delivered to me now, or at any Time hereafter, except it be to a true and lawful Brother, or in a just and lawful Lodge of Brothers and Fellows, him or them whom I shall find to be such, after just Trial and due Examination. I furthermore do swear, that I will not write it, print it, cut it, paint it, or stint it, mark it, stain or engrave it, or cause it so to be done, upon any thing moveable or immoveable, under the Canopy of Heaven, whereby it may become legible or intelligible, or the least Appearance of the Character of a Letter, whereby the secret

183

Art may be unlawfully obtained. All this I swear, with a strong and steady Resolution to perform the same, without any Hesitation, mental Reservation, or Self-Evasion of Mind in me whatsoever; under no less Penalty than to have my Throat cut across, my Tongue torn out by the Root, and that to be buried in the Sands of the Sea, at Low-Water Mark, a Cable's Length from the Shore, where the Tide ebbs and flows twice in twenty-four Hours. So help me God, and keep me steadfast in this my Entered Apprentice's Obligation.

(He kisses the Book.)

Funde merum Genio!

N.B. After this Obligation they drink a Toast to the Heart that conceals, and to the Tongue that never reveals. The Master in the Chair gives it, and they all say Ditto, and they draw the Glasses across their Throats, as aforesaid.

Mas. Now, Brother, after you received this Obligation, what was the first that was said to you?

Ans. I was asked what I most desired?

Mas. What was your Answer?

Ans. To be brought to Light.

Mas. Who brought you to Light?

Ans. The Master and the rest of the Brethren.

Mas. When you was thus brought to Light, what were the first Things you saw?

Ans. The Bible, Square, and Compass.

Mas. What was it they told you they signified?

Ans. Three great Lights in Masonry.

Mas. Explain them, Brother.

Ans. The Bible, to rule and govern our Faith; the Square, to square our Actions; the Compass to keep us within Bounds with all Men, particularly with a Brother.

Mas. What were the next Things that were shewn to you?

Answer. Three Candles, which I was told were three lesser Lights in Masonry.

Mas. What do they represent?

Ans. The Sun, Moon, and Master-Mason.

Mas. Why so, Brother?

Ans. There is the Sun to rule the Day, the Moon to rule the Night, and the Master-Mason his Lodge, or at least ought so to do.

Mas. What was then done to you?

Ans. The Master took me by the Right-hand, and gave me the Grip and Word of an Entered Apprentice, and said, Rise, my Brother JACHIN.

N.B. Sometimes they shew you the Sign before the Grip and Word is given, which is JACHIN: It is the Entered Apprentice's Word, and Grip thereto belonging is to pinch with your Right Thumb Nail upon the first Joint of your Brother's Right-hand.

Mas. Have you got this Grip and Word, Brother?

Ans. I have, Worshipful.

Mas. Give it to your next Brother.

N.B. Then he takes his next Brother by the Right-hand, and gives him the Grip and Word, as before described, he tells the Master, that is right.

According to the following Proof.

The 1st. Brother gives him the Grip.

The 2d. Brother says, What's this?

1st. Bro. The Grip of an Entered Apprentice.

2d. Bro. Has it got a Name?

1st. Bro. It has.

2d. Bro. Will you give it me?

1st. Bro. I'll letter it with you, or halve it.

2d. Bro. I'll halve it with you.

1st. Bro. Begin.

2d. Bro. No, you begin first.

1st. Bro. JA—

2d. Bro. CHIN.

1st. Bro. JACHIN.

2d. Bro. It is right, Worshipful Master.

Mas. What was the next Thing that was shewn to you?

Ans. The Guard or Sign of an Entered Apprentice.

N.B. The Guard or Sign, as they call it, is by drawing your Right Hand across your Throat edgeways; which is to remind you of the Penalty of your Obligation, that you would sooner have your Throat cut across, than discover the Secrets of Masonry.

Mas. Have you got the Guard, or Sign, of an Entered Apprentice?

N.B. He draws his Right-hand across his Throat (as aforesaid), to shew the master that he has.

Mas. After all this, what was said to you?

Answer. I was ordered to be taken back, and invested with what I had been divested of; and to be brought again to return Thanks, and to receive the Benefit of a Lecture, if Time would permit.

Mas. After you was invested of what you had been divested of, what was done to you?

Ans. I was brought to the North-West Corner of the Lodge, in order to return thanks.

Mas. How did you return Thanks?

Ans. I stood in the North-West Corner of the Lodge, and, with the Instruction of a Brother, I said, Master, Senior and Junior Wardens, Senior and Junior Deacons, and the rest of the Brethren of this Lodge, I return you Thanks for the Honour you have done me, in making me a Mason, and admitting me a Member of this worthy Society.

Mas. What was said to you then?

Ans. The Master called me up to the North-East Corner of the Lodge, or at his Right-hand.

Mas. Did he present you with any Thing?

Ans. He presented me with an Apron, which he put on me; he told me it was a Badge of Innocency, more ancient than the Golden Fleece or the Roman Eagle; more honoured than the Star and Garter, or any other Order under the Sun, that could be conferred upon me at that Time, or any Time hereafter.

Mas. What were the next Things that were shewn to you?

Ans. I was set down by the Master's Right-hand, who shewed me the working Tools of an Entered Apprentice.

M. What were they?

Ans. The 24 Inch Gauge, the Square, and common Gavel, or Setting Maul.

Mas. What are their Uses?

Ans. The Square to square my Work, the 24 Inch Gauge to measure my work, the common Gavel to knock off all superfluous Matter, whereby the Square may set easy and just.

Mas. Brother, as we are not all working Masons, we apply them to our Morals, which we call spiritualizing: explain them.

Ans. The 24 Inch Gauge represents the 24 Hours of the Day.

Mas. How do you spend them, Brother?

Ans. Six Hours to work in, Six Hours to serve God, and Six to serve a Friend or a Brother, as far as lies in my Power, without being detrimental to myself or Family: and Six Hours to Sleep in.

The rite continues in this vein at some length. For the full version, see Krause.

Notes

PREFACE

1. Günter Grass, *Dog Years* (Neuwied: Luchterhand, 1963), 337.

2. Thomas Mann, *Gesammelte Werke* (Frankfurt/M: S. Fischer, 1960), III, 700.

3. Karl Gutzkow, *The Knights of Spirit*, 2d ed. (Leipzig: Brockhaus, 1852), VIII, 297–298.

4. For a more detailed, more comprehensive history of the Freemasonic movement than can be given in this book there are many sources available. One might well begin with the Eleventh Edition of the *Encyclopaedia Britannica*. Roberts's *The Mythology of the Secret Societies* (New York: Charles Scribner's Sons, 1972) provides a readable and scholarly introduction to the order in the context of the conspiracy theories which grew up around it. D. Knoop and G. P. Jones's *The Genesis of Freemasonry* is good on origins. Mackey's *Encyclopaedia of Freemasonry* (Manchester, 1947), especially the later editions, is a good source for English speakers. For German Freemasonry, among the most helpful works are Eugen Lennhoff and Oskar Posner's *Internationales Freimaurer-Lexikon* (1932), J. G. Findel's groundbreaking *Geschichte der Freimaurerei* (Leipzig, 1870), and F. J. Schneider's *Die Freimaurerei und ihr Einfluss auf die geistige Kultur in Deutschland am Ende des XVIII. Jahrhunderts* (Prag: Taussig and Taussig, 1909).

5. The following studies of Freemasonry and of Masonic novels are among the most interesting:

1959   Reinhart Koselleck, *Kritik und Krise* (extremely influential) (Freiburg, 1959)

1962   Jürgen Habermas: *Strukturwandel der Öffentlichkeit* (Darmstadt: Luchterhand, 1962)

1968   Ion Contiades, ed., *Ernst und Falk. Mit den Fortsetzungen Johann Gottfried Herders und Friedrich Schlegels* (Frankfurt/M.: Insel, 1968) Hans Grassl, *Aufbruch zur Romantik* (Munchen: C. H. Beck, 1968)

1970   Jacob Katz, *Jews and Freemasons in Europe 1723–1939* (Cambridge: Harvard University Press, 1970)

1972   J.M. Roberts, *The Mythology of the Secret Societies* Jacques Chailly, *The Magic Flute, Masonic Opera* (London: Victor Gollancz, 1972) Frances Yates, *The Rosicrucian Enlightenment* (London: Routledge and Kegan Paul, 1972)

1975   Richard van Dülmen, *Der Geheimbund der Illuminaten* (Stuttgart: Friedrich Frommann, 1975)

1976   Johannes Rogalla von Bieberstein, *Die These von der Verschwörung 1776–1945* (Bern: Herbert Lang and Peter Lang, 1976)

1979   Peter Christian Ludz, ed., *Geheime Gesellschaften* (Heidelberg: Lambert Schneider, 1979)

1980   Helmut Neuberger, *Freimaurerei und Nationalsozialismus* (Hamburg: Bauhutten, 1980)

1981   Margaret Jacob, *The Radical Enlightenment* (London: Allen and Unwin, 1981)

1982   Adrian von Buttlar, *Der Englische Landsitz 1715–1760* (Mittenwald: Mäander, 1982)

1984   Manfred Agethen, *Geheimbund und Utopie* (München: Oldenbourg, 1984)

1985   Gerhard Steiner, *Freimaurer und Rosenkreuzer: Georg Forsters Weg durch Geheimbünde* (Weinheim: Acta humaniora, 1985)

1987   Michael Voges, *Aufklärung und Geheimnis* (Tübingen: Niemeyer, 1987)

CHAPTER ONE

1. William James Hughan, "Freemasonry," *The Encyclopaedia Britannica*, 11th ed., XI, 78.

2. Lennhoff and Posner, *Internationales Freimaurer-Lexikon*, 707; as also the next quotation.

3. For an excellent study of the Illuminati see Richard van Dülmen, *Der Geheimbund der Illuminaten*. Also R. Le Forestier, *Les Illuminés de Bavière et la franc-maçonnerie allemande* (Paris: Hachette, 1914).

4. Roberts's *The Mythology of the Secret Societies* examines the conspiracy theory in detail. See also Rogalla von Bieberstein's *Die These von der Verschwörung 1776–1945*.

5. Johann Gottlob Fichte, *Gesamtausgabe*, II/3, ed. Reinhard Lauth and Hans Jacob (Stuttgart, Bad Cannstatt: Friedrich Frommann, 1971), 371–372.

6. Fichte's lectures were published, with editorial additions, in the Masonic journal *Eleusinien des 19. Jahrhunderts,* 1802–1803.

7. Johann Gottlob Fichte, *Philosophie der Maurerei,* ed. Wilhelm Flitner (Leipzig: Felix Meiner, 1923), 17.

8. A mid nineteenth-century description of Freemasonry supplies a corroborative inside view of what the fraternity offers its members, again emphasizing the cosmopolitan character of the order, its democratic nature, the commitment to support both state and religion, and the education given through Masonic ritual:

> Der Freimaurerbund . . . ist ein auf freie Vereinigung begründeter, über die ganze Erde verbreiteter Bruderbund von Männern, die sich bei ihrer feierlichen Aufnahme aufs Heiligste verpflichten, den Cultus oder die Kunst der Freimaurerei zu erlernen, geheim zu halten und im Stillen auszuüben, die unter allen Zonen an gewissen, ebenfalls geheim zu haltenden, Merkmalen und Zeichen sich als Glieder des Bundes erkennen, und ohne Rücksicht auf Stand und äusseres Verhältniss, unberührt von den Zerwürfnissen der Zeit, aber unterthan dem Gesetze, der Sitte und Humanität sich als Freunde und Brüder untereinander betrachten. Diese Kunst der Freimaurerei, . . . seit der Aufnahme Wilhelm's III. von England im J. 1693 "königliche Kunst" genannt, besteht in der Ausübung gewisser, theils von den Werkmaurern und Steinmetzen, theils aus der biblischen Geschichte, theils auch wol von ältern, wissenschaftliche und religiöse Ziele verfolgenden Geheimbündnissen entlehnter symbolischer Gebräuche und ethische, Menschen erziehende und beglückende Zwecke befördernder Mittel.

August Wilhelm Müller, "Freimaurerei," *Allgemeine Encyklopädie der Wissenschaften und Künsten,* 1849.

9. Reinhart Koselleck, *Kritik und Krise: Eine Studie zur Pathogenese der bürgerlichen Welt* (Freiburg: Karl Alber, 1959; rpt. Frankfurt/M: Suhrkamp, 1973), 49. Michael Voges gives a good summary of recent critiques of Koselleck's work in *Aufklärung und Geheimnis,* 15 ff.

10. Koselleck does not cite this example, but it strongly supports his argument.

11. See Adrian von Buttlar, *Der Landschaftsgarten* (München: Wilhelm Heyne, 1980); also his *Der Englische Landsitz 1715–1760.*

12. There were links to fiction as well. Buttlar points out that the garden *Sanspareil* near Zwernitz in Franken was built in imitation of Fénelon's novel *Les Aventures de Télémaque* (1699). The visitor walking through the garden passed through landscapes made (through monuments, inscriptions, decorations, and the like) to represent scenes from the novel (*Der Landschaftsgarten,* 114).

13. In *Der Landschaftsgarten* Buttlar describes the garden:

> Von der *Bethöhle des Eremiten* gelangt der Wanderer zur *Zelle des Mystagogen,* hinter der sich der Weg aufteilt: "Der eine, nach rechter Hand zu, ist gleichsam der gedankenlose mühselige Steig des Menschen ohne Kenntnis

> und Geisteskultur, der andere Weg zur Linken ist der geheimnisreiche Pfad der Mysten, der Lehrlinge erhabener Weisheit, welche ihren Anhängern über Hier und Dort geheime Aufschlüsse erteilt," berichtet Rode. In Anlehnung an die Einweihungsriten freimaurerischer und anderer geheimer Gesellschaften sollte hier Aufstieg und Initiation des einsam Gottsuchenden nachvollzogen werden, der sich aus dem feuchten Dunkel der Grotte über den schmalen Grat des Felsens—"Grenzscheide zwischen Leben und Tod"—zum Tempel von Licht, Liebe und Schönheit . . . hinauftastet. (124)

Cf. the Masonic, English garden in Illustration I, where the symbolic journey from grotto to the top of Mount Parnassos could be made.

14. Friedrich Schlegel, *Philosophy of History*, trans. James Burton Robertson, 7th ed. (London: Bell & Daldy, 1873), 456.

15. July 8, 1796. *Goethes Werke*, 6th ed. (Hamburg: Christian Wegner, 1950), VIII, 539–540.

16. Koselleck, *Kritik und Krise*, 114. A final example of Koselleck's thesis can be seen in the growth of Freemasonry in prerevolutionary France. After the American revolution, Benjamin Franklin became head of the lodge "Les Neuf Soeurs" in Paris (lodge of several of the Encyclopedists, and the lodge into which Franklin introduced the young Georg Forster and the aged Voltaire). Since 1773 Masons of the Grand Orient of France had looked on themselves as belonging to a Masonic democracy; and the republican principles Franklin brought from North America intensified those feelings. From 1772 to 1789, the number of lodges in France grew from 164 to 629, one indication that Freemasonry was indeed a political antipode to the system of absolutism. See Koselleck, 64.

17. Karl Krause, *Die drei ältesten Kunsturkunden der Freimaurerbrüderschaft* (Dresden: Arnold, 1810).

18. See Krause's "Entered Apprentice's Lecture" in the Appendix.

19. Alice Kuzniar, "Philosophic Chiliasm: Generating the Future or Delaying the End?" *Eighteenth-Century Studies*, 19 (1985), 16–17.

20. Michel Foucault, *The Order of Things* (New York: Vintage Books, 1973); a translation of *Les Mots et les choses* (Paris: Gallimard, 1966).

21. David Wellbery, *Lessing's "Laocoon": Semiotics and Aesthetics in the Age of Reason* (Cambridge: Cambridge University Press, 1984), 36.

22. J. G. Fichte, *Gesamtausgabe*, III/4, ed. Reinhard Lauth und Hans Gliwitzky (Stuttgart-Bad Cannstatt: Friedrich Frommann, 1973), 245–270.

23. E. M. Butler, *The Myth of the Magus* (Cambridge: The University Press, 1948), 218.

24. Cagliostro was arrested again in Rome in 1789 and for being a heretic was condemned to death, a sentence ultimately commuted to life imprisonment.

25. Andreae had it himself from earlier sources. His work is part of a tradition of utopian literature that includes Andreae's own *Christianopolis*, Bacon's *New Atlantis*, More's *Utopia*, and Hartlib's *Macaria*.

26. Yates, *The Rosicrucian Enlightenment* , 50.

27. Perhaps the most interesting example of the extent and result of this furor appears in Adrien Baillet's biography of Descartes. While wintering near the Danube in 1619, the young Descartes searched for the much-talked-about Rosicrucians. In 1623 when he returned to Paris, he met rumors that he had enrolled in the Fraternity. Other rumors claimed that six Rosicrucian deputies had taken up secret lodging in Paris and that they could only be communicated with through a kind of telepathy. Descartes found it necessary to show himself in public, thus proving that even if there were invisible Rosicrucians in the city as rumor would have it, he was not one of them. That Descartes would have to prove himself visible to dispel rumors about his Rosicrucian involvement is a fine indication of just how passionately the Rosicrucian fictions were received throughout Europe. For more on this see chapters VII and VIII in Yates, *The Rosicrucian Enlightenment*, which document "The Rosicrucian Furore in Germany" and "The Rosicrucian Scare in France," and the following chapters about England and Italy.

28. Andrew Ramsay's *Cyrus* was extremely popular, with many editions and translations. There were German translations in 1728, 1745, 1779, and 1780 (the last by Matthias Claudius).

29. Terrasson's *Sethos* was translated into German in 1732 and then again in 1777–1778, this time by Matthias Claudius.

30. Ivan Nagel has recently interpreted *The Magic Flute* in part as a "Masonic" text manifesting Koselleck's theory of Masonry as a response to absolutist governments. *Autonomie und Gnade: Über Mozarts Opern* (München, Wien: Carl Hanser, 1985).

31. Carl Bahrdt, as quoted in Sten Flygt, *The Notorious Dr. Bahrdt* (Nashville, Tenn.: Vanderbilt University Press, 1963), 254.

32. For modern versions of Bahrdt's story linking Jesus and secret societies, see Hugh J. Schonfield, *The Passover Plot* (New York: Bernard Geis Associates, 1966); and Michael Baigent, Richard Leigh, and Henry Lincoln, *Holy Blood, Holy Grail* (London: Jonathan Cape Ltd., 1982; New York: Dell, 1983). Albert Schweitzer's *The Quest of the Historical Jesus* (New York: MacMillan Co., 1961; originally published as *Von Reimarus zu Wrede*, 1906) gives an informative account of Bahrdt's work.

33. Johann Heinrich Jung-Stilling, *Lebensgeschichte* (Frankfurt/M: Insel, 1983), 480-481.

34. Habermas, *Strukturwandel der Öffentlichkeit* (Darmstadt: Luchterhand, 1962), 58–59. The negative campaign to be described here, however, contributed not to a further opening of the public sphere but rather to paranoia and reaction.

35. Other articles include, for example, translations from Greek texts, essays about witch trials, capital punishment and marriage, a discussion of the Montgolfier brothers and balloons, an article on the relationship between architecture and garden art, an exposé of female suicide as the consequence of "secret vice," an essay on the expression "Freudenmädchen," news of the Russian sea war against the Turks from 1769 to 1773, a discussion of the problems arising because too many young people are studying at universities and there are not enough jobs available for such highly trained people, a series on the financial status of the new French government after the revolution, news of the establishment of the first morgue in Berlin, an essay on the influence of the moon on the weather (by Kant), "Negotiations of the Chiefs of the Seneca Nation in North America with President Washington concerning a land sale in the years 1790 and 1791," and so on.

36. *Vollendeter Aufschluss des Jesuitismus und des wahren Geheimnisses der Freimaurer, Ans Licht gestellt von dem Herausgeber der Enthüllung der Weltbürger-Republik* (Rom, 1787). (The authorship and place of publication are parts of the parody.)

CHAPTER TWO

1. Leo Tolstoy, *War and Peace*, trans. Rosemary Edmonds (Baltimore: Penguin Books, 1969), 419–420.

2. Two recent works take the novel seriously: Michael Voges's *Aufklärung und Geheimnis* (Tübingen: Max Niemeyer, 1987), 343–398 investigates the novel as a text caught between essay and novel; and Liliane Weissberg's productive rhetorical approach views *Der Geisterseher* as a popular novel which turns into a philosophical dialogue (*Geistersprache: philosophischer und literarischer Diskurs im späten achtzehnten Jahrhundert* [Würzburg: Königshausen and Neumann, 1990]).

3. Borcherdt's introduction to the novel in the *Nationalausgabe* ends with a discussion of the connection between morality and power developed in the philosophical conversation (NA XVI, 394). Staiger discusses the same concept in his book *Friedrich Schiller* (Zürich: Atlantis, 1967) 62–65, and in his introduction to the novel in Insel Verlag's five-volume edition of *Schillers Werke* (Frankfurt/M: Insel, 1966), III, 516–519.

4. Cf. the excellent introduction to the novel in the *Säkular-Ausgabe*, II, XXII–XXXVIII, or Benno von Wiese's *Friedrich Schiller* (Stuttgart: J. B. Metzler, 1959), 314–329, or again the *Nationalausgabe*, XVI, 390–392, or Adalbert von Hanstein's *Wie entstand Schillers Geisterseher?* (Berlin: Alexander Kuncker, 1903; rpt. Hildesheim: Gerstenberg, 1977).

5. Cf. Marianne Thalmann's ground-breaking *Der Trivialroman des 18. Jahrhunderts und der romantische Roman: Ein Beitrag zur Entwicklungsgeschichte der Geheimbundmystik* (Berlin: Emil Ebering, 1923); or Wal-

ter Bussman's "Schillers 'Geisterseher' und seine Fortsetzer: Ein Beitrag zur Struktur des Geheimbundromans" (Ph.D. diss., Göttingen, 1961); or Rosemarie Haas's *Die Turmgesellschaft in "Wilhelm Meisters Lehrjahren": Zur Geschichte des Geheimbundromans und der Romantheorie im 18. Jahrhundert* (Bern: Herbert Lang, 1975), 10–13.

6. Gert Ueding has recognized the novel as a self-reflexive portrayal of aesthetic problems, declaring that it is not only the exciting story of battle between Enlightenment reason and ghost-seeing swindlers but also the "theoretische Auseinandersetzung mit zentralen Problemen der zeitgenössischen Aesthetik." "Die Wahrheit lebt in der Täuschung fort: Historische Aspekte der Vor-Schein-Aesthetik," in *Literatur ist Utopie*, ed. Gert Ueding (Frankfurt/M.: Suhrkamp, 1978), 90.

7. Richard Weissenfels, introducing *Der Geisterseher* in the Säkular-Ausgabe, points to articles in the *Berlinische Monatsschrift* disclosing Cagliostro's elaborate frauds, one written by Elisabeth von der Recke, a woman whom Schiller's and Körner's aquaintances would have met during her visits to Leipzig and Dresden during this time. He notes the letter written by Garve, one of Schiller's favorite popular philosophers, attacking Biester's fanatical war on Jesuits and Freemasons. He mentions Körner's role as a "liberal Freemason," Wieland's literary interest in ghosts and secret societies, and Bode's intense involvement with Freemasonic realities and rumors, and shows that all three men had close contacts with Schiller during this time.

8. Letter to Henriette von Wollzogen, Mannheim d. 11./12. Septb, 1783. NA XXIII, 112-113.

9. Weimar, 10. September 1787.

10. Cf. E. F. W. E. Folenius, *Der Geisterseher: Aus den Memoiren des Grafen von O: Zweyter und dritter Theil von X. .Y. .Z...* (Leipzig: Barth, 1796–1797), and Hanns Heinz Ewers, *Der Geisterseher: Aus den Papieren des Grafen O...* (München: Georg Müller, 1922).

11. Thalmann, *Der Trivialroman des 18. Jahrhunderts und der romantische Roman*.

12. The *Bundesroman* has been defined variously as follows:

> Der Genius und die Bundestochter sind also die zwei vom Orden ausgesandten Schergen, welche die Willensfreiheit ihrem Opfer zu rauben und alle Handlungen desselben nach dem Zwecke zu leiten haben, dem sie dienen sollen. Der Held ist fast in allen Fällen ein unerfahrener Optimist und Idealist, der schon von Jugend auf seine angeborene Neigung für alles Dunkle und Rätselhafte durch Lektüre und geistiges Nacherleben grotesker Wundergeschichten genährt hat, mit einem Wort: er ist, ob er nun in dieser oder jener Maske auftritt, dieser oder jener Nation angehört, immer der leicht lenkbare deutsche Schwärmer am Ende des 18. Jahrhunderts.

Schneider, *Die Freimaurerei und ihr Einfluss auf die Geistige Kultur in Deutschland am Ende des XVIII. Jahrhunderts*, 213.

Was sowohl für F.J. Schneider als auch für Marion Beaujean die Gemein-
samkeit dieser Romane ausmacht, ist die Tatsache, dass in all diesen Romanen ein Geheimbund sein Wesen treibt, der es versteht, den Helden in
seine Netze zu ziehen und ihn mit Hilfe oft dunkler Machenschaften wie
der Inszenierung von Geistererscheinungen nach einem ganz bestimmten
Plan zu einem ganz bestimmten Ziel zu lenken. Dieser Plan ist zwar oft,
aber nicht notwendig verbrecherisch, wie auch das Ziel für den Helden
nicht unbedingt verderblich zu sein braucht. Immer jedoch ist es ihm un-
bekannt, hat der Held selbst keine Einsicht in das, was mit ihm vorgenom-
men wird, und ist er überhaupt dem Bund—mag dieser nun Gutes oder
Böses mit ihm vorhaben—als einer unbekannten, für ihn auf keine Weise
durchschaubaren Macht ausgeliefert.

Jürgen Viering, *Schwärmerische Erwartung bei Wieland, im Trivialen Geheimnisroman, und bei Jean Paul* (Köln, Wien: Böhlau, 1976), 13.

13. Counting the German entries in Taute's bibliography of *Or-
dens- und Bundesromane* (Frankfurt/M: Mahlau & Waldschmidt, 1907), a
haphazard collection in some ways, but still the best of its kind, one finds
an enormous increase in league novels at the end of the eighteenth and beginning of the nineteenth century:

years	no. of novels
1728–1770	6
1771–1780	9
1781–1785	14
1786–1790	31
1791–1795	41
1796–1800	32
1801–1805	39
1806–1810	11
1811–1815	11
1816–1820	9
1821–1825	16
1826–1830	12
1831–1835	14
1836–1840	17
1841–1845	11
1846–1850	9
1851–1855	11
1856–1860	13

14. Oskar Seidlin has commented on a related topic: "I suggest
that the motif 'letter' seems to release in Schiller a compulsive mechanism.
'Letter' always points, as I am trying to show, to a break of immediacy, to
something impenetrable, to an existential situation in which man is prone
to deception, and becomes uncertain concerning the true *données* and con-
catenations." "Schiller's 'Treacherous Signs': The Function of the Letters in

His Early Plays," in *Essays in German and Comparative Literature* (Chapel Hill: University of North Carolina Press, 1961), 127.

15. Cf. the following:

> Er lebte hier unter dem strengsten Inkognito, weil er sich selbst leben wollte. . . . Den Aufwand vermied er, mehr aus Temperament als aus Sparsamkeit. Er floh die Vergnügungen; in einem Alter von fünfunddreissig Jahren hatte er allen Reizungen dieser wollüstigen Stadt widerstanden. . . . Seine Neigungen waren still . . . zufrieden, von keinem fremden Willen abzuhängen, fühlte er keine Versuchung, über andere zu herrschen. . . . Er las viel, doch ohne Wahl; eine vernachlässigte Erziehung und frühe Kriegsdienste hatten seinen Geist nicht zur Reife kommen lassen. (NA XVI, 45–46)

Elisabeth von der Recke's account of her own life before she was deluded by Cagliostro may have served Schiller as a source here:

> Seit meinem sechzehnten Jahre ward ich aus dem Geräusche der grossen Welt in stille Einsamkeit auf dem Lande, durch meine Heurath, versetzt. Da entstand aus Mangel anderer Geschäfte bey mir ein Hang zur Leserey, ohne Plan, Ordnung und Auswahl. Wielands frühere Schriften, besonders seine Sympathien, Cronegks Einsamkeiten, Youngs Nachtgedanken, und Lavaters Schriften, waren mir die liebste Lektur, durch welche meine Seele sehr bald eine religiöse-schwärmerische Stimmung erhielt.

Nachricht von des berüchtigten Cagliostro Aufenthalt in Mitau im Jahre 1779 und von dessen dortigen magischen Operationen (Berlin: Friedrich Nicolai, 1787), 5.

16. This corresponds perfectly to the effect of the ornate church (and other cleverly employed artifacts) on the prince later in the novel.

17. "'Ich stellte mich in die Mitte des Doms und überliess mich der ganzen Fülle dieses Eindrücks; allmählich traten die grossen Verhältnisse dieses majestätischen Baues meinen Augen bemerkbar hervor, ich verlor mich in ernster ergetzender Betrachtung'" (NA XVI, 129–30).

18. Staiger argues that this statement indeed comes down on the side of history. See *Schillers Werke* (Insel, 1966), III, 515.

19. Elisabeth von der Recke characterizes Cagliostro in similar terms:

> Sein Vortrag war sehr heftig, und hatte eine gewisse hinreissende Beredsamkeit; dazwischen aber sagte er so viel plattes. . . . (112)
> Cagliostro setzte sich an einen grossen Tisch, wir alle um ihn, und wir hatten die Erlaubniss so schnell wir konnten, seine Vorlesungen nachzuschreiben. In dem Tone eines Begeisterten trug er sie vor. Ob er gleich keiner Sprache recht mächtig war, so machte doch die Heftigkeit mit der er redete und das Galimathias von fremden und zum Theil geheimnissreichen Worten, auf uns, in der Stimmung der Seele in welcher wir damals waren, einen grossen Eindruck. Den alltäglichsten Dingen wusste er durch Ton und durch geheimnissvollen Anstrich, Gewicht zu geben; aber sehr oft sagt' er auch etwas ganz plattes mit unter. (127)

195

20. We further question the Graf's straightforwardness when we see him concealing names, dates, and places—"Graf von O. .," the "Baron von F. . .," "im Jahr 17. .," "in . .schen Kriegsdienst," etc. —as does the Sicilian—"'Aber es muss mir erlaubt sein' setzte er hinzu, 'einige Namen dabei zu verschweigen'" (NA XVI, 76).

21. The prince's quick condemnation of the Sicilian's story ("'Verdient ein Mensch, der mich mehrmal betrogen, der den Betrug zu seinem Handwerk gemacht hat, in einer Sache gehört zu werden, wo die aufrichtigste Wahrheitsliebe selbst sich erst reinigen muss, um Glauben zu verdienen?'" (NA XVI, 91)) should also warn the reader, who is in a similar circumstance. The Sicilian has hoped to evoke this very response in the prince in order to set him up for a more important fraud. By analogy, then, the reader should beware of simply pointing to the Graf as a conniving artist; for who knows to what real end the Graf has constructed his text?

22. Herbert Kraft refers to this chain of narrators and sees in it an expression of the relative inscrutability of events:

> Wo die Darstellung von Geschehen formal immer indirekter erfolgt, spiegelt im sich verundeutlichenden Inhalt das Werk die Verhältnisse wider, unter denen der politische Betrug ungehindert durchgeführt werden kann, weil die Betrugsfälle im scheinbar Privaten nicht mehr erkennbar sind. Unter der Tarnung des Privaten werden politische Veränderungen programmierbar.

Um Schiller betrogen (Pfullingen: Günther Neske, 1978), 111.

23. In addition, the Sicilian calls his own story into question. The prince's reflections add to that doubt. We suspect Civitella as a conspirator in the grand plot, so his story immediately invites scrutiny. While the prince tells his story the baron repeatedly questions the prince's ability to rationally report the event he has just experienced. The count, just before printing the baron's first letter, states that he and the baron see things differently and that the reader will have to seek the truth in the letters. And as I have already shown, the count is far from a trustworthy narrator/editor.

24. He began the book with the words "Ich erzähle eine Begebenheit"—so with the words "die unerhörte Geschichte" he is once again in his opening narrative position, and we expect a manipulative novella in place of historical truth.

25. See Roberts, *The Mythology of the Secret Societies*, 9–16.

CHAPTER THREE

1. Karl Philipp Moritz, *Andreas Hartknopf*, ed. Hans Joachim Schrimpf (Stuttgart: J. B. Metzler, 1968), Nachwort, 33. For a discussion of the novel in a Masonic context, see Voges, *Aufklärung und Geheimnis*, 472–536.

2. Goethe, *Wilhelm Meisters Wanderjahre oder Die Entsagenden* (Erster Theil, 1821). This version is reprinted in the *Gedenkausgabe* (1949), VIII, 8.

3. Two usages from a contemporary dictionary: "Eine Seite, einen Bogen setzen"; "so werden im Hüttenbaue die Erze gesetzt, wenn sie geschlemmt oder gewaschen werden, so dass sich das gepochte Erz zu Boden setzt." Joachim Heinrich Campe, *Wörterbuch der Deutschen Sprache* (Braunschweig, 1810).

4. *Goethes Werke*, "Hamburger Ausgabe," XIV, 78. Hereafter refered to in the text as HA, with Roman numeral for volume and Arabic numeral for page.

5. Felix immediately pulls out a kind of pine cone and asks what it is. Wilhelm's answer demonstrates his ability to extrapolate analogically ("eine Frucht . . . und nach den Schuppen zu urteilen, sollte sie mit den Tannenzapfen verwandt sein"); but Felix's reply shows that he still needs to learn the skill ("das sieht nicht aus wie ein Zapfen, es ist ja rund").

6. September 10, 1823; *Goethes Briefe*, "Hamburger Ausgabe" (Hamburg: Christian Wegner, 1967), IV, 90.

7. Cf. Goethe's poem "Der Schatzgräber" (1798), in which a poor man tries to sell his soul for the magic formula that will lead him to "dem alten Schatze." Fortunately (or unfortunately) for him, a "heavenly" messenger appears and counsels him to go back to work: "'Grabe hier nicht mehr vergebens! / Tages Arbeit, abends Gäste! / Saure Wochen, frohe Feste! / Sei dein künftig Zauberwort'" (HA, I, 265–266).

8. Cf. the following careful formulation:

> Es wäre einer besonderen Untersuchung wert, einmal den Schlüssel, den Goethe im Roman abbilden ließ, auf seine Form hin zu überprüfen, wobei freilich höchste Vorsicht bewahrt werden muss. Der untere Schlüsselteil mit seinen 'Haken' erinnert auffälig an ein griechisches CH, und der obere geht wahrscheinlich auf Freimaurersymbole zurück (Quadrat mit drei Kreisen an den oberen Ecken, innerer durchkreuzter Kreis). Doch müsste eine solche Untersuchung sich vor eindeutigen Festlegungen und vor allem vor mystischen Auslegungen hüten.

Wilhelm Emrich, "Das Problem der Symbolinterpretation im Hinblick auf Goethes *Wanderjahre*," *Deutsche Vierteljahresschrift*, 26 (1952): 348.

9. Friedrich Ohly, "Goethes Ehrfurchten—ein ordo caritatis," *Euphorion*, 55 (1961): 419–423.

10. Cf. the quotations from Emrich in HA,VIII, 616–617.

11. *Goethes Briefe*, HA, I, 294. The facts concerning Goethe's relationship to Freemasonry are well known, but for the purpose of my argument I repeat them here.

12. *Goethes Werke*, "Weimarer Ausgabe" (Weimar, 1889), IV, 5, 342.

13. March 15, 1783; *Goethes Briefe*, HA, I, 422.

14. April 6, 1789; "Weimarer Ausgabe" (1891), IV, 9, 101.

15. In the play a Cagliostro figure swindles members of the French nobility with promises of spiritual visitations, the opening of all of nature's secrets, eternal youth, and constant health. He claims to have his secrets from ancient India and Egypt and belongs, he says, to a secret society of men scattered around the world. The Gross-Cophta leads his gullible followers through ritual dialogues, through ever higher levels until they reach his Egyptian lodge where the ultimate secret lies hidden. For the audience, the ultimate secret is obvious—it lies in the ability of a brilliant confidence man to dupe a public frantic for supernatural knowledge.

16. For a more complete account of Goethe's ties to Freemasonry see Lennhoff and Posner, *Internationales Freimaurer-Lexikon*, 616–619; and Haas, *Die Turmgesellschaft in 'Wilhelm Meisters Lehrjahren,'* 21–28. Although I emphasize Goethe's involvement in the Freemasonry of the Enlightenment, there is another side to the story. How deeply Goethe was influenced by the hermetic tradition—the Gold- and Rosenkreuzer—is made apparent by Rolf Christian Zimmermann in his two-volume *Das Weltbild des jungen Goethe: Studien zur hermetischen Tradition des deutschen 18. Jahrhunderts* (München: Wilhelm Fink, 1969, 1979).

17. Anthony Vidler, "The Architecture of the Lodges," *Oppositions* 5 (Summer 1976): 75–97.

18. J. W. Oliver, *The Life of William Beckford* (London: Oxford University Press, 1937), 172–181.

19. Neil M. Flax, "The Presence of the Sign in Goethe's *Faust*," *PMLA* 98 (1983): 183–203.

20. Trunz's notes in the HA point out the following Freemasonic allusions: "die Grade *(Schrittweis)*, der Teppich bzw. Vorhang *(Hülle)*, der *Stern*, der Zuruf des 'Meisters vom Stuhl'; vielleicht auch die Gräber." (HA, I, 658).

21. *Ehrfurcht* proves to be an important lesson of the *Wanderjahre*, whose ritual routes I describe later. The covering, here identified with *Ehrfurcht*, bears symbolic representations of the stars above and the graves below. Compare, from the *Wanderjahre*: "Ehrfurcht vor dem, was über uns ist," and "Ehrfurcht vor dem, was unter uns ist."

22. The best recent discussion of the Tower Society is Wilfried Barner's "Geheime Lenkung. Zur Turmgesellschaft in Goethes *Wilhelm Meister*," in *Goethe's Narrative Fiction: The Irvine Goethe Symposium* (Berlin: Walter de Gruyter, 1983), 85–109.

23. July 8, 1796. *Goethes Werke*, VIII, 539–540.

24. Tolstoy's description of the Freemason Pierre meets on the road in *War and Peace* seems to be drawn in part from this description of Jarno:

> Pierre looked at him, and had not time to turn away when the old man opened his eyes and fastened his severe, resolute gaze directly on Pierre's face.

Pierre felt confused, and tried to escape that searching look, but the brilliant old eyes drew him irresistibly. . . .

The stranger's face was not genial, it was even cold and severe, but in spite of this, to Pierre both the speech and the face of his new acquaintance were irresistibly attractive. (409)

25. On the subject of the Society of the Tower and this initiation rite as they relate to the theater that Wilhelm has just forsaken, see Haas, *Die Turmgesellschaft in 'Wilhelm Meisters Lehrjahre,'* and David Roberts, *The Indirections of Desire: Hamlet in Goethe's "Wilhelm Meister"* (Heidelberg: Carl Winter, 1980), 181–187.

26. Again the *Ehrfurcht* so prominent in the *Wanderjahre*.

27. Also found in the *Gedenkausgabe* (1949), VIII, 8.

28. Cf. Trunz's notes to "Die Geheimnisse": "Manches, was in den Geheimnissen unausgeführt blieb, kam in den Wanderjahren zur Sprache: Verschiedene religiöse Wege, die alle letztlich zum gleichen Ziele führen; bildliche Darstellungen, die symbolisch eine Urreligion aussprechen; ein Kreis weiser Männer, der solches esoterische Wissen bewahrt und pflegt" (HA, II, 595).

29. The charcoal burner's trade, like the mason's, is one long associated with secret societies. Cf. Italy's Carbonari.

30. To argue against this view of the Pedagogical Province one could use the description of how Wilhelm judges the paintings in the Province's octagonal hall: "Er betrachtete diese Bilder zuletzt nur aus den Augen des Kindes, und in diesem Sinne war er vollkommen damit zufrieden" (HA, VIII, 161).

31. Wilhelm Vosskamp, "Utopie und Utopiekritik in Goethes Romanen *Wilhelm Meisters Lehrjahre und Wilhelm Meisters Wanderjahre*," in *Utopieforschung: Interdisziplinäre Studien zur neuzeitlichen Utopie*, ed. Wilhelm Vosskamp (Stuttgart: Metzler, 1982), III, 227–249.

32. In the Province the only mention of a garden is in connection with a "Galerie . . . die, an der einen Seite offen, einen geraumigen, blumenreichen Garten umgab. Die Wand zog jedoch mehr als dieser heitre, natürliche Schmuck die Augen an sich" (HA, VIII, 158). Another reason, perhaps, to reject this as "die geistig reine Mitte."

33. A final note on the successive realms: it seems that Wilhelm's route alternates between the natural/unbounded and the artificial/ bounded. He moves from the mountain to the "umschlossenes Tal" of St. Joseph, from Montan's peak where he feels threatened to the "beschränkter Waldraum" of the charcoal burner, from the *Riesenschloss* on a wild peak to the extraordinary order of the Oheim's, from the frightening openess of Makarie and her tower to the pedantic order of the Province, and finally from the open Italian lake to the self-imposed order of the Tower Society.

34. Quoted in Joseph Strelka, *Esoterik bei Goethe* (Tübingen: Niemeyer, 1980), p. 84, note 5. Originally in *Blätter für literarische Unterhaltung*, Nr. 264–266, September 21–23, 1830.

CHAPTER FOUR

1. Julian Schmidt, quoted in *Karl Gutzkow: Liberale Energie*, Peter Demetz, ed. (Frankfurt/M: Ullstein, 1974), 328; originally published in *Die Grenzboten* 11 (1852/2), 41–63.

2. Robert Prutz, quoted in Claus Richter, *Leiden an der Gesellschaft: Vom literarischen Liberalismus zum poetischen Realismus* (Kronberg/Ts.: Athenäum, 1978), 193; originally published in Robert Prutz, *Die deutsche Literatur der Gegenwart 1848–1858* (Leipzig, 1859).

3. See Jeffrey Sammons's comments on the censors' campaign against Gutzkow after the 1835 ban. *Six Essays on the Young German Novel* (Chapel Hill: University of North Carolina Press, 1972), 27.

4. Other readers reacted positively to the novel. Theodor Storm, for example, liked the idea of a secret society:

> ich habe die *Ritter vom Geiste* jetzt zu Ende gelesen und bin jetzt von bewundernder Hochachtung und Sympathie für den Verfasser erfühlt. . . . Es ist wirklich eine That, dies Buch, wie sie die Zeit verlangte. Ein Bund der Geister gegen den Missbrauch der Gewalt von oben und unten. . . . Ob der Verfasser an praktische Folgen gedacht, ob das Buch schon solche gehabt, ich weiss es nicht.

Theodor Storm, Sept. 11, 1852, letter to Hartmuth Brinkmann (quoted in Friesen, 131).

5. The powerful mother lodge "Zu den drei Weltkugeln" in Berlin documents its own rise from sixteen lodges with 763 members in 1788 to 96 lodges with 8,589 members in 1848 and finally to 122 lodges with 13,524 members in 1889. *Geschichte der Grossen National-Mutterloge in den Preussischen Staaten genannt zu den drei Weltkugeln* (Berlin: W. Büxenstein, 1890), 470–471.

6. Findel, *Geschichte der Freimaurerei*, 535, 544.

7. Findel seems tentatively to approve of this development, for he castigates a reactionary statement from a Breslau lodge which proudly claims that not a single Mason had been involved in the recent movements to undermine the rule of law (544–545). He also quotes with approval an 1835 statement by a Freiberg lodge that encouragingly speaks of a coming renewal in Masonry and at the same time sees a positive sign in present public activities:

> Um so eher wird dies erfolgen [a return to work in the lodges], da die Veränderungen, welche jetzt im äussern Leben vorgehen und die unsere Aufmerksamkeit so auf sich und von dem stillen Bunde hinweg zogen, dem wahren Sinne der Maurerei nicht entgegen, ihm vielmehr entsprechend sind, da die Umänderung, welche jetzt in dem politischen Ganzen und in dem einzelnen vorgeht, eher eine Entwickelung des maurerischen Geistes ausserhalb der Grenzen des Freimaurerbundes, als ein sich ihr entgegenstemmendes Streben genannt werden kann. (546)

This conscious linking of private Freemasonic principles and practice with liberal public advances occurs in later years as well.

8. See Johannes Rogalla von Bieberstein's "Geheime Gesellschaften als Vorläufer politischer Parteien," in *Geheime Gesellschaften*, ed. Peter Christian Ludz, 429–460.

9. In *Internationales Freimaurer-Lexikon*: "Mit Lessing ist daher Krause der eigentliche Begrunder jener humanitär denkenden Freimaurerei, die ein spezifisch deutsches Produkt ist" (875).

10. Such Masonic patriotism evidently made its mark. Wilhelm I became a Mason in 1840 and was especially active in defending Freemasonry during times of sharp attack. In 1851 he wrote a letter of explanation to Ministerpräsident Manteuffel: "Die Freimaurerlogen sind die wirksamsten Pflanzstätten wahrer Gottesfurcht, christlicher Frömmigkeit, sittlicher Tugenden, echter Vaterlandsliebe, zuverlässigster Untertanentreue, aufrichtigster Ehrfurcht und Ergebenheit gegen den Landesherrn. . . . Übrigens sind die Verleumdungen gegen den Freimaurerorden nicht neu, sie sind so alt als er selbst und wiederholen sich nur von Zeit zu Zeit" (*Internationales Freimaurer-Lexikon*, 709).

11. The *Freimaurer-Zeitung*, first published in January 1847 in Leipzig, was one of the most important Freemasonic publications of the nineteenth century, matched as a weekly only by the later *Bauhütte*, first published in 1858.

12. The lead essay was unsigned, but it bore striking similarites to August Wilhelm Muller's article on Freemasonry in Ersch and Gruber's *Allgemeine Encyklopädie der Wissenschaften und Künste* (Leipzig: Johann Friedrich Gleditsch, 1849).

13. R. R. Fischer writes:

> Dunkler aber, als alles Andre, schwebt aus der Ferne eine Wolke herauf, die schweres Unheil droht; Das ist das immer mehr sich zerklüftende Missverhältniss zwischen den Arbeitern und Brotherren und die mit Schrecken zunehmende Zahl der Menschen, die von der Hand in den Mund, nur für die eben vorhandne Stunde leben und Nichts zu verlieren haben. In ihnen entwickelt sich ein Bestandtheil der menschlichen Gesellschaft, der höchst gefährlich erscheint. Hungrig und unzufrieden, besitzlos und unstät, von der Not unablässig zur Untreue versucht, unter der Last des Daseins finster und mürrisch gestimmt . . . stehen sie da, ausgeschlossen vom Reiche der Liebe, von den Festen des Lebens. Immer grösser wird die Kluft, welche sie von den Begüterten scheidet, immer bitterer und schneidender wird der Ton, der ihre Stimmung verräth; und niedergehalten, zusammengepresst von der äussern Gewalt und von der Gewöhnung an Unterwürfigkeit, glüht der Unmuth und Hass, wie ein Feuer, das aus dem verschlossnen Raum den Ausweg sucht und mit Dampf und Flamme das hemmende Gewölbe zu brechen droht.

14. Kotzebue was special envoy for Russia, a Freemason, and the author of many popular plays, among which is the rather silly *Der Freimaurer* (1818).

15. During this same time Goethe wrote to Fritz von Stein (March 11, 1819) that the evident proclivity to form such societies proved that needs were present that the current governments could not satisfy (quoted in Rogalla von Bieberstein, *Die These von der Verschwörung*, 153).

16. Marchangy was quoted in ibid.

17. Eitel Wolf Dobert, *Karl Gutzkow und seine Zeit* (Bern, München: Francke, 1968).

18. Peter Demetz, *Marx, Engels and the Poets*, trans. Jeffrey Sammons (Chicago: University of Chicago Press, 1967), 12.

19. See Rogalla von Bieberstein, *Die These von der Verschwörung*, 190.

20. Ibid.

21. *Freimaurerei und Sozialdemokratie, oder, Ist ausser der Sozialdemokratie auch die Freimaurerei nachweisbar Religions-, Staats- und Gesellschaftsgefährlich?* 4th ed. (Stuttgart: Süddeutscher Verlagsbuchhandlung, 1891). Cf. also Karl Didler's *Freimaurer-Denkschrift über die politische Wirksamkeit des Freimaurer-Bundes als der unter verschiedenen Namen und Formen unter uns im Finstern schleichenden Propaganda zum Sturz der legitimen Throne und des positiven Christenthum*, "Vor Nachdruck wird gewarnt! Als Geheimschrift gedrückt" 2d ed. (Berlin, 1864–1871).

22. In his biography of Börne, Karl Gutzkow retells a story about an ongoing Masonic conflict concerning whether or not Jews should be allowed membership in the lodges. One Frankfurt lodge, Sokrates zur Standhaftigkeit, excluded Jews by requiring an affirmative answer to the question: Are you a Christian? Börne replied to this, Gutzkow writes, by pointing out that Socrates himself would have been turned away at the door of this lodge named after him. Karl Gutzkow, *Gesammelte Werke* (Frankfurt/M: Literarische Anstalt, 1845), VI, 88.

23. Börne, *Sämtliche Schriften* (Düsseldorf: Joseph Melzer, 1964), I, 130–131.

24. Achim von Arnim, *Sämtliche Romane und Erzählungen*, ed. Walther Migge (München: Carl Hanser, 1962), I.

25. *Ludwig Tieck's Schriften*, XXIII (Berlin: Reimer, 1853; rpt. Walter de Gruyter, 1966).

26. Freemasons were also popular in French literature of the time. Balzac's *Histoire des Treize* (1833–1835), for example, consists of three stories about a secret society formed by thirteen criminals. Balzac relates the order to the workers' guilds supposedly stemming from Solomon's temple and to Freemasons. These men, he says, have reconstituted the Society of Jesus for the profit of the devil (see the preface). During the same period he also published "Seraphita," the story of a girl whose father is a true disciple of Swedenborg, the eighteenth-century Swedish scientist and mystic who influenced some branches of Masonry and who ranks with Lavater, Mesmer, and Cagliostro as one of the extraordinary figures of the age.

27. Karl Immermann: *Werke*, ed. Benno von Wiese (Frankfurt/M: Athenäum, 1971), II.

28. Sammons, *Six Essays on the Young German Novel*, 137–138. Hans Asbeck, in his notes to the novel, discusses the radical student movement and specifically Karl Follen as a partial model for Menon (*Werke*, II, 687–688).

29. Immermann also includes a humorous account of popular theories of conspiracy. After Hermann is arrested he listens to his two guards discussing the subject:

> "Weisst du," sagte der eine zum andern, "woher all die Teufelei rührt? Ich kann's dir sagen. Die Juden stiften den ganzen Spektakel an."
>
> "Nicht möglich!" rief der andre. "Ich dachte, die Franzosen steckten dahinter."
>
> "Franzosen hin, Franzosen her!" sagte der erste. "Das ist ja eben die Sache. Die Franzosen sind auch alle heimliche Juden. Dazumal in Aegypten hat der Bonaparte seine ganze Armee dazu herumgekriegt, und die Soldaten haben dann nach ihrer Rückkehr das Judentum weiter gestiftet, und auch bei uns ausgebreitet, bis der Krieg kam, und davon rühren die Demagogen her."
>
> "Drum assen auch die Kerle so viel Knoblauch," sagte der zweite Gendarm.
>
> "Richtig," verstezte der erste. "Der Knoblauch ist der erste Grad im Judentum. Der Bart ist der zweite. (341)

30. Georg Büchner, *Woyzeck*, ed. Hans Meyer (Frankfurt/M: Ullstein, 1974), 8–9. Büchner published *Dantons Tod* in Gutzkow's *Phönix* in 1835. This paranoia is not only a literary creation, but was a factor in the insanity of the historical Woyzek: "Im Gefängnis hatte der Verurteilte dem Geistlichen von Gesichten erzählt, die er gehabt hat; Stimmen habe er gehört, Träume erlebt, die ihm die geheimen Erkennungszeichen der Freimaurer entschleiert hätten, er habe daraus gefolgert, daß er von den Freimaurern verfolgt werde." Hans Mayer, *Georg Büchner und seine Zeit* (Suhrkamp, 1972), 334 f.

31. Or secret societies' rituals can soothe shell-shocked soldiers as they do in later stories by Rudyard Kipling.

32. After his initiation in Worms, Freiligrath appears never to have returned to the lodge, despite repeated requests. Perhaps he hoped to find a more political organization than he found. See Wilhelm Muchner, *Ferdinand Freiligrath: Ein Dichterleben in Briefen* (Lahr: Moritz Schauenburg, 1882), I, 400–401.

33. Consuelo is a talented Spanish singer who travels through Europe while gaining a threefold education: 1. She advances musically until she becomes a composer. 2. She becomes aware of despotism. 3. She dedicates herself to helping the poor and suffering. When she is imprisoned in Berlin for conspiracy, the secret society of Invisibles helps her escape.

They initiate her into their order, and she learns to value their doctrine of absolute equality between sexes and classes.

Strangely enough, Gutzkow, who had earlier supported women's rights, saw no need to follow Sand's lead in this matter. His Knights of Spirit are all male.

34. George Sand, *Isolde*, trans. Dr. Scherr (Stuttgart: Franck, 1850).

35. Die Geheimbünde sind bisher eine Nothwendigkeit der Staatsgesellschaften gewesen. Weil in diesen Staatsgesellschaften die Ungleichheit herrschte, so musste sich die Gleichheit schlechterdings in Dunkel und Geheimniss hüllen, um ihr göttliches Werk zu fördern.(1)

Wie könnte man sich den Fall der römischen Republik und aller Reiche erklären, wenn nicht durch die Existenz aller Arten von geheimen Gesellschaften, welche an die Stelle der offen anerkannten zu treten suchen, schweigend in dem Schoosse der letzteren wühlen und ihre Fundamente unterhöhlen? (2)

Bis jetzt glichen die Geschichtschreiber nur allzusehr einem Beobachter, dessen Auge nur die Oberfläche der Dinge streift. . . . Warum suchen sie nicht das zu erforschen, was heute für die Gesellschaft den Tod verursacht, während es morgen das Prinzip ihres Lebens sein wird? Es gibt in der Geschichte der Staaten Augenblicke, wo die allgemeine Gesellschaft nur dem Namen nach besteht und wo das wahrhaft Lebende nur die in ihrem Schoosse verborgenen Sekten sind. (2–3)

36. Cf. also Eugéne Sue's novel *Le Juif errant* (1844–1845), with which Gutzkow's novel has often been compared. The novel depicts a diabolical Jesuit plot against a brave and innocent family. The Society of Jesus appears as a manipulative secret society with emissaries in all parts of the world, with a most extraordinary archive bursting with useful biographical information about friends and enemies, and with a leader (with brilliant, piercing eyes) who can say that from a single room he governs the whole world. Opposed to the evil Jesuits is the immortal Jew, the emissary of a supernatural power, cursed to wander through the centuries in service of others.

Gérard de Nerval's *Voyage en Orient* (1851) is one more French work of the time to deal extensively with Freemasonry. It is, in part, a lengthy retelling of the story of Hiram, chief builder of Solomon's temple and the "patron saint" of Freemasonry.

37. Herbert Kaiser, *Studien zum deutschen Roman nach 1848* (Duisburg: Walter Braun, 1977), 50.

38. Hier sind alle Illusionen der Vorreiter der liberalen Intelligenz versammelt, die ihre Isolation und politische Verzichtserklärung noch feiert. Die Abwendung von Gesellschaft und Öffentlichkeit und der Aufruf zur individuellen Läuterung bleiben das Vermächtnis der Rit-

ter. Bei ihrem konstituierenden Treffen auf dem "Tempelstein" bes-
chliessen sie ihre Riten und geheime Symbolik. Sie wollen hinfort
dem Geist einer Schöpfung leben, von der sie nicht wissen, wie sie
aussieht. Sie stiften einen neuen Mythos wider besseres Wissen.

Claus Richter, *Leiden an der Gesellschaft*, 197.

39. Siegbert makes this explicit: "Mein Bruder . . . beneidet sehr
oft die Jesuiten um ihre Organisation. Er behauptet, der Jesuitenorden in
seiner Form, aber mit einem edlen Inhalte, könnte die Welt erlösen" (V:
281).

40. Dankmar later returns to this condemnation of Freemasonry
as an organization that denies all its considerable political potential by focusing on charitable works: "Die moralische Dehnkraft dieses weltlichen
Ordens ist aber sehr gering. Sie geht über einen gewissen anständigen
Egoismus nicht hinaus. Anständigen Egoismus nenn' ich Den, der seinem
Jahrhundert nichts Anderes als Wohltätigkeiten spendet. Eine rüstige po-
lemische Kraft liegt in der Freimaurerei nirgends" (VI, 324–325).

41. Harder continues: "Man hat Diejenigen steinigen wollen, die
wie einst Bruder Krause und Mossdorf unsere Geheimnisse verriethen, aber
man ist hinter diesen, die nur zur Reform unsres Bundes Öffentlichkeit
wollten, weit zurückgeblieben. Wohl weiss ich, dass das graue Alter unsrer
Kunsturkunden nicht zu ermitteln ist" (IX, 174).

42. See the first epigraph to this chapter.

43. Claus Richter judges this return to Enlightenment strategies
harshly: "War die Moral für die bürgerliche Intelligenz der Aufklärung eine
politische Waffe gegen den Staat, so ist sie bei Gutzkow Ausdruck des
Rückzugs vor der Gesellschaft, der politischen Wendung zur Unpolitik"
(193).

44. Dankmar's insistence on gaining political power through
proof of inherited right contrasts, however, with Louis Armand's view of
the right of inheritance. Armand, a French artisan, Communist, and
staunch friend of Prince Egon and the Wildungen brothers, argues from the
point of view of people who have suffered as the upper classes have passed
on property and privileges through the centuries. After Leidenfrost states
that *Erbrecht*, although sometimes unjust, gives necessary cohesion to life,
Armand argues (in Gutzkow's own words) against him: "das Erbrecht wäre
doch der eigentliche Grund aller Leiden der Menschheit. Ihm verdanke
man die Aufhäufungen der Kapitalien, ihm die ungerechte Vertheilung der
Lebensgüter, ihm den Fluch, der auf ganzen Generationen läge. Das Erbrecht wäre ein fortlaufender Protest gegen das Glück der Menschheit" (VI,
241–242). Cf. Gutzkow's own statement in his *Säkularbilder*:

"Unwiderleglich ist der tiefe Widerwille, den wir gegen überlieferte oder
angeborne gesellschaftliche Vorzüge, Privilegien und Kastenvorrechte
empfinden. . . . Unwiderleglich ist das schreiende Unrecht jenes Vor-
sprunges, welchen bei allem Fleiss, aller Bildung, allem Talent des Nichts-

besitzenden der Capitalist bei jeder Unternehmung vor dem Capitallosen voraus hat." (*Gesammelte Werke*, IX, 207–208).

But after attacking inherited goods and privileges, Gutzkow defends a certain kind of inheritance: "Wir erkennen eine Errungenschaft, ein Eigenthum an; aber nur ein allgemeines, an welches Jeder Ansprüche machen darf, ein Eigenthum, das sich nicht auf Einzelne, sondern auf Generationen vererbt!" (*GW*, IX, 209).

    45. While building up the tradition of ideas to which the Knights of Spirit are heir, the novel undercuts the tradition of aristocratic familial *Erbrecht*, a right supposedly based on birth, but as the plot discloses, riddled with illegitimacy.

    Murray (Friedrich Zeck) is an interesting mixture of the legitimate and illegitimate, first as a counterfeitor, and then, after moral renewal in America, the legitimate engraver of plates from which the money for the Wildungen's material inheritance is made.

    Rodewald/Ackermann sees a paradox in the fact that his illegitimate son is working to strengthen the established, supposedly legitimate order: "Ihm schilderte sein Verhältniss zu Egon das Verhältniss der ganzen Zeit zu ihren Verfechtern oder Anklägern. Er sagte sich: Das ist Euer Adel, Eure Erbberechtigung, Eure Monarchie, Eure Kirche, Eure Sitte, Euer Glaube, Eure Konvention" (IX, 407–408). Part of what Egon has inherited as the supposed son of Waldemar von Hohenberg are the Hohenberg lands. They are in disarray, and Egon has little interest in them; but Ackermann, who has learned progressive agriculture in America, takes over managing the property from Schlurck, and it begins to prosper. Once again a spiritual inheritance gained in America, when applied to a German inheritance previously in the hands of selfish and visionless caretakers, proves productive.

    46. Alexander Jung, *Briefe über Gutzkow's Ritter vom Geiste* (Leipzig: Brockhaus, 1856).

    47. At one point Dankmar compares Olga Wäsämskoi and a white-bearded musician to Mignon and the old harpist in the *Lehrjahre* (VI: 125). The riding instructor Lassally and Olga's mother are both negatively characterized by their shallow reactions to *Wilhelm Meister*, while the long-suffering and likeable Anna von Harder defends the "Bekenntnisse einer schonen Seele." See Gerhard Friesen, *The German Panoramic Novel of the 19th Century* (Berne and Frankfurt/M: Herbert Lang, 1972), 111–112.

    48. Letter to Levin Schücking, August 5, 1850; quoted in Friesen, 19. Cf. also, "Ich wollte wieder an Goethe, Tieck, Immermann anknüpfen."

    49. Cf. the passage about the ground undermined by Freemasons in *Woyzeck*.

        50. Ich überlasse es jedem Unparteiischen, zu entscheiden, ob die allerdings absolute Unmöglichkeit jenes Mechanismus, den ich mit dem alten Templerorden, mit dem Process der Brüder Wildungen, dem

> Schrein, dem Bilde, den alten Documenten anlegte, sich auch, was ich leugnen muss, mitgetheilt habe dem durch diese mechanischen Hebel hervorgerufenen individuellen Leben. Dass diese Hebel willkürlich sind, dieser Mechanismus oft klappert, schon weil er oft geradezu von Holz ist, darüber möge man doch nicht die Stirn zu sehr in aristarchische Falten ziehen. Man möge darüber lächeln. Jeder vernünftige Beurtheiler wird einsehen, dass der Zweck des Dichters auf die Gährungen und Zersetzungen, die er schilderte, gerichtet war; die Säure, womit er diese Zersetzungen hervorbrachte, ist ein zufälliges Reagens, eine humoristische Nachahmung der Weltkomödie, wie sie der Allphantasie Gottes gegenüber eben anders die Menschenphantasie nicht geben kann.

See foreword to 3d ed., Gutzkow, *Die Ritter vom Geiste*, fifth ed. (Berlin: Otto Janke, 1869), I, XVI–XVII.

51. Mundt's contribution is the least interesting, involving a Masonic conversation between Count Mirabeau and General von Bischoffswerder in the "historical" novel *Graf Mirabeau* (1860) and a depiction of *Cagliostro in Petersburg* (1858).

52. In 1855 Breier published another novel about Freemasons (*Pandur und Freimaurer*), this time featuring Emanuel von Swedenborg as a powerful emissary traveling through Austria to expand Freemasonry.

53. Wolfstieg identifies the author of *The Three Freemasons* as Jos. v. Rathewitz (Hamburg: J.F. Richter, 1855 and 1856). Republished by the same publisher as *Die Braut des Freimaurers*, 1874.

54. See Gerhard Friesen's discussion of Oppermann in *The German Panoramic Novel of the 19th Century*, and Heiko Postma's informative afterword to Oppermann's novel *Hundert Jahre: 1770–1870* (Frankfurt/M.: Zweitausendeins, 1982).

CHAPTER FIVE

1. Disraeli's speech quoted in Roberts, *The Mythology of the Secret Societies*, 7.

2. Rogalla von Bieberstein, *Die These von der Verschwörung*, 193 ff.

3. For a more complete account see the *Internationales Freimaurer-Lexikon*, 1558 ff., and Rogalla von Bieberstein, *Die These von der Verschwörung*, 195 f.

4. See Norman Cohn, *Warrant for Genocide: The Myth of the Jewish World Conspiracy and the Protocols of the Elders of Zion* (New York: Harper & Row, 1967), and Jacob Katz, *Jews and Freemasons in Europe 1723–1939*, trans. Leonard Oschry (Cambridge: Harvard University Press, 1970).

5. And their influence continues. Joan Didion quotes a poem by Roque Dalton Garcia which begins with reference to the contemporary

influence of the *Protocols*: "In San Salvador / in the year 1965 / the best sellers / of the three most important / book stores / were: / The Protocols of the Elders of Zion;" etc., *The New York Review of Books*, November 4, 1982, 14.

6. Trotsky's own statement:

> In einzelnen Zweigen der Freimaurerei waren die Elemente der offen feudalen Reaktion noch stark, wie zum Beispiel in dem schottischen System. Im 18. Jahrhundert füllen sich die Formen der Freimaurerei in einer Reihe von Ländern mit kriegerischem Kulturträgertum, politischer und religiöser Aufklärung, die eine vorrevolutionäre Rolle spielen und deren linker Flügel in die Bewegung der Karbonari überging. *Leo Trotzki: Mein Leben* (Frankfurt/M: Fischer, 1974), 113.

7. Trotsky's notebook was subsequently lost, but he looked back on his first work as an early test of his own thoughts.

8. Hansjürgen Linke, *Das Kultische in der Dichtung Stefan Georges und seiner Schule* (München: Helmut Küpper vormals Georg Bondi, 1960), 155.

George's work reflects this repeatedly. His *Der Stern des Bundes* (1914), for example, is a semi-secret book for initiates of the cult. And in the poem "Der Eid," published in *Der Siebente Ring* (1907), a prophetic leader who alone knows the goal of history gathers chosen ones and through their blood oath gains power to use against the enemies of the secret society.

9. Fritz Stern, *The Politics of Cultural Despair* (1961; rpt. Berkeley: University of California Press, 1974).

10. *Der Roman der XII* (Berlin: Konrad W. Mecklenburg, vormals Richter, 1909).

11. Another novel written by a consortium of authors was published a century earlier in Berlin: *Die Versuche und Hindernisse Karls* (1808) by Varnhagen, Neumann, Bernhardi, and Fouqué. This novel fragment, product of Berlin romanticism and a parody of *Wilhelm Meisters Lehrjahre*, features Jean Paul as a character who speaks with Wilhelm Meister about the young man's creator, Goethe.

12. Felix Hollaender, *Der Weg des Thomas Truck* (Berlin: Bruno Cassirer, 1902).

13. Hanns Heinz Ewers, *Der Geisterseher* (München: Georg Müller, 1922).

14. Meyrink was a product of the same turn-of-the-century Prague that influenced Kafka, Rilke, and Werfel. Peter Demetz writes that "the real historic heritage which this town bestowed upon its poets was mystic ecstasy . . . ranging from the humanitarian rapture of Werfel to the occult horror tales of Gustav Meyrink." *René Rilkes Prager Jahre* (Düsseldorf: Diederichs, 1953), 109. Werfel's drama *Der Spiegelmensch*, a drama of initiation into a secret order, is one more example of the new century's fascination with secret societies and the occult.

15. Eduard Frank, "L'Ésotériste Gustav Meyrink," in *Gustav Meyrink*, ed. Yvonne Caroutch (Paris: Editions de l'Herne, 1976), 130–131.

16. Carl Vogl, *Aufzeichnungen und Bekenntnisse eines Pfarrers* (Wien, Berlin: Aegis, 1930); quoted in Lennhoff and Posner, *Internationales Freimaurer-Lexikon*, 1034.

17. Friedrich Wichtl, *Weltfreimaurerei, Weltrevolution, Weltrepublik* (München: J. F. Lehmann, 1919).

18. Meyrink edited a series of books called *Romane und Bücher der Magie* which included *Eliphas Levi, der grosse Kabbalist und seine magischen Werke* (1922); and among his many translations is one of Kipling's "Masonic stories," "Der Mann der König sein wollte."

19. Meyrink, *Der Engel vom westlichen Fenster* (Leipzig: Grethlein, 1927).

20. The novel's narrator discovers while going through papers of John Dee, an English ancestor, that he himself is an incarnation of Dee. His own experiences are then interwoven with those of Dee (one of the magi E. M. Butler discusses), who sought the philosopher's stone—not to transform base materials into gold, but to transform his own body and thus achieve eternal life. Dee, in both incarnations, is influenced by emissaries from the black Isais and an order called the *Weiss-Alben*, who are "die Diener einer Unsichtbaren, die Geschichte der Menschheit leitenden Brüderschaft, genannt 'Die Gärtner.'" With the help of his earlier wife, Dee is able to extricate himself from the hold of the powers of darkness, to pass through death a number of times, and finally to attain eternal life, becoming a "Gardener," joining the "Kette des Lichts . . . den Ring der Verketteten," whose purpose is to increase light in the world.

21. See Manfred Lube, *Gustav Meyrink: Beiträge zur Biographie und Studien zu seiner Kunsttheorie* (Graz: dbv Verlag fur die Technische Universität Graz, 1980), 133.

22. Ferdinand Maack, *Zweimal gestorben!* (Leipzig: Wilhelm Heims, 1912).

23. When he writes about contemporary practitioners of Rosicrucianism he discusses Rudolf Steiner at some length, especially his supposed claims to belong to a cosmic secret society whose emissaries direct world affairs; and he blasts Steiner as a supposed "Jesuitenzögling"! Just as Jesuits took over Freemasonry at the end of the eighteenth century in order to destroy it, he writes, they are now attempting to infiltrate twentieth-century Rosicrucianism through Steiner. The same rumors, again and again.

24. Herbert Silberer, *Probleme der Mystik und Ihrer Symbolik* (Wien; rpt. Darmstadt: Wissenschaftliche Buchgesellschaft, 1961).

25. Theodor Wieser, "Der Malteser in Hofmannsthals *Andreas*," *Euphorion*, 51 (1957): 409. This is the best discussion of Sacramozo's role in the novel yet written; and my understanding of Sacramozo owes much to Wieser's account.

26. In 1912 Hofmannsthal included *Der Geisterseher* in his anthology of German prose works.

27. David Miles discusses this in his *Hofmannsthal's Novel 'Andreas'* (Princeton: Princeton University Press, 1972), 110, 174 ff.

28. "Motto zu diesem Capital ["Der Malteser"]: Ich sehe nicht, rief Wilhelm aus, wozu ich, (wenn ich einmal mein Vaterland sehen will,) einen Italiener zur Gesellschaft brauche! Weil ein junger Mensch, versetzte der Abbé mit einem gewissen improvisierenden Ernst, immer Ursache hat, sich anzuschließen. Wilhelm Meisters Lehrjahre." Hofmannsthal, *Sämtliche Werke*, XXX, ed. Manfred Pape (Frankfurt/M.: S. Fischer, 1982), 31. See Pape's "Aurea Catena Homeri. Die Rosenkreuzer-Quelle der 'Allomatik' in Hofmannsthals *Andreas*," *Deutsche Vierteljahresschrift* 4 (1975): 686.

29. Cf. the following:

> In der Gesellschaft des Maltesers, ja nur durch einen Bezug auf diesen verfeinert und sammelt sich Andres Existenz. Begegnet er diesem, so kann er sicher sein, nachher etwas Merkwürdiges oder wenigstens Unerwartetes zu erleben. Seine Sinne verfeinern sich, er fühlt sich fähiger, im andern das Individuum zu geniessen, fühlt sich selber mehr und höheres Individuum. Liebe und Hass sind ihm näher. Die Bestandtheile der eigenen Natur sind ihm interessanter er ahnt hinter ihnen das Schöne. In dem Malteser ahnt er eine Meisterschaft im Spiel von dessen eigener Rolle. Es gibt keine Situation in der er ihn sich nicht vorstellen könnte. An dem Malteser tritt ihm höchste Empfänglichkeit für eigene Natur entgegen. (31–32)

> Er fühlt wie der Malteser ihn trägt und hebt, jedes Wort von ihm releviert —er kommt sich ganz als Geschöpf Sacramozos vor, aber ohne Gedrücktheit." (110) "Die Erziehung durch den Malteser: Was dieser Mensch mit einem Blick mit einem Wort über ihn vermag: es ist Sclaverei und Freiheit was er von ihm empfängt." (160)

Cf. also 164.

30. Ibid.; see also 185.

31. Hofmannsthal, *Gesammelte Werke in zehn Einzelbänden*, VII, ed. Bernd Schoeller (Frankfurt/M.: Fischer, 1979), 464–465.

32. Hofmannsthal uses several spellings of this name.

33. Quoted in Pape's notes to *Andreas*, p. 421.

CHAPTER SIX

1. For a detailed account of the relationship between Thomas Mann and Heinrich Mann in these years, see Peter De Mendelssohn's *Der Zauberer: Das Leben des deutschen Schriftstellers Thomas Mann, Erster Teil: 1875–1918* (Frankfurt/M: S. Fischer, 1975), especially the subchapter "Anti-Heinrich," 647ff.; or Nigel Hamilton's *The Brothers Mann* (New Haven: Yale University Press, 1979).

2. Part of *The Subject* was serialized in the journal *Zeit im Bild* (1914), and the novel itself was first published in German in a small, private printing in 1916 by Kurt Wolff Verlag, which also printed a much larger edition in 1918. There were also Russian printings in a journal and as a book in 1914 and 1915.

3. Thomas Mann, *Betrachtungen eines Unpolitischen*, in Gesammelte Werke in zwölf Bänden (Frankfurt/M.: S. Fischer, 1960), XII, 120.

4. Fabrikbesitzer Dr. Diederich Hessling, Pastor Zillich und Assessor Dr. Jadassohn von der Staatsanwaltschaft bogen in die Kaiser- Wilhelm-Strasse ein und hatten verschiedene Herren zu grüssen, die eben das Haus der Loge betraten. Als sie die tief gezogenen Hüte wieder aufgesetzt hatten und vorüber waren, sagte Jadassohn: "Man wird sich die Herrschaften merken müssen, die den freimaurerischen Unfug noch mitmachen. Seine Majestät missbilligt ihn entschieden.

"Von meinem Schwager Heuteufel wundert mich auch das gefährlichste Sektenwesen nicht," erklärte der Pastor. "Nun, und der Herr Lauer?" meinte Diederich. "Ein Mensch, der sich nicht entblödet, seine Arbeiter am Gewinn zu beteiligen? Dem ist alles zuzutrauen!"

"Das Unerhörteste," behauptete Jadassohn, "ist doch, dass Herr Landgerichtsrat Fritzsche sich in dieser Judengesellschaft zeigt: ein königlicher Landgerichtsrat, Arm in Arm mit dem Wucherer Cohn. Wie haisst, Cohn," machte Jadassohn und steckte den Daumen unter die Achsel.

Diederich sagte: "Da er ja mit der Frau Lauer—". Er brach ab und erklärte, dann begreife er allerdings, dass diese Leute vor Gericht immer recht bekämen. "Sie halten zusammen und schanzen einander den Profit zu." Pastor Zillich murmelte sogar etwas von Orgien, die sie in dem Haus dort drüben feiern sollten, und bei denen schon unaussprechliche Dinge vorgekommen waren. Aber Jadassohn lächelte bedeutsam.

5. André Banuls speculatively attributes this positive portrayal of Freemasonry to Heinrich's supposed membership in an Italian lodge: "Echte Bruderschaft unter Gleichgesinnten hatte er wohl vielmehr in der Freimaurerei gefunden. Darüber fehlt jedes Dokument, aber mehrere Anspielungen Thomas Manns zeigen deutlich, dass Heinrich dem Bund beigetreten war." Banuls refers here to several statements by Thomas in *Betrachtungen eines Unpolitischen* (ambiguous proof at most). *Heinrich Mann* (Stuttgart: W. Kohlhammer, 1970), 88.

More convincingly, Banuls continues with reference to Heinrich's autobiography, *Ein Zeitalter wird besichtigt*: "Er selbst wird in seinen Memoiren die Freimaurerei als 'eine andere Form des Bekenntnisses zur göttlichen Vernunft' bezeichnen: 'Von den jungen Tagen dieser Menschengläubigkeit, ihrer gloire premiere, zeugte die 'Zauberflöte' des wunderbaren Mozart. Kein anderes Credo kann höher, edler, reiner gewesen sein'" (88–89).

6. Thomas Mann writes that at its center was to be a choice between virtuous, rational life and creative sympathy with death: "'Sympathie mit dem Tode'—ein Wort der Tugend und des Fortschritts ist das nicht. Ist es nicht vielmehr, wie ich sagte, Formel und Grundbestimmung aller Romantik?" (*Betrachtungen*, XII, 424).

7. München, February 12, 1918; in *Dichter über ihre Dichtungen, 1889-1917*, ed. Hans Wysling (München: Ernst Heimeran, 1975), 457.

8. Hofmiller, "Combinazioné," in *Kriegshefte der Süddeutschen Monatshefte*, München, June 1915, 471–477.

9. Heinz Brauweiler, "Vatikan und Loge im Weltkrieg," in *Kriegshefte der Süddeutschen Monatshefte*, München, March 1917, 735–746.

10. For a more complete discussion of Mann's interest in a Freemasonic political conspiracy against Germany, see Klaus Urner, "Thomas Mann und die Freimaurerei," *Neue Zürcher Zeitung*, September 30, 1973, 51–52.

11. Letter from Thomas Mann to Julius Bab, München, September 5, 1920; in *Dichter über ihre Dichtungen*, 461.

12. "Leo Naphta, ein halbjüdischer Jesuitenzögling mit krassen Anschauungen, ist aufgetaucht und liegt beständig mit Herrn Settembrini in scharfen Disputen, die eines Tages zum pädagogischen Duell führen werden." *Dichter über ihre Dichtungen*, 466.

13. Thomas Mann, "The Making of *The Magic Mountain*," in *The Magic Mountain*, trans. H. T. Lowe-Porter (New York: Modern Library College Editions), 726.

14. Letter from Thomas Mann to Joseph Angell, Küsnacht, May 11, 1937, in *Dichter über ihre Dichtungen*, 547.

15. Fritz Ballin, "Thomas Mann und die Freimaurerei," in *Eklektisches Bundesblatt* (July/August 1930): 237–242.

> Ist es Zufall oder Absicht, dass Thomas Mann die Freimaurerei von zwei grotesk-extremen Standpunkten aus beleuchtet? Naphta als Interpret eines spekulativen Mystizismus der Hochgradmaurerei, eines Produktes der freim. Verfallzeit. Settembrini, der Exponent maurerischer Politik, wie sie in den romanischen Logen gang und gäbe. Aber zugunsten der echten humanitären, der deutschen Freimaurerei, hat sich kein Fürsprecher finden wollen. Weiss Thomas Mann nichts von jenem edlen Menschenbunde, für den Männer wie Goethe, Herder, Fichte, Mozart und andere mehr begeistert und mit reinstem Herzen sich einsetzten? Oder will Thomas Mann hiervon nichts wissen?

16. *Die Bruderschaft*, published by the Vereinigten Grosslogen von Deutschland (Juni/Juli 1961): 209–215.

17. Hans Bürgin and Hans-Otto Mayer, *Thomas Mann: Eine Chronik seines Lebens* (Frankfurt/M: S. Fischer, 1965), 62.

18. Other borrowings show a slight reworking:

Thalmann: "Dieses Rosenfest geht leicht ins Bacchantische über, wie ja die Bacchusmysterien selbst in Orgien ausliefen. Es eröffnet der Frau ihren Wirkungskreis, die von diesen Bündnissen doch vielfach ausgeschlossen bleibt. . . . Auch die Bedeutung der Rose ist in den Rosenfesten besonders herangezogen. Drei blaue Rosen prangten bezeichnenderweise auf der Maurerschürze." (81)

Mann: "Es gab da Logenfeste, Feste der eleusischen Mysterien und der aphrodiesischen Geheimnisse, bei denen dann endlich doch die Frau ins Spiel trat,—Rosenfeste, auf die jene drei blauen Rosen der Maurerschürze anspielten und die, wie es scheint, ins Bacchantische auszulaufen pflegten." (III, 708)

19. Thalmann may have recognized her work in Mann's novel. She sent Mann a letter expressing her admiration for *Der Zauberberg* (January 16, 1925); and later she sent him a copy of an article she had written on his *Tod in Venedig: Germanisch-Romanisch Monatsschrift* 15 (Okt. 1927)— both in the Thomas-Mann-Archiv in Zürich. But out of respect for Mann, through humility, or perhaps because she did not notice, Thalmann never mentioned in print the wholesale borrowings Mann made from her book.

20. "Es ist der Beachtung wert, wie sehr Thomas Mann gerade in den zweiten Band des *Zauberbergs* direkt Tageserlebnisse und Lesefrüchte hineinnahm, wahrend er in dem *Doktor Faustus* und *Die Bekenntnisse des Felix Krull* viel mehr lebenslang Bewahrtes verarbeitete." Heinz Saueressig, "Die Entstehung des Romans *Der Zauberberg*," in *Besichtigung des Zauberbergs*, ed. Heinz Saueressig (Biberach an der Riss: Wege und Gestalten, 1974), 40.

21. Ibid., 23ff.

22. Among many others: Fessler's *Marc Aurel*, Vulpius's *Rinaldo*, Grosse's *Genius*, Knigge's *Peter Clausen*, Meyern's *Dya Na Sore*, Tschink's *Geisterseher*.

23. Herbert Lehnert, *Thomas-Mann-Forschung: Ein Bericht* (Stuttgart: J. B. Metzler, 1969), 141.

24. Compare also the following passage from *Der Zauberberg* and its source in Thalmann:

"Um so weniger, als es sich da um eine Führung zum Letzten handelt, zum absoluten Bekenntnis des Übersinnlichen und damit zum Ziele. Die alchimistische Logenobservanz hat viele edle, suchende Geister in späteren Jahrzehnten zu diesem Ziele geführt,—ich muss es nicht nennen, denn es kann Ihnen nicht entgangen sein, dass die Rangstufenfolge der schottischen Hochgrade nur ein Surrogat ist der Hierarchie, dass die alchimistische Weisheit des Meister-Maurers sich im Mysterium der Wandlung erfüllt, und dass die geheime Führung, die die Loge ihren Zöglingen angedeihen liess, sich ebenso deutlich in den Gnadenmitteln wiederfindet, wie die sinnbildlichen Spielereien des Bundes-zeremoniells in der liturgischen und baulichen Symbolik unserer heiligen katholischen Kirche. (III, 707)

Diese letzte Beichte romantischer Adeptenfrömmigkeit ist eine bedingte
Entwicklung, die Auflösung der Disharmonie in ein absolutes Bekenntnis
des Übersinnlichen. Der Traum aller Alchymisten, die Wundersehnsucht
aller geheimen Gesellschaften entzaubert sich in der romantischen Einkehr
in den Katholizismus. Die wunderlichen blauen und roten Grade der Orden verklären sich in der Hierarchie der Kirche, die Weisheit des Meisters
in der Verwandlung der Hostie, die geheime Führung in den Gnadenmitteln und der ästhetische Formtrieb in der liturgischen und baulichen Symbolik, in der sich sinnhaft Beschwertes in bildhafte Geistigkeit wandelt.
(320–321)

25. Letter from Thomas Mann to Ernst Bertram, München, February 19, 1924, in *Dichter über ihre Dichtungen*, 476.
26. T. J. Reed, *Thomas Mann: The Uses of Tradition* (London: Oxford University Press, 1974), 258.
27. See also E. M. Butler's *The Myth of the Magus* (New York:
Macmillan Company, 1948), which discusses St. Germain and Cagliostro as
such magi.
28. Zum erstenmal stand er unter der unmittelbaren Einwirkung von Pee-
perkorns wuchtiger Persönlichkeit . . . , und seine schwanken Jün-
glingsjahre fühlten sich erdrückt von dem Gewicht dieser breitschul-
trigen, rotgesichtigen, weissumlohten Sechzig, mit dem weh
zerrissenen Munde und Kinnbart, der lang und schmal auf die geist-
lich geschlossene Weste niederhing. Übrigens war Peeperkorn die
Artigkeit selbst. (III, 775–776)

29. Compare the following:

Wie seltsam, diese Zweideutigkeit von einem König zu betrachten, als die
Streiter auf Ehe und Sünde kamen, auf das Sakrament der Nachsicht, auf
Schuld und Unschuld der Wollust. Er neigte das Haupt zur Schulter und
Brust, die wehen Lippen taten sich voneinander, schlaff-klagend klaffte
der Mund, die Nüstern spannten und verbreiterten sich wie in Schmerzen,
die Falten der Stirne stiegen und weiteten die Augen zu blassem Leidens-
blick,—ein Bild der Bitternis. Und siehe, im selben Nu erblühte die Marter-
miene zur Üppigkeit! Die schräge Neigung des Hauptes deutete sich um in
Schalkheit, die Lippen, noch offen, lächelten unsittsam, das sybaritische
Grübchen, bekannt von früheren Gelegenheiten, erschien in einer Wange,
—der tanzende Heidenpriester war da. (III, 819)

30. A few pages later Peeperkorn is again referred to as a *Magne-
tiseur:* "und wenn diejenigen, die ihn umstanden, ursprünglich nur durch
das Gerücht seines Reichtums mochten angezogen worden sein, so war es
doch sehr bald seine Persönlichkeit selbst und allein, an der sie hingen:
lächelnd standen sie und nickten ihm zu, ermunternd und selbstvergessen;
gebannt durch sein fahles Auge unter den mächtigen Stirnfalten" (III, 770).
31. Jill Kowalik has recently argued that Peeperkorn is not a synthesis of opposites (the opposites supposedly represented by Settembrini

and Naphta) as critics have so often assumed, but rather that he helps rein-state and heighten Hans Castorp's sympathy with death. "'Sympathy with Death': Hans Castorp's Nietzschean Resentment," *The German Quarterly* 58 (Winter 1985): 27–48.

32. Letter from Thomas Mann to Arthur Schnitzler, München, January 9, 1925, in *Dichter über ihre Dichtungen*, 487.

CHAPTER SEVEN

1. Theodore Ziolkowski, *The Novels of Hermann Hesse* (Prince-ton: Princeton University Press, 1965), 255–261.

2. Hermann Hesse, "Kindheit des Zauberers," first printed in *Corona* 7 (1937); in *Eigensinn* (Frankfurt/M: Suhrkamp, 1972), 156.

3. Hermann Hesse, *Gesammelte Schriften* (Frankfurt/M: Suhrk-amp, 1958), VI, 327.

4. Ziolkowski, *Novels of Hesse*, 264.

5. See Christiane Völpel, *Hermann Hesse und die deutsche Jug-endbewegung* (Bonn: Bouvier, 1977).

6. Joseph Mileck sees the order as basically trivial:

Credibility is most immediately strained by the narrative's outmoded derivative form. Its prototype was clearly the rather trivial league novel (*Bundesroman*) vogue in Germany during the second half of the eighteenth century. The exclusive Order, its parareligious structure and atmosphere . . . and its emissary Leo are all standard trappings of a genre passé.

Hermann Hesse: Life and Art (Berkeley: University of California Press, 1980), 221.

7. Ziolkowski discusses this in detail, *Novels of Hesse*, 255–261.

8. André Gide, preface to *Journey to the East*, in *Hesse, A Collection of Critical Essays*, ed. Theodore Ziolkowski (Englewood Cliffs, N.J.: Prentice-Hall, 1973), 23–24.

9. But even while recognizing how closely Hesse has recon-structed the romantic structures of this subgenre, one must take issue with Gide when he calls the novel's form specious and with Joseph Milek's as-sessment of the "narrative's outmoded derivative form . . . [whose] proto-type was clearly the rather trivial league novel." By now it should be clear that the romantic league novel can be a marvelously expressive form in the hands of a good writer. And in fact, Gide himself wrote a witty league novel, *Les Caves du Vatican*.

10. For a postwar league novel influenced very strongly by *Die Morgenlandfahrt*, see Ernst Kreuder's *Die Unauffindbaren* (Stuttgart: Ro-wohlt, 1948; rpt. Frankfurt/M.: Europäische Verlagsanstalt, 1965). Like H. H., Kreuder's hero is in contact with emissaries of a secret society represent-ing a fantastic spiritual realm. He loses his vision, struggles through a nor-

mal life for seven years, and then is led by emissaries of the order through an elaborate initiation sequence back into contact with the higher existence they represent.

11. See also Rogalla von Bieberstein, *Die These von der Verschwörung.*

12. Neuberger, *Freimaurerei*, 115.

13. Ibid.

14. Mathilde Ludendorff, *Der ungesühnte Frevel an Luther, Lessing, Mozart und Schiller* (München, 1928).

15. Adolf Bartels, *Freimaurerei und Literatur* (München: F. Eher Nachfolger, 1929). This same house published *Mein Kampf, Die jüdische Weltpest*, and *Die Geheimnisse der Weisen von Zion.*

16. Tucholsky, "Ludendorff oder der Verfolgungswahn," in *Gesammelte Werke in 10 Bänden* (Reinbek bei Hamburg: Rowohlt, 1960), VI, 296–297.

17. Compare also the lines in Ernst Toller's play *Pastor Hall* (1939):

> Paul von Grotjahn (geht auf Ida zu, küsst ihr die Hand): . . . Nicht wahr, lieber Friedrich, strahlt sie nicht wie eine Rose im Mai? "Im wunderschönen Monat Mai, da alle Knospen sprangen, da ist in meinem Herzen die Liebe aufgegangen." Dichter unbekannt, wie es heute heisst.
>
> Friedrich Hall: Du irrst Dich, lieber Paul, das Gedicht ist von Goethe, nicht von Heine.
>
> Paul von Grotjahn: Der Goethe war auch nicht stubenrein. Erstens war er Freimaurer, zweitens war er ein Kosmopolit.

Gesammelte Werke (München: Carl Hanser, 1978), III, 266.

18. Several books have been written about connections between the Nazis and secret societies, many of them more sensational than scholarly. Cf. Heinz Höhne, *Der Orden unter dem Totenkopf* (Gütersloh: Sigbert Mohn, 1967), René Alleau, *Hitler et les Sociètes Secrétes* (Paris: Editions Bernard Grasset, 1969), Jean-Michel Angebert, *Hitler et la Tradition Cathare* (Paris: Editions Robert Laffont, S.A., 1971), and Trevor Ravenscroft, *The Spear of Destiny* (New York: Putnam, 1973).

19. Alfred Rosenberg, *Der Deutsche Ordenstaat* (München: Zentralverlag der NSDAP, Franz Eher nachf., 1934), 17. Cf. Dankmar's assertions in *Die Ritter vom Geiste* that his order must develop symbols and a ritual to attract and hold new members.

20. Arno Schmidt, "Dya Na Sore: Blondeste der Bestien," in *Dya Na Sore: Gespräche in einer Bibliothek* (Karlsruhe: Stahlberg, 1958).

21. Arno Schmidt, *Die Ritter vom Geist* (Karlsruhe: Stahlberg, 1965).

22. Martin Walser, *Ehen in Philippsburg* (Frankfurt/M: Suhrkamp, 1957).

23. A Jesus figure—thirty-three years old, named Christlieb or Schäfler. For Walser, the hope for the future obviously lies among the proletariat.

24. The novel has reminded at least one critic of Schiller's *Ghost-Seer*. Martin Greiner compares novels like Schiller's with works like Walser's, and sees a likeness between eighteenth-century Jesuitical Freemasons and twentieth-century capitalists and communists, especially as they are portrayed in literature. *Die Entstehung der modernen Unterhaltungsliteratur. Studien zum Trivialroman des 18. Jahrhunderts*, ed. Therese Poser (Reinbeck b. Hamburg: Rowohlt, 1964), 130.

25. Quotations from Grass's *Die Blechtrommel* (Frankfurt/M.: Fischer, 1962), 299–316.

26. Ibid., 434. Symbolically numbered steps are an important part of Freemasonic rites.

27. Ann Mason discusses Bebra in these terms: "In terms of the traditional *Bildungsroman*, Bebra represents a parodic variation on the familiar guide figure; he appears at important moments to counsel Oskar, leading him gradually out of private life into varied forms of involvement with the public world." Ann L. Mason, *The Skeptical Muse: A Study of Günter Grass' Conception of the Artist* (Bern: Herbert Lang, 1974), 42.

28. Compare the allusion to Christ in Bebra's geneology: "ein Spross aus dem Stamme Prinz Eugens" (253).

29. Grass, *Hundejahre* (Neuwied am Rhein, Berlin: Hermann Luchterhand, 1963).

30. *Revised Freemasonry Illustrated* (Chicago: Ezra A. Cook, 1919), 331. Also see "The Entered Apprentice's Lecture" in the Appendix. An 1838 German exposé of the ritual reproduces the passage as follows: "Buchstabiert ihn und fanget an. / Nein, Ihr fanget an. / Nein, fanget Ihr an." *Ritual und Aufdeckung der Freimaurerei*, 61.

31. Of such criticism, Michael Harscheidt's *Günter Grass: Wort-Zahl-Gott* (Bonn: Bouvier, 1976), a 758-page numerological/theological interpretation, is the most conspicuous.

32. Grass, "Menschen in Auschwitz," in *Der Bürger und seine Stimme: Reden, Aufsätze, Kommentare* (Darmstadt: Hermann Luchterhand, 1974), 89.

33. Grass, in *New York Times, Book Review* December 17, 1978, 14.

34. Grass, "Unser Grundübel ist der Idealismus," *Der Spiegel*, August 11, 1969, 94.

35. Claude Lévi-Strauss, *Structural Anthropology* (New York: Basic Books, 1963), 207, 229.

36. Ibid., 209.

37. It is somewhat surprising that such congruence between seemingly opposed positions exists, but Grass approaches Lévi-Strauss's position even more closely in a later novel. After making his point about

the dangers inherent in mythical thinking in *Hundejahre* and *Aus dem Tagebuch einer Schnecke*, Grass, in *Der Butt*, appropriates large portions of Lévi-Strauss's *The Raw and the Cooked* to develop a myth of cooking as an antidote to the *Weltgeist* Flounder. See my "The Raw and the Cooked: Claude Lévi-Strauss and Günter Grass," in *"Of the Fisherman and his Wife": Günter Grass's 'The Flounder' in Critical Perspective*, ed. Siegfried Mews (New York: AMS Press, 1982), 107–120.

38. Ernst Cassirer, *The Philosophy of Symbolic Forms, Volume Two: Mythical Thought*, trans. Ralph Manheim (New Haven: Yale University Press, 1975), 235.

39. Ernst Cassirer, *The Myth of the State* (New Haven: Yale University Press, 1971), 278.

40. Cf. also the statement by Mircea Eliade on Marxism, myth, and history: "It is indeed significant that Marx turns to his own account the Judaeo-Christian eschatological hope of an *absolute (end to) History*; in that he parts company from the other historical philosophers (Croce, for instance, and Ortega y Gasset), for whom the tensions of history are implicit in the human condition, and therefore can never be completely abolished." *Myth and Reality* (New York: Harper & Row, 1968), 184.

41. "Green Years for Grass," *Life*, 4 June 1965, 56.

42. Grass, "Unser Grundübel ist der Idealismus," 94.

43. The narratively serious but ultimately satirical worm dialectic has an analogue in Störtebeker's use of Heideggerian language in speaking of and to rats: "'Die Ratte entzieht sich, indem sie sich in das Rattige entbirgt. . . . Denn das Rattige ist in die Irre ereignet, in der es die Ratte umirrt und so den Irrtum stiftet. Er ist der Wesensraum aller Geschichte!'" (367).

44. John Reddick, *The 'Danzig Trilogy' of Günter Grass* (New York: Harcourt Brace Jovanovich, 1975), 239–266.

45. "Studienrat Oswald Brunies—das Autorenkollektiv hat vor, ihm ein Denkmal zu bauen—" (108).

46. Fredric Jameson, *Marxism and Form: Twentieth-Century Dialectical Theories of Literature* (Princeton: Princeton University Press, 1974), 66–67.

AFTERWORD

1. Ludwig Tieck, *Der gestiefelte Kater*, in *Ludwig Tiecks Schriften* (Berlin: Georg, 1853; rpt. Walter de Gruyter, 1966), V, 167.

2. See Karl Olbrich, *Die Freimaurer im deutschen Volksglauben* (Breslau: Verlag von M. & H. Marcus, 1930).

3. Masonic fiction is, naturally, broader than the German novel. English, French, Russian, American, Italian, and Spanish novels should be included in the discussion as well. The Freemasonic sections of Tolstoy's *War and Peace*, for instance, fairly cry out for analysis in terms of German

literary models. André Gide's *Les Caves du Vatican* (1914), with its swindlers (led by a quite traditional emissary figure) who fleece gullible Catholics of huge sums of money by claiming that Freemasons have kidnaped the
Pope, would likewise provide an interesting chapter in a broader study. So
too would Kipling's "The Man Who Would be King" (1889), John Fowles's
The Magus (1965, 1978), and Lawrence Durrell's *Avignon Quincunx* (1974–
1985). Similarly, it would be informative to work with the Masonic passages in Melville's *Moby Dick* (1851), with Nerval's Masonic myth in *Voyage
en Orient* (1851), with references to Freemasonry in Dostoevsky's fiction,
and with Yeats's Rosicrucian stories. Parodies like *The Illuminatus Trilogy*
by Robert Shea and Robert Anton Wilson (1975) would add still another
dimension to such a study. And most recently, Umberto Eco's *Foucault's
Pendulum* mixes contemporary theory and Freemasonry as its narrator jok-
ingly combines Templar, Rosicrucian, and Masonic ritual and history to create meaning in a postmodern world of surfaces.

Bibliography

LITERARY WORKS

Andreae, Johann Valentin. *Fama Fraternitatis*. Cassel: Wilhelm Wessell, 1614.

————. *Confessio Fraternitatis*. Cassel: Wilhelm Wessel, 1615.

————. *Chymische Hochzeit Christiani Rosenkreutz: Anno 1459*. Strassburg: L. Zetzner, 1616.

Arnim, Achim von. *Die Kronewächter*. Vol. 1 of *Sämtliche Romane und Erzählungen*. Ed. Walther Migge. München: Carl Hanser, 1962.

Bahr, Hermann, et al. *Der Roman der XII*. Berlin: Konrad W. Mecklenburg vormals Richter, 1909.

Bahrdt, Carl Friedrich. *Ausführung des Plans und Zwecks Jesu, in Briefen*. 12 vols. Berlin, 1784–1793.

Breier, Eduard. *Pandur und Freimaurer: Historischer Roman*. 4 vols. Leipzig, 1855.

————. *Die Rosenkreuzer in Wien: Sittenroman aus der Zeit Kaiser Joseph II*. 4 vols. Wien: Kober, 1852.

Büchner, Georg. *Woyzeck*. Ed. Hans Meyer. Frankfurt/M.: Ullstein, 1974.

Durrell, Lawrence. *The Avignon Quincunx*. London: Faber, 1974–1985.

Eco, Umberto. *Foucault's Pendulum*. Trans. William Weaver. New York: Harcourt Brace Jovanovich, 1989.

Ewers, Hanns Heinz. *Der Geisterseher: Aus den Papieren des Grafen O*. München: Georg Müller, 1922.

Fénelon, Francois de Salignac de La Mothe-. *Les aventures de Télémaque, fils d'Ulysse*. Paris, 1699. Reprint. Paris: Garnier-Flammarion, 1968.

221

Fessler, Ignatz Aurelius. *Marc-Aurel.* 4 vols. Breslau, 1789–1792.

Folenius, E. F. W. E. *Der Geisterseher: Aus den Memoiren des Grafen von O: Zweyter und dritter Theil von X. .Y. .Z. . .* Leipzig: Barth, 1796–1797.

Fowles, John. *The Magus.* Boston: Little, Brown, 1965.

Gide, André. *Les Caves du Vatican: Sotie.* Paris: Gallimard, 1967.

Goethe, Johann Wolfgang. *Goethes Briefe.* "Hamburger Ausgabe." 4 vols. Hamburg: Christian Wegner, 1967.

————. *Goethes Werke.* "Gedenkausgabe." Ed. E. Beutler. Zürich: Artemis, 1949.

————. *Goethes Werke.* "Hamburger Ausgabe." 14 vols. Ed. Erich Trunz. 6th ed. Hamburg: Christian Wegner, 1964.

————. *Goethes Werke.* "Weimarer Ausgabe." 143 vols. Weimar, 1887–1919.

————. *Wilhelm Meisters Lehrjahre: Ein Roman.* 4 vols. Berlin: J. F. Unger, 1795–1796.

————. *Wilhelm Meisters Wanderjahre oder die Entsagenden. Erster Teil.* Stuttgart: Cotta, 1821.

————. *Wilhelm Meisters Wanderjahre oder die Entsagenden.* Vols. 21–23 of *Goethes Werke: Ausgabe letzter Hand.* Stuttgart: Cotta, 1829.

Grass, Günter. *Die Blechtrommel.* Neuwied am Rhein and Berlin-Spandau: Luchterhand, 1959. Reprint Frankfurt/M.: Fischer, 1962.

————. *Der Bürger und seine Stimme: Reden, Aufsätze, Kommentare.* Darmstadt: Luchterhand, 1974.

————. *Hundejahre.* Neuwied am Rhein: Luchterhand, 1963.

————. "Unser Grundübel ist der Idealismus." In *Der Spiegel.* August 11, 1969, 94.

Grosse, Karl. *Der Genius: Aus den Papieren des Marquis C* von G**.* 4 vols. Halle: Hendel, 1791–1794.

Gutzkow, Karl. *Gesammelte Werke.* 13 vols. Frankfurt/M.: Literarische Anstalt, 1845–1852.

————. *Karl Gutzkow. Liberale Energie: Eine Sammlung seiner kritischen Schriften.* Ed. Peter Demetz. Frankfurt/M.: Ullstein, 1974.

————. *Die Ritter vom Geiste.* 9 vols. Leipzig: Brockhaus, 1850–1851.

————. *Die Ritter vom Geiste.* 9 vols. 2d ed. Leipzig: Brockhaus, 1852.

————. *Die Ritter vom Geiste.* 5th ed. Berlin: Otto Janke, 1869.

Hesse, Hermann. *Gesammelte Schriften.* Frankfurt/M.: Suhrkamp, 1958.

————. "Kindheit des Zauberers." In *Eigensinn.* Frankfurt/M.: Suhrkamp, 1972.

————. *Die Morgenlandfahrt: Erzählung.* Berlin: S. Fischer, 1932.

Hippel, Theodor Gottlieb von. *Kreuz- und Querzüge des Ritters A. bis Z.* 2 vols. Berlin: Voss, 1793-1794. Reprint. Leipzig: Göschen, 1860.

Hölderlin, Friedrich. *Hyperion oder der Eremit in Griechenland.* 2 vols. Tübingen: J. G. Cotta. 1797, 1799.

Hofmannsthal, Hugo von. *Andreas oder die Vereinigten: Fragmente eines Romans.* Berlin: S. Fischer, 1932.

————. Vol. 7 of *Gesammelte Werke in zehn Einzelbänden.* Ed. Bernd Schoeller. Frankfurt/M.: Fischer, 1979.

————. Vol. 30 of *Sämtliche Werke.* Ed. Manfred Pape. Frankfurt/M.: S. Fischer, 1982.

Hollaender, Felix. *Der Weg des Thomas Truck: Ein Roman in vier Büchern.* 2 vols. Berlin: Bruno Cassirer, 1902.

Immermann, Karl. *Die Epigonen: Familienmemoiren in neun Büchern 1823-1835.* Vols. 5–7 of Karl Immermanns Schriften. Düsseldorf: J. E. Schaub, 1836.

————. *Werke.* 5 vols. Ed. Benno von Wiese. Frankfurt/M.: Athenäum, 1971.

Jung-Stilling, Johann Heinrich. *Das Heimweh.* 4 vols. Marburg: Krieger, 1794–1797. Reprint. Stuttgart, 1836.

————. *Lebensgeschichte.* Frankfurt/M.: Insel, 1983.

————. *Theobald oder die Schwärmer.* 2 vols. Leipzig, 1784–1785.

Kipling, Rudyard. *Debits and Credits.* Garden City, N. Y.: Doubleday, 1926.

————. *The Phantom Rickshaw.* New York: Nottingham Society, 1909.

Knigge, Adolf Freiherr von. *Geschichte Peter Clausens.* 3 vols. 1783–1785. Reprint. 3 vols. Frankfurt/M. 1794.

————. *Der Roman meines Lebens.* 4 vols. Riga, 1781–1783.

————. *Sämtliche Werke.* Ed. Paul Raabe. 24 vols. Nendeln, Liechtenstein: KTO Press, 1978.

Kotzebue, August Friedrich. *Der Freimaurer: Lustspiel in einem Akt,* 1818. In Vol. 8 of *Dramatische Spiele.* Stuttgart: A. F. Macklot, 1822.

Kreuder, Ernst. *Die Gesellschaft vom Dachboden.* Hamburg: Rowohlt, 1946.

————. *Die Unauffindbaren: Roman.* Stuttgart: Rowohlt, 1948.

Kühne, Gustav. *Die Freimaurer: Eine Familiengeschichte aus dem vorigen Jahrhundert.* Frankfurt/M.: Meidinger Sohn, 1855.

Lessing, Gotthold Ephraim. *Ernst und Falk. Mit den Fortsetzungen Johann Gottfried Herders und Friedrich Schlegels.* Ed. Ion Contiades. Frankfurt/M.: Insel, 1968.

Lytton, Edward Bulwer. *Zanoni.* In the *Monthly Chronicle,* 1841. Reprint. Estes and Lauriat: Boston, 1892.

Mann, Heinrich. *Der Untertan.* Leipzig and Wien: Kurt Wolff, 1918.

Mann, Thomas. *Dichter über ihre Dichtungen: 1889–1917.* Ed. Hans Wysling. München: Ernst Heimeran, 1975.

————. *Gesammelte Werke in zwölf Bänden.* Frankfurt/M.: S. Fischer, 1960.

————. "The Making of *The Magic Mountain."* In *The Magic Mountain.* Trans. H. T. Lowe-Porter. New York: Modern Library College Editions, 1969.

————. *Der Zauberberg.* Berlin: S. Fischer, 1924.

Meyern, Friedrich Wilhelm von. *Dya-Na-Sore oder Die Wanderer: Eine Geschichte aus dem Samskritt übersetzt.* 3 vols. Wien & Leipzig: Stahel, 1787–1791.

Meyrink, Gustav. *Der Engel vom westlichen Fenster: Roman.* Leipzig, Zürich: Grethlein, 1927.

Moritz, Karl Philipp. *Andreas Hartknopf. Eine Allegorie.* Berlin, 1786. Reprint. Stuttgart: J. B. Metzler, 1968.

Mozart, Wolfgang Amadeus and Emanuel Schikaneder. *Die Zauberflöte.* [First performed in Vienna, 1791.] Vienna: J. Alberti, 1791 (original libretto).

Mundt, Theodor. *Cagliostro in Petersburg: Historische Novelle.* Prag: J. L. Kober, 1858.

———. *Graf Mirabeau.* 2d rev. ed. 4 vols. Berlin: Janke, 1860.

Nerval, Gérard de. *Voyage en Orient.* 2 vols. Paris: Charpentier, 1851.

Oppermann, Heinrich Albert. *Hundert Jahre 1770–1870: Zeit- und Lebensbilder aus drei Generationen.* Leipzig: Brockhaus, 1871. Reprint. Frankfurt/M.: Zweitausendeins, 1982.

Ramsay, Andrew Michael. *Les Voyages de Cyrus, avec un discours sur la mythologie et une lettre de M. Fréret sur la chronologie de cet ouvrage.* 2 vols. Paris: Guillau, 1727.

Rathewitz, Jos. v. *Die drei Freimaurer: Enthüllungen aus dem Leben und Treiben derselben seit dem Revolutionsjahr 1848. Als Seitenstück zu dem Leben und Treiben der Jesuiten. Aus den hinterlassenen Papieren eines verstorbenen Freimaurers.* 2 vols. Hamburg: J. F. Richter, 1855–1856. Republished as *Die Braut des Freimaurers.* Hamburg, J. F. Richter, 1874.

Richter, Johann Paul Friedrich (Jean Paul). *Die Unsichtbare Loge: Eine Biographie.* 2 vols. Berlin: Matzdorf, 1793.

———. *Titan.* 4 vols. Berlin: Matzdorf, 1800–1803.

Sacher-Masoch, Leopold von. *Maria Theresia und die Freimaurer.* Leipzig: Günther, 1873.

Sand, George. *Le Compagnon du Tour de France.* Paris: Perrotin, 1840. Translated into German as *Isolde.* "Deutsch von Dr. Scherr." Stuttgart: Franck, 1850.

———. *Consuelo.* In *Revue indépendant,* 1842–1843.

———. *La Comtesse de Rudolstadt.* In *Revue indépendante,* 1843–1844.

Schiller, Friedrich. *Der Geisterseher: Eine Geschichte aus den Memoires des Grafen von O.* In *Thalia,* nos. 4–8, 1787–1789. Reprint [book]. Leipzig: Göschen, 1789.

———. *Sämtliche Werke.* "Säkular-Ausgabe." 16 vols. Stuttgart: J. G. Cotta'sche Buchhandlung Nachfolger, 1904.

———. *Schillers Werke. Nationalausgabe.* Weimar: Böhlau, 1943 ff.

———. *Schillers Werke.* Frankfurt/M.: Insel, 1966.

Schmidt, Arno. "Dya Na Sore: Blondeste der Bestien." In *Dya Na Sore: Gespräche in einer Bibliothek.* Karlsruhe: Stahlberg, 1958.

———. *Die Ritter vom Geist.* Karlsruhe: Stahlberg, 1965.

Shea, Robert, and Robert Anton Wilson. *The Illuminatus Trilogy.* New York: Dell, 1975.

Sue, Eugéne. *Le Juif errant*. In *Constitutionnel*. Paris, 1844–1845. Reprint. Paris: Robert Laffont, 1983.

Terrasson, Jean. *Sethos, histoire ou vie tirée des monuments anecdotes de l'ancienne Egypte*. Paris: Guerin, 1731. [German translations in 1732–1737 and 1777–1778.]

Tieck, Ludwig. *Der gestiefelte Kater*. In Vol. 5 of *Ludwig Tieck's Schriften*. Berlin: Reimer, 1828. Reprint. Walter de Gruyter, 1966.

―――. *Die Wundersüchtigen*. In *Novellenkranz auf das Jahr 1831*. Berlin: Reimer, 1831.

―――. *Die Wundersüchtigen*. In Vol. 23 of *Ludwig Tieck's Schriften*. Berlin: Reimer, 1853. Reprint. Walter de Gruyter, 1966.

Toller, Ernst. *Pastor Hall: Schauspiel*. 1939. In Vol. 3 of *Gesammelte Werke*. Ed. John M. Spalek and Wolfgang Frühwald. München: Carl Hanser, 1978.

Tolstoy, Leo. *War and Peace*. 1865. Trans. Rosemary Edmonds. Baltimore: Penguin Books, 1969.

Tschink, Cajetan. *Geschichte eines Geistersehers: Aus den Papieren des Mannes mit der eisernen Larve*. Leipzig: Böhme, 1797.

Tucholsky, Kurt. "Ludendorff oder der Verfolgungswahn." 1928. In Vol. 6 of *Gesammelte Werke in 10 Bänden*. Ed. Mary Gerold-Tucholsky and Fritz J. Raddatz. Reinbek bei Hamburg: Rowohlt, 1960.

Vulpius, Christian Aug. *Aurora: Ein Romantisches Gemälde der Vorzeit*. 2 vols. Leipzig: Gräff, 1794–1795.

Walser, Martin. *Ehen in Philippsburg: Roman*. Frankfurt/M: Suhrkamp, 1957.

Wieland, Christoph Martin. *Agathodämon*. Leipzig: Göschen, 1799.

HISTORICAL AND SECONDARY LITERATURE

Agethen, Manfred. *Geheimbund und Utopie: Illuminaten, Freimaurer und deutsche Spätaufklärung*. München: Oldenbourg, 1984.

Alleau, René. *Hitler et les Sociètes Secrèts*. Paris: Bernard Grasset, 1969.

Allgemeine Encyklopädie der Wissenschaften und Künste. Ed. J. S. Ersch and J. G. Gruber. Leipzig: Johann Friedrich Gleditsch, 1849.

Angebert, Jean-Michel. *Hitler et la Tradition Cathare*. Paris: Robert Laffont, 1971.

Baigent, Michael, Richard Leigh, and Henry Lincoln. *Holy Blood, Holy Grail*. New York: Dell, 1983.

Baillet, Adrien. *La Vie de Monsieur Descartes*. Paris, 1691.

Ballin, Fritz. "Thomas Mann und die Freimaurerei." In *Eklektisches Bundesblatt*. Juli/August 1930, 237–242.

Banuls, André. *Heinrich Mann*. Stuttgart: W. Kohlhammer, 1970.

Barner, Wilfried. "Geheime Lenkung. Zur Turmgesellschaft in Goethes *Wilhelm Meister*." In *Goethe's Narrative Fiction: The Irvine Goethe Symposium*. Berlin: Walter de Gruyter, 1983.

Bartels, Adolf. *Freimaurerei und Literatur: Feststellungen und Vermutungen*. München: F. Eher Nachfolger, 1929.

Beaujean, Marion. *Der Trivialroman in der zweiten Hälfte des 18. Jahrhunderts: Die Ursprünge des modernen Unterhaltungs-romans*. 2d rev. ed. Bonn: H. Bouvier, 1969.

Beck, Angelike. *"Der Bund ist Ewig": Zur Physiognomie einer Lebensform im 18. Jahrhundert*. Erlangen: Palm & Enke, 1982.

Berlinische Monatsschrift. Ed. Friedrich Gedike and Johann Erich Biester. Berlin, 1786–1793.

Bieberstein, Johannes Rogalla von. *Die These von der Verschwörung 1776–1945*. Bern: Herbert Lang and Peter Lang, 1976.

Börne, Ludwig. *Sämtliche Schriften*. Düsseldorf: Joseph Melzer, 1964.

Brauweiler, Heinz. "Vatikan und Loge im Weltkrieg." In *Kriegshefte der Süddeutschen Monatshefte*, München, Juni 1917, 735–746.

Bürgin, Hans, and Hans-Otto Mayer. *Thomas Mann: Eine Chronik seines Lebens*. Frankfurt/M.: Fischer, 1965.

Bussmann, Walter. "Schillers 'Geisterseher' und seine Fortsetzer: Ein Beitrag zur Struktur des Geheimbundromans." Ph.D. diss. Göttingen, 1961.

Buttlar, Adrian von. *Der Englische Landsitz 1715–1760*. Mittenwald: Mäander, 1982.

———. *Der Landschaftsgarten*. München: Wilhelm Heyne, 1980.

Butler, E. M. *The Myth of the Magus*. New York: MacMillan, 1948.

Campe, Joachim Heinrich. *Wörterbuch der Deutschen Sprache*. Braunschweig, 1810.

Cassirer, Ernst. *The Myth of the State*. New Haven: Yale University Press, 1971.

———. *Mythical Thought*. Vol. 2 of *The Philosophy of Symbolic Forms*. Trans. Ralph Manheim. New Haven: Yale University Press, 1975.

Chailly, Jacques. *The Magic Flute, Masonic Opera*. London: Victor Gollancz, 1972.

Cohn, Norman. *Warrant for Genocide: The Myth of the Jewish World Conspiracy and the Protocols of the Elders of Zion*. New York: Harper & Row, 1967.

Darnton, Robert. *Mesmerism and the End of the Enlightenment in France*. Cambridge: Harvard University Press, 1968.

Das Freimaurermuseum. Zeulenreude: Bernhard Sporn, 1928.

Demetz, Peter. *Marx, Engels and the Poets*. Trans. Jeffrey Sammons. Chicago: University of Chicago Press, 1967.

———. *René Rilkes Prager Jahre*. Düsseldorff: Diederichs, 1953.

Der verklärte Freymaurer. Vienna, 1791.

Didion, Joan. "Salvador." *The New York Review of Books.* October and November, 1982. Reprint. New York: Simon and Schuster, 1983.

Didler, Karl. *Freimaurer-Denkschrift über die politische Wirksamkeit des Freimaurer-Bundes als der unter verschiedenen Namen und Formen unter uns im Finstern schleichenden Propaganda zum Sturz der legitimen Throne und des positiven Christenthum.* "Vor Nachdruck wird gewarnt! Als Geheimschrift gedrückt." 2. Aufl. Berlin, 1864–1871.

Dobert, Eitel Wolf. *Karl Gutzkow und seine Zeit.* Bern: Francke, 1968.

Dülmen, Richard van. *Der Geheimbund der Illuminaten: Darstellung, Analyse, Dokumentation.* Stuttgart: Friedrich Frommann, 1975.

Eliade, Mircea. *Myth and Reality.* New York: Harper & Row, 1968.

Emrich, Wilhelm. "Das Problem der Symbolinterpretation im Hinblick auf Goethes *Wanderjahre.*" *Deutsche Vierteljahresschrift* 26 (1952): 331–352.

Fichte, Johann Gottlob. *Gesamtausgabe.* Vol. II/3. Ed. Reinhard Lauth und Hans Jacob. Stuttgart: Friedrich Frommann, 1971.

———. *Gesamtausgabe.* Vol. III/4. Ed. Reinhard Lauth and Hans Gliwitzky. Stuttgart: Friedrich Frommann, 1973.

———. *Philosophie der Maurerei.* Ed. Wilhelm Flitner. Leipzig: Felix Meiner, 1923.

Findel, J. G. *Geschichte der Freimaurerei.* 3d ed. Leipzig: J. G. Findel, 1870.

Flax, Neil M. "The Presence of the Sign in Goethe's *Faust.*" *PMLA* 98 (1983): 183–203.

Flygt, Sten. *The Notorious Dr. Bahrdt.* Nashville, Tenn.: Vanderbilt University Press, 1963.

Foucault, Michel. *The Order of Things: An Archeology of the Human Sciences.* New York: Vintage, 1973. Originally *Les Mots et les choses.* Paris: Gallimard, 1966.

Frank, Eduard. "L'Ésotériste Gustav Meyrink." In *Gustav Meyrink.* Ed. Yvonne Caroutch. Paris: Editions de l'Herne, 1976.

Freimaurerei und Sozialdemokratie, oder, Ist ausser der Sozialdemokratie auch die Freimaurerei nachweisbar Religions-, Staats- und Gesellschaftsgefährlich? 4th ed. Stuttgart: Süddeutscher Verlagsbuchhandlung, 1891.

Das Freimaurermuseum. Zeulenroda: Bernhard Sporn, 1928.

Freimaurer-Zeitung. Ed. R. R. Fischer. Leipzig: Heinrich Weinedel, 1847–1848.

Frick, Karl R. H. *Die Erleuchteten.* Graz: Akademische Druck- und Verlagsanstalt, 1973.

Friesen, Gerhard. *The German Panoramic Novel of the 19th Century.* Bern: Herbert Lang, 1972.

Geschichte der grossen National-Mutterloge in den Preussischen Staaten genannt zu den drei Weltkugeln. Berlin: W. Büxenstein, 1890.

Göchhausen, Ernst August Anton von. *Enthüllung des Systems der Weltbürger-Republik.* Rome [Leipzig], 1786.

Grassl, Hans. *Aufbruch zur Romantik: Bayerns Beitrag zur deutschen Geistes-geschichte 1765–1785.* München: C. H. Beck, 1968.

Greiner, Martin. *Die Entstehung der modernen Unterhaltungsliteratur. Studien zum Trivialroman des 18. Jahrhunderts.* Ed. Therese Poser. Reinbeck b. Hamburg: Rowohlt, 1964.

Haas, Rosemarie. *Die Turmgesellschaft in "Wilhelm Meisters Lehrjahren": Zur Geschichte des Geheimbundromans und der Romantheorie im 18. Jahrhun-dert.* Bern: Herbert Lang, 1975.

Habermas, Jürgen. *Strukturwandel der Öffentlichkeit: Untersuchungen zu ei-ner Kategorie der bürgerlichen Gesellschaft.* Darmstadt: Luchterhand, 1962.

Hamilton, Nigel. *The Brothers Mann.* New Haven: Yale University Press, 1979.

Hanstein, Adalbert von. *Wie entstand Schillers Geisterseher.* Berlin: Alexan-der Kuncker, 1903. Reprint. Hildesheim: Gerstenberg, 1977.

Harscheidt, Michael. *Günter Grass: Wort-Zahl-Gott.* Bonn: Bouvier, 1976.

Hesse. A Collection of Critical Essays. Ed. Theodore Ziolkowski. Englewood Cliffs, N.J.: Prentice-Hall, 1973.

Höhne, Heinz. *Der Orden unter dem Totenkopf.* Gütersloh: Sigbert Mohn, 1967.

Jacob, Margaret. *The Radical Enlightenment: Pantheists, Freemasons, and Re-publicans.* London: Allen & Unwin, 1981.

Jameson, Fredric. *Marxism and Form: Twentieth-Century Dialectical Theories of Literature.* Princeton: Princeton University Press, 1974.

Jolles, Matthijs. *Dichtkunst und Lebenskunst: Studien zum Problem der Sprache bei Friedrich Schiller.* Ed. Arthur Groos. Bonn: Bouvier, 1980.

Jung, Alexander. *Briefe über Gutzkow's Ritter vom Geiste.* Leipzig: Brock-haus, 1856.

Kaiser, Herbert. *Studien zum deutschen Roman nach 1848.* Duisburg: Walter Braun, 1977.

Katz, Jacob. *Jews and Freemasons in Europe 1723–1939.* Trans. Leonard Os-chry. Cambridge: Harvard University Press, 1970.

Kestner, August. *Die Agape oder der geheime Weltbund der Christen.* Jena: A. Schmid, 1819.

Knoop, D. and G. P. Jones. *The Genesis of Freemasonry: An Account of the Rise and Development of Freemasonry in its Operative, Accepted and Early Speculative Phases.* Manchester, 1947.

Koselleck, Reinhart. *Kritik und Krise: Eine Studie zur Pathogenese der bürger-lichen Welt.* Freiburg, 1959. Reprint. Frankfurt/M.: Suhrkamp, 1973.

Kowalik, Jill. " 'Sympathy with Death': Hans Castorp's Nietzschean Resent-ment." *The German Quarterly* 58 (1985): 27–48.

Krause, Karl Christian Friedrich. *Die drei ältesten Kunsturkunden der Frei-maurerbruderschaft.* Dresden: Arnold, 1810.

Kraft, Herbert. *Um Schiller betrogen.* Pfullingen: Günther Neske, 1978.

Kuzniar, Alice. "Philosophic Chiliasm: Generating the Future or Delaying the End?" *Eighteenth-Century Studies* 19, no. 1 (1985): 1–20.

Larudan, Abbé. *Les Francs-Macon Écrasés*. Amsterdam, 1747.

Le Forestier, René. *Les Illuminés de Bavière et la franc-maçonnerie allemande*. Paris: Hachette, 1914.

Lehnert, Herbert. *Thomas-Mann-Forschung: Ein Bericht*. Stuttgart: J. B. Metzler, 1969.

Lennhoff, Eugen, and Oskar Posner. *Internationales Freimaurer-Lexikon*. 1932. Reprint. Wien, München: Amalthea, 1980.

Lévi-Strauss, Claude. *Structural Anthropology*. New York: Basic Books, 1963.

Lindner, Erich J. *Freimaurerisches Brauchtum in Bildern 1730–1840*. Bayreuth, 1969.

Linke, Hansjürgen. *Das Kultische in der Dichtung Stefan Georges und seiner Schule*. München: Helmut Küpper vormals Georg Bondi, 1960.

Lube, Manfred. *Gustav Meyrink: Beiträge zur Biographie und Studien zu seiner Kunsttheorie*. Graz: dbv Verlag für die Technische Universität Graz, 1980.

Ludendorff, Erich. *Vernichtung der Freimaurerei durch Enthüllung ihrer Geheimnisse*. München: 1927.

Ludendorff, Mathilde. *Der ungesühnte Frevel an Luther, Lessing, Mozart und Schiller*. München, 1928.

Ludz, Peter Christian, ed. *Geheime Gesellschaften*. Heidelberg: Lambert Schneider, 1979.

Maack, Ferdinand. *Zweimal gestorben! Die Geschichte eines Rosenkreuzers aus dem XVIII. Jahrhundert*. Leipzig: Wilhelm Heims, 1912.

Mackey, Albert G. *An Encyclopaedia of Freemasonry*. Chicago: Masonic History Company, 1927.

Mason, Ann L. *The Skeptical Muse: A Study of Günter Grass' Conception of the Artist*. Bern: Herbert Lang, 1974.

Mayer, Hans. *Georg Büchner und seine Zeit*. Frankfurt/M.: Suhrkamp, 1972.

Mendelssohn, Peter De. *Der Zauberer: Das Leben des deutschen Schriftstellers Thomas Mann, Erster Teil: 1875–1918*. Frankfurt/M.: S. Fischer, 1975.

Mileck, Joseph. *Hermann Hesse: Life and Art*. Berkeley: University of California Press, 1980.

Miles, David H. *Hofmannsthal's Novel 'Andreas': Memory and Self*. Princeton: Princeton University Press, 1972.

Muchner, Wilhelm. *Ferdinand Freiligrath: Ein Dichterleben in Briefen*. Lahr: Moritz Schauenburg, 1882.

Nagel, Ivan. *Autonomie und Gnade: Über Mozarts Opern*. München: Carl Hanser, 1985.

Neuberger, Helmut. *Freimaurerei und Nationalsozialismus: Die Verfolgung der deutschen Freimaurerei durch völkische Bewegung und Nationalsozialismus 1918–1945*. Hamburg: Bauhütten, 1980.

Ohly, Friedrich. "Goethes Ehrfurchten—ein ordo caritatis." *Euphorion* 55 (1961): 113–145, 405–448.

Olbrich, Karl. *Die Freimaurer im deutschen Volksglauben.* Breslau: M. & H. Marcus, 1930.

Oliver, J. W. *The Life of William Beckford.* London: Oxford University Press, 1937.

Pape, Manfred. "Aurea Catena Homeri: Die Rosenkreuzer-Quelle der 'Allomatik' in Hofmannsthals *Andreas.*" *Deutsche Vierteljahresschrift* 4 (1975): 680–693.

Prutz, Robert. *Die deutsche Literatur der Gegenwart 1848–1858.* Leipzig, 1859.

Ravenscroft, Trevor. *The Spear of Destiny.* New York: Putnam, 1973.

Recke, Elisabeth von der. *Nachricht von des berüchtigten Cagliostro Aufenthalt in Mitau im Jahre 1779 und von dessen dortigen magischen Operationen.* Berlin: Friedrich Nicolai, 1787.

Reddick, John. *The 'Danzig Trilogy' of Günter Grass.* New York: Harcourt Brace Jovanovich, 1975.

Reed, T. J. *Thomas Mann: The Uses of Tradition.* London: Oxford University Press, 1974.

Reinalter, Helmut, ed. *Freimaurer und Geheimbunde im 18. Jahrhundert in Mitteleuropa.* Frankfurt: Suhrkamp, 1983.

Rennert, M. "Die Freimaurer in Italien." *Kriegshefte der Süddeutschen Monatshefte.* München, Juni 1915, 471–477.

Richter, Claus. *Leiden an der Gesellschaft: Vom literarischen Liberalismus zum poetischen Realismus.* Kronbert/Ts.: Athenäum, 1978.

Ritual und Aufdeckung der Freimaurerei, der Gesellschaften der Oranienmänner und seltsamen Gesellen; mit vielen Bildern, einem Schlüssel zu dem Phi Beta Kappa so wie auch einer Darstellung des, an William Morgan, wegen Enthüllung der Geheimnisse der Maurerei begangenen Menschenraubes und Mordes. Aus englischen Schriften gezogen von Einem Freunde des Lichts. Leipzig: Leopold Michelsen, 1838.

Roberts, David. *The Indirections of Desire: Hamlet in Goethes "Wilhelm Meister."* Heidelberg: Carl Winter Universitätsverlag, 1980.

Roberts, J. M. *The Mythology of the Secret Societies.* New York: Charles Scribner's Sons, 1972.

Rosenberg, Alfred. *Der Deutsche Ordenstaat: Ein neuer Abschnitt in der Entwicklung des nationalsozialistischen Staatsgedanken.* München: Zentralverlag der NSDAP, Franz Eher nachf., 1934.

———. *Das Verbrechen der Freimaurerei.* 1921. Reprint. In Vol. 1 of *Schriften und Reden.* München: Hoheneichen, 1943.

Runkel, Ferdinand. *Geschichte der Freimaurer in Deutschland.* 3 vols. Berlin: Reimar Hobbing, 1932.

Sammons, Jeffrey. *Six Essays on the Young German Novel.* Chapel Hill: University of North Carolina Press, 1972.

Saueressig, Heinz. "Die Entstehung des Romans *Der Zauberberg*." *Besichtigung des Zauberbergs.* Ed. Heinz Saueressig. Biberach an der Riss: Wege und Gestalten, 1974.

Schlegel, Friedrich. *Philosophy of History.* Trans. James Burton Robertson. 7th ed. London: Bell & Daldy, 1873.

Schneider, Ferdinand Josef. *Die Freimauerei und ihr Einfluss auf die Geistige Kultur in Deutschland am Ende des XVIII. Jahrhunderts.* Prag: Taussig und Taussig, 1909.

Schneider, Heinrich. *Quest for Mysteries: The Masonic Background for Literature in Eighteenth-Century Germany.* Ithaca: Cornell University Press, 1947.

Schonfield, Hugh J. *The Passover Plot.* New York: Bernard Geis Associates, 1966.

Schweitzer, Albert. *The Quest of the Historical Jesus.* New York: MacMillan, 1961. [Originally *Von Reimarus zu Wrede*, 1906.]

Seidlin, Oskar. "Schiller's 'Treacherous Signs': The Function of the Letters in His Early Plays." In *Essays in German and Comparative Literature.* Chapel Hill: University of North Carolina Press, 1961.

Sewell, William H., Jr. *Work and Revolution in France: The Language of Labor from the Old Regime to 1848.* Cambridge: Cambridge University Press, 1980.

Silberer, Herbert. *Probleme der Mystik und Ihrer Symbolik.* Wien, 1914. Reprint. Darmstadt: Wissenschaftliche Buchgesellschaft, 1961.

Staiger, Emil. *Friedrich Schiller.* Zürich: Atlantis, 1967.

Starck, Johann August Freiherr von. *Saint Nicaise oder eine Sammlung merkwürdiger maurerischer Briefe, für Freymäurer und die es nicht sind. Aus dem Französischen übersetzt.* Frankfurt/M.: Fleischer, 1785.

———. *Über die alten und neuen Mysterien.* Berlin, 1782.

———. *Über den Zweck des Freymäurerordens.* Berlin: Germanien, 1781.

Steiner, Gerhard. *Freimaurer und Rosenkreuzer: Georg Forsters Weg durch Geheimbünde.* Weinheim: Acta humaniora, 1985.

Stern, Fritz. *The Politics of Cultural Despair.* 1961. Reprint. Berkeley: University of California Press, 1974.

Strelka, Joseph. *Esoterik bei Goethe.* Tübingen: Niemeyer, 1980.

Taute, Reinhold. *Ordens- und Bundes-Romane: Ein Beitrag zur Bibliographie der Freimaurerei.* Frankfurt/M.: Mahlau & Dschmidt, 1907.

Thalmann, Marianne. *Der Trivialroman des 18. Jahrhunderts und der romantische Roman: Ein Beitrag zur Entwicklungsgeschichte der Geheimbundmystik.* Berlin: Emil Ebering, 1923.

Trotzki, Leo. *Leo Trotzki: Mein Leben.* Frankfurt/M.: Fischer, 1974.

Ueding, Gert, ed. *Literatur ist Utopie.* Frankfurt/M.: Suhrkamp, 1978.

Urner, Klaus. "Thomas Mann und die Freimaurerei." *Neue Zürcher Zeitung,* Sept. 30, 1973, 51–52.

Der verklärte Freymaurer. Eine Schrift, worinn ihre hieroglyphische Zeichen, Worte, Werke, wie sie sollen verstanden, und soweit es thunlich ist, ausgedeutet werden. Wien: Pazowski, 1791.

Vidler, Anthony. "The Architecture of the Lodges: Ritual Form and Associational Life in the Late Enlightenment." *Oppositions.* 5 (Summer 1976): 75–97.

Viering, Jürgen. *Schwärmerische Erwartung bei Wieland, im trivialen Geheimnisroman, und bei Jean Paul.* Köln: Böhlau, 1976.

Voges, Michael. *Aufklärung und Geheimnis: Untersuchungen zur Vermittlung von Literatur- und Sozialgeschichte am Beispiel der Aneignung des Geheimbundmaterials im Roman des späten 18. Jahrhunderts.* Tübingen: Niemeyer, 1987.

Vollendeter Aufschluss des Jesuitismus und des wahren Geheimnisses der Freimaurer. Ans Licht gestellt von dem Herausgeber der Enthüllung der Weltbürger-Republik. Rom (!), 1787.

Vöpel, Christiane. *Hermann Hesse und die deutsche Jugendbewegung.* Bonn: Bouvier, 1977.

Vogl, Carl. *Aufzeichnungen und Bekenntnisse eines Pfarrers.* Wien: Aegis, 1930.

Vosskamp, Wilhelm. "Utopie und Utopiekritik in Goethes Romanen *Wilhelm Meisters Lehrjahre und Wilhelm Meisters Wanderjahre.*" In Vol. 3 of *Utopieforschung: Interdisziplinäre Studien zur neuzeitlichen Utopie.* Ed. Wilhelm Vosskamp. Stuttgart: Metzler, 1982.

Weissberg, Liliane. *Geistersprache: philosophischer und literarischer Diskurs im späten achtzehnten Jahrhundert.* Würzburg: Königshausen and Neumann, 1990.

Wellbery, David E. *Lessing's "Laocoon": Semiotics and Aesthetics in the Age of Reason.* Cambridge: Cambridge University Press, 1984.

Wichtl, Friedrich. *Weltfreimaurerei, Weltrevolution, Weltrepublik. Eine Untersuchung über Ursprung und Endziele des Weltkrieges.* München: J. F. Lehmann, 1919.

Wiese, Benno von. *Friedrich Schiller.* Stuttgart: J. B. Metzler, 1959.

Wieser, Theodor. "Der Malteser in Hofmannsthals *Andreas.*" *Euphorion* 51 (1957): 397–421.

Wilkinson, Lynn R. "Balzac, Baudelaire, and the Popularization of Swedenborgianism in France." Ph.D diss., Berkeley, 1983.

Wolfstieg, August. *Bibliographie der freimaurerischen Literatur.* Leipzig: Karl W. Hiersemann, 1923.

Yates, Frances A. *The Rosicrucian Enlightenment.* London: Routledge and Kegan Paul, 1972. Reprint. Boulder: Shambhala, 1978.

Der Ziegeldecker im Osten von Altenburg. Published from 1837–1847. Ed. Bernhard Lützelberger. [In 1848 the journal became known as *Bruderblätter für Freimaurer.*]

Zimmermann, Rolf Christian. *Das Weltbild des jungen Goethe: Studien zur hermetischen Tradition des deutschen 18. Jahrhunderts.* 2 vols. München: Wilhelm Fink, 1969, 1979.

Ziolkowski, Theodore. *The Novels of Hermann Hesse.* Princeton: Princeton University Press, 1965.

Index

235